SEX, LIES AND DEMOCRACY

The Press and the Public

edited by
Michael Bromley and Hugh Stephenson

LONGMAN
London and New York

Addison Wesley Longman Limited
Edinburgh Gate
Harlow
Essex CM20 2JE
United Kingdom
and Associated Companies throughout the world

*Published in the United States of America
by Addison Wesley Longman, New York*

© Addison Wesley Longman Limited 1998

The right of Michael Bromley and Hugh Stephenson
to be identified as authors of this work has been asserted
by them in accordance with the Copyright, Designs and
Patents Act 1988.

First published 1998

ISBN 0 582 29332 4 PPR

British Library Cataloguing-in-Publication Data

A catalogue record for this book is available from the British Library

Library of Congress Cataloging-in-Publication Data

Sex, lies, and democracy: the press and the public / edited by
  Michael Bromley and Hugh Stephenson.
    p. cm.
  Includes bibliographical references and index.
  ISBN 0-582-29332-4 (pbk.)
  1. Press–Great Britain. I. Bromley, Michael, 1947–
II. Stephenson, Hugh, 1938–
PN5114.S48 1998
072–dc21   97-26175
                                                                   CIP

Set by 7 in 10/11 pt Palatino
Produced through Longman Malaysia, LSP

Contents

CONTENTS

Contributors

Claude-Jean Bertrand is Professor Emeritus at the Institut français de presse (Université de Paris-2). He has specialized in the fields of 'world media' and 'media ethics' and has authored, co-authored or edited a dozen books devoted to Anglo-American civilization in general, to religion but mainly to media. He has published some 80 articles in Arabic, Chinese, English, French, Italian, Japanese, Russian, Spanish and eight other languages.

Michael Bromley is Director of the postgraduate programme in International Journalism, and deputy director of the Communications Policy and Journalism Research Unit at City University.

Andrew Calcutt is a former record producer. He has contributed to various publications, including *Arena, Esquire, futures, The Idler, Living Marxism, The Modern Review* and BBC2's *The Net*. His critical essay on the 'culture of crime' was published by Macmillan. He is currently a commissioning editor at Channel Cyberia.

Walter Jaehnig is a faculty member at Southern Illinois University, Carbondale. He is a former newspaper reporter and editor and holds a doctorate in sociology from Essex University.

Tom O'Malley is Senior Lecturer in Media Studies at the University of Glamorgan, Wales. Recent publications include *Closedown? The BBC and Government Broadcasting Policy* (Pluto, 1994); with Michael Harris (eds) *Studies in Newspaper and Periodical History* (Greenwood, 1996 and 1997) and with Michael Bromley (eds) *A Journalism Reader* (Routledge, 1997). He is co-editor of the journal *Media History*, and a member of the Campaign For Press and Broadcasting Freedom.

Adrian Page is Principal Lecturer in Media at the University of Luton.

Hugh Stephenson has been Professor of Journalism at City University since 1986. He was previously editor of the *New Statesman* from 1982 to 1986, and editor of *The Times Business News* from 1972 to 1982.

Christophe Texier is at the Institute for the Study of Language and Society at Aston University, Birmingham, and has also worked in the Department of Languages and European Studies. He has also taught at Leeds and Warwick Universities. His research and teaching areas are Media and Cultural Studies.

Barbara Thomaß is at the Institut für Politische Wissenschaft at the University of Hamburg.

John Tulloch is Associate Head of the School of Communication, University of Westminster and a member of the Centre for Communication and Information Studies.

Robert M. Worcester is chairman of MORI (Market and Opinion Research International), visiting Professor in the Department of Journalism at City University and Governor at the London School of Economics.

Acknowledgements

We are grateful to the following for permission to reproduce copyright material:

National Union of Journalists for 'National Union of Journalists' Code of Conduct'; Press Complaints Commission for a Table and 'The Press Complaints Commission Code of Practice, 1995'.

Introduction

It is instructive to observe, year on year, thirty or more young people from around the world, who either are or intend to be journalists, and who come to study journalism for a year at City University, encountering the British press at first hand for the first time. Their reactions are invariably ones of disbelief, dismay and, occasionally, disgust – in tabloid terms, one might say SHOCK HORROR. Their overwhelming view is that no press is as intrusive, offensive, quasi-pornographic, arrogant, inaccurate, salacious and unprincipled. The press in other cultures shares many of these traits, of course. The 'tabloid' weekly magazine is largely a continental European product, and two of the three publications of this type with the largest UK circulations are owned by non-British companies. Rarely, however, does the press elsewhere appear to have all of these characteristics together: *Bild Zeitung* in Germany may be one of the partial exceptions (Weymouth 1996: 45–6). Where sections of the press in other cultures can be said to be as 'tabloid' in their approach, they are often marginalized, as in the USA where they have been moved symbolically from the news-stand to the supermarket shelf. In the UK, even the *Sport* titles, which, in keeping with common practice, are largely excluded from consideration in this volume because they don't seem to fit comfortably under the category 'press', nonetheless take their place alongside titles such as the *Financial Times* and *The Economist*.

Moreover, and almost incidentally, the British national press is also steadfastly metropolitan, unashamedly partisan, and controlled by an almost unhealthy oligopoly. Thus, the impression may be gained that the press in Britain is shaped exclusively by a mainstream, national 'tabloid' culture, emanating from London and exemplified by *The Sun* newspaper's populist conservatism and preoccupation with sex, sport, chauvinism, celebrity, competitions, free offers, and more sex. The relationship of the 'tabloid' press to the 'quality' press could be summed up no more succinctly than it was in *The Sun*'s advertising campaign which parodied that of the *Financial Times*: 'No *FT*, no comment', said one – 'No *Sun*, no fun', the other.

The readership for national tabloid newspapers – The *Mirror* and the *Daily Star*, and the Sunday titles the *News of the World*, *People* and *Sunday Mirror*, as well as *The Sun* – is considerably greater than for any other single, identifiable section of the British press. Each weekday and every Sunday more than 20 million people read at least one of these papers (*Press Gazette*, 14 Feb. 1997).[1] The 'tabloid' concentration on sex and celebrity, also dominates much of the magazine market. As well as a still-expanding 'celebrity' weekly sector more traditional women's magazines have increasingly turned to celebrities to maintain sales, while a reliance on sex has permeated even so-called women's fashion titles, and has been the basis for establishing a men's lifestyle sector (Jaynes and Smallman 1997). As many as two-thirds of British adults probably read a weekly magazine carrying substantial amounts of material on sex, television and celebrities (Cutts 1997).

By comparison, the market for the 'serious' press is small. The five broadsheet daily newspapers sell fewer than 3 million copies between them. The sales of the four 'quality' Sunday papers are about the same. This suggests a total readership for this type of press of no more than 7.5 million. No substantial weekly news magazine sector exists in the UK, except for *The Economist*, more than half of whose circulation is outside Britain. The so-called political weeklies – the *New Statesman* and *Spectator* – have struggled for many years even to survive. Given these statistics, there has been a great deal of pessimism about the future of the 'serious' press, in Britain as elsewhere (Dahlgren 1992: 7). This has tended to mask the underlying trends. The 'tabloid' national press, in fact, has been in steeper decline in terms of circulation since 1988 than the 'quality' press. This has been only partially mitigated by a policy of crude price-cutting introduced by News International in 1993 (McNair 1996: 9). The number of Britons reading a 'popular' newspaper, in the widest sense of the term, has probably almost halved from 45 million in 1959 (McNair 1996: 159–60). It is this secular decline which has provided the backdrop to the circulation 'wars' and editorial excesses among the tabloids since the 1970s. Furthermore, it became received wisdom that the key readership was young and in the lower social class groups, a target pursued by the *Daily Mirror* since the mid-1930s. This readership – classified by a process of reduction in the 1970s and 1980s to C_2s, but undoubtedly a far more diverse and vague grouping than that – was preponderantly a mid-market one until perhaps the early 1960s (Tunstall 1996: 9–10). Particularly after 1945, the *Mirror* attracted many of these readers away from mid-market newspapers: its 'high point' has been put in the period 1953 to 1961, although its circulation peaked in the mid-1960s. All the same, the mid-market contained both the 'mass' readership of the *Daily Express*, whose circulation reached 4 million in 1949, and left-of-centre titles such as the *Daily Herald*, which was outselling the *Daily Mail* in 1945, and the *News Chronicle* (Engel 1996: 174, 182–3). In 1965 mid-market titles still accounted for 49 per cent of national daily newspaper sales. This 'old popular market' withered away thereafter (Bromley 1995: 21–2).

There was one major underlying reason for this: a significant working-class readership for far more sensational, scandal-mongering and salacious Sunday newspapers had existed since the mid-nineteenth century. The *Daily Mirror* had gone only so far in transferring this approach to the daily press (Tunstall 1996: 11). When Rupert Murdoch bought *The Sun* in 1969, the paper at first attempted to imitate the *Mirror*; then in the 1970s it adopted far more fully the values of the 'popular' Sunday press. Since *The Sun* had originally replaced the *Herald*, at a stroke about 5 million readers were moved out of the mid-market sector. Coincidentally, the number of national newspapers published in tabloid format rose from only three in 1962 to eleven in 1990 (Bromley 1995: 22). These changes did indeed prove attractive to younger, more working-class readers: in the mid-1970s 45 per cent of 15–24-year-olds read *The Sun* (Christmas 1997: 19). In 1995, *The Sun*, the *Mirror* and the *Daily Star* still attracted, in that order, younger and lower social class readerships. Not surprisingly, the broadsheet *Daily Telegraph* conversely had the oldest and a far higher social class readership. The distribution of readers among the rest of the national daily press did not follow as simple a pattern, however.

Two of the remaining mid-market titles, the *Daily Mail* and *Daily Express*, had older and more 'upmarket' appeal than their designation might suggest: the third title in that sector, *Today* (which closed in 1995) a younger and more 'downmarket' one. The three other broadsheets, *The Times*, *The Guardian* and *The Independent* were predictably 'upmarket', but each had younger readerships than the *Mirror*, and *The Guardian*'s readership was proportionately younger than that of *The Sun* (Tunstall 1996: 93). Undoubtedly there had been shifts in reading habits. By 1997 the number of 15–24-year-olds reading *The Sun* had fallen by more than one-third to 29 per cent, and the *Mirror* was attracting only 13 per cent of this age group: a decline of 60 per cent on the mid-1970s. On the other hand, the number of 18–24-year-olds reading broadsheet daily papers rose in the same period from 6 per cent to 14 per cent (Christmas 1997: 19).

The statistical evidence suggests that while, as a rule, there is direct correlation between tabloid and broadsheet formats and values, and the age and social class of readerships, the relationship is not fixed. In other words, this relationship between the press and its readers is not determined solely by 'the market'.

More than political economy

Intercourse between the press and its readers is rarely a private matter: it is nearly always moderated on behalf of some notion of 'the public interest', a factor enshrined in the code of practice of the Press Complaints Commission (PCC). The focus of this book is this intercession, which takes two principal forms: regulation and control, which is usually compulsory and commonly at least underwritten, if not enforced, by the State; and accountability, in which the consenting parties enter into voluntary arrangements. More often than not, the two work in tandem: the imposition of broad formal controls alone tends to prove counter-productive as it risks stripping the press of the credibility of critical independence. Effective 'answerability' of the press is dependent on a complex matrix of interconnected actions, processes and people, which facilitates criticism, monitoring, access and greater awareness. While Britain arguably has the most sophisticated press in Europe, it can be said that in practice press 'answerability' works at a rather primitive level. A main conclusion to be drawn from this book is that, while many of the necessary processes and procedures for ensuring press 'answerability' exist, few operate successfully, and for little of the time. The two main problems identified in the chapters which follow are: (i) a lack of individuals and groups willing systematically to utilize the means and measures available; and (ii) overlapping this, the inaccessibility of the press which may be said to be overly protective of its so-called editorial integrity.

In giving weight to each element which makes up an 'answerability' system, every press culture develops its own framework, which is also constitutive of that culture. A society whose legal system traditionally emphasizes the public responsibility of individual participation in society, while developing statutory and case law specifically exempting powerful groups and individuals from the requirement of disclosure, is likely to encourage a press which almost randomly intrudes into personal privacy but is disabled in pursuing malfeasance among those holding power. A system of 'answerability' which challenged such fundamental precepts would inevitably sit uneasily within the broader culture. The intense variability of media accountability systems (MAS) is a clear manifestation of the cultural basis of 'answerability': Bertrand counts more than thirty (Chapter 8). It is surely here that we can begin to outline the peculiar configuration of the British press which is so noticeable to outsiders. The idea that the primacy of 'the market' by itself will superimpose uniformity and priority is demonstrably untenable (Hetherington 1989).

There is no longer any serious debate about whether the press functions better in some kind of idealized Fourth Estate role under the conditions of either a 'free' market or an interventionist state. Nor are the values of the press any longer measured in terms of its constancy and comprehensiveness which were so prized by eighteenth-century bourgeois readers. Distinctions are far more rarely drawn between 'argument [and] persuasion' and 'influence and interest' (Harris 1996: 106–7). The so-called 'freeing' of the press to act as an independent critic and formulator of public opinion in the mid-nineteenth century was driven by an ideology comprised of both philosophy and commercial opportunism (Boyce 1978: 24–5). The abolition of the 'taxes on knowledge' began with Gladstone's 'free trade' Budget of 1853 as part of the removal of duty on hundreds of consumer goods. The result was that, whereas the 'mass' press came to depend on promoting its own self-interests as an increasingly industrialized enterprise, the 'quality' press relied on political sponsorship, subsidy and patronage (Boyce 1978: 28–9). Critics of both the left and the right have subsequently argued that the press has been too much a hostage of either the corporatist state or corporate capital (Whittam Smith 1989; Curran and Seaton 1991). Yet, rather than seeking a more delicate balance of forces, in the 1980s it was widely assumed that the market alone could deliver a press responsive to both its own readers and the wider public.

In many respects the apogee of this experiment was the removal of the national newspaper industry from its traditional location in Fleet Street and its complete restructuring as a business in 1986–7. An essential precondition was a further concentration of the ownership of titles and the emergence of a new group of press barons, epitomized both in practice and symbolically by Rupert Murdoch. The favourable political and economic context was provided by the Thatcher government after 1979. After Murdoch had removed his four newspapers from Fleet Street to Wapping making more than 5000 print workers redundant, Margaret Thatcher claimed, rather ambiguously, 'We have brought sanity to Fleet Street.' The 'Wapping revolution' was widely hailed as a liberation of the national newspaper industry, which would lead to a flowering of responsible, quality journalism and a greater diversity of choice. This optimistic view received support initially from the launch of new broadsheet titles, such as *The Independent* in 1989. In practice, however, the main consequence of the breaking of the power of the London print unions by Murdoch over Wapping was to open the eyes of national newspaper managements to the potential for profitability of already well-established titles, if they were managed and marketed aggressively with the aim of maximizing revenues and minimizing costs.

The immediate consequence was, in fact, a crisis in what used to be Fleet Street. At no time since the end of the Second World War did it seem more likely that explicit statutory control of the press would be introduced in response to a series of misdemeanours committed by tabloid newspapers. The crisis can be dated with some precision as lasting from 1987 until 1993. In 1987 the *Daily Star* embarked on its notorious foray into 'bonk journalism', and the first of a number of MPs made an attempt to introduce legislation to control the activities of the press. There followed a series of press outrages – including the misreporting of the Hillsborough football-stadium disaster and intrusions into the privacy of members of the royal family – matched almost step-by-step by warnings from government ministers, an inquiry chaired by David Calcutt, who later produced a follow-up report, a National Heritage select committee report, a White Paper on privacy legislation from the Lord Chancellor, and a number of high profile libel cases. Moreover, the heyday of the tabloid press had already passed: the height of the popularity of the best-selling national daily newspaper of the 1970s and 1980s, *The Sun*, came in the early years of the decade (Church 1997: 218).

For the most part the crisis seemed to pass, ironically, when, after the re-election of John Major's government in 1992, much of the tabloid national press began to abandon its traditional support for the Conservative Party in general, and Major in particular, and to pursue a new theme of political 'sleaze', exposing a number of ministers' and MPs' sexual and financial embarrassments. It can be argued that the press itself responded to the 'formidable backlash of opinion' generated at this time through a commitment to making the PCC, introduced in 1991 as a successor body to the much criticized Press Council, an effective self-regulatory instrument. All the same, there was little evidence, until at least 1995, of the tabloid press recognizing a need to change its journalistic values (McNair 1996: 165–77). Indeed, it is argued by Bromley (Chapter 2) that a legacy of this period has been the adoption of many of those values by other sectors of the press. In broader terms, the late 1980s and the early 1990s hold the key to understanding the mutual relationship between the press and its audiences, and they are a major concern of this book.

What has emerged from this period of crisis is a renewal of the commitment to voluntarism, a reiteration of the distaste of jurisprudence, and a restatement of the liberal belief that the considerable disadvantages do not outweigh the often hidden benefits of tolerating a largely unfettered press. The place of the reader and the public in this arrangement, however, is uncertain and problematical.

Privacy and citizenship

Invasions of privacy appear more important to the press than they are to the public at large. Britain in the mid-1990s is a more invasive society, as Worcester's data show (Chapter 3). It remains an open question whether the press is the cause or effect of this. What is undeniable is that in the course of the past century the press has reported more fully and more deeply into the realm of private life. As Stephenson (Chapter 1) points out, the public fascination with revelations of the lives of the rich and famous has a relatively long history. This has played a role, too, in the process of democratization, and the conspiracy of silence entered into by the press and others over the relationship between the King and Mrs Simpson in the 1930s remains a potent symbol of the demeaning and damaging nature of secrecy and deference in the British system of governance. Yet such arguably beneficial exposés have traditionally been accompanied by more prurient journalism fixated with sex, and dubious journalistic methods which have not fallen short of telling lies.

Thus, while particularly since the late 1980s there has been a burgeoning of titles whose primary purpose is to expose what was once considered to be wholly private, as Bromley argues (Chapter 2), there is an honourable tradition to both sensationalism and press exposé. Moreover, many of the 'victims' of this press treatment not only willingly collaborate in their own exposure, but often exist, to solicit it. Celebrity journalism would hardly flourish if there were not people deliberately seeking iconization. Yet one aspect of such trivialization of the press, Bromley suggests, is the undermining of journalists' perceptions of their role as quasi-professionals guided in their work by what is in 'the public interest'. Worcester's poll results give credence to this insecurity: public trust in journalists reached a particularly low point at the time when a tolerance of invasions of privacy was increasing.

It also coincided with the emergence of journalism as a graduate profession. By 1996 more than 80 per cent of new entrants into journalism had completed a university education.[2] Since 1970, journalism has been taught as a university subject, chiefly at postgraduate level until a large number of undergraduate courses were introduced in the early 1990s. Nevertheless, the development of an ethos of professionalism has been slow. Thomaß's survey of British journalism schools (Chapter 10) discovered a new, although as yet inchoate, movement to integrate ethics into a curriculum until now largely prescribed by industrial bodies, particularly employers. Despite the continued opposition of the industrial training bodies and the resistance of students, the possibility of a new generation of more reflective practitioners emerging from journalism schools is now a real one. Many of the university lecturers and tutors interviewed gave the impression that this was a project initiated by the universities as part of their wider remit to develop critical reflection in their students. The 'real world', Page suggests (Chapter 9), is having an impact, too, however. The increased reliance on codes of conduct and practice which has resulted from the establishment of the PCC – although the National Union of Journalists' code dates back to 1936 – has begun to set new paradigms, affecting the assumptions made about the role of journalists in society. The need for reflection is greater and more urgent, as the idea diminishes that a journalist need only 'publish and be damned'.

The main outcome of such heightened awareness of the consequences of publication ought to be a greater protection for the public as a whole. However, Stephenson argues, that as the 'public service' remit of the press has diminished, to be replaced by aggressive marketing driven by business objectives, readers have become consumers of leisure products devoid of any meaningful moral dimension. The PCC does not, and cannot, adequately perform the role of protector of the general public in its present form, Tulloch claims (Chaper 5). Its existence is too closely woven into the complex web of patronage and subservience which characterizes 'the Establishment'. In practice its interests lie, as exemplified by its adjudications, with the 'rich and famous' rather than the ordinary citizen. Behind this inactivity on behalf of the public at large lies an inability to tackle the core problem of the lack of accountability of powerful personal ownership. O'Malley produces evidence (Chapter 6) that public concern over such matters intensified in the 1940s, and that demands for greater and more transparent public responsibility in the press grew into the 1970s and possibly beyond. That on three occasions between 1947 and 1974 governments saw fit to set up Royal Commissions on the press indicates the extent to which they took public disquiet seriously. This break with the nineteenth century liberal tradition towards 'freedom of the press' was itself significant. In the end, however, it proved impossible to institute greater 'answerability' of the press in the face of alarms raised by proprietors and managers about the threat of state interference.

Deploying a business term – 'quality control' – Bertrand proposes (Chapter 8) the adoption of a multiplex system of media accountability centrally involving active citizens in partnership with media profession-als. Elements of such a system have enjoyed some success in the USA and attracted interest in the UK, as Thomaß's research confirms. Never-theless, active citizenship, although it may often find expression in con-sumer activism, remains a more potent concept on the other side of the Atlantic. This does not mean that the greater European inclination to rely on the collectivist response of state regulation is a manifestation of the inability of individuals and groups to act effectively in the event of media abuses. Indeed, as Calcutt argues (Chapter 12), given the in-ability or unwillingness of the British State over fifty years to confront the consequences of the concentration of ownership of the press, ordinary citizens can expect little effective protection from that quarter. The decline in newspaper readerships charted by Worcester is perhaps one indica-tion of citizens calling the press to account. Another, Calcutt suggests, is cultural resistance to the images and messages purveyed by the press.

More interactively readers have demanded the press account for it-self in print through the mechanism of letters to the editor. Correspond-ence columns meet many of the criteria set by Bertrand for media accountability: ideally, they are open for criticism and monitoring. They may also indirectly serve the function of sensitizing both media profes-sionals and citizens. In so far as national daily newspapers, as busi-nesses, have adopted the notion of 'giving the customers what they want', they have to varying degrees modified their approaches to corre-spondence with their readers to meet their changing expectations. Bromley (Chapter 11) suggests that this has not resulted in greater ac-countability or transparency, however. On the contrary, editorial con-trol over access to correspondence columns may have further marginalized readers as potential watchdogs of the press.

There is little evidence, despite cultural stereotyping, that the British public has been unduly passive in its relationships with the press. As Texier points out (Chapter 4), there is a tendency to view the British press as exceptional. This may have derived from the idea that Britain occupied a place in respect of its press somewhere between the more highly regulated systems of continental Europe and the libertarianism of the US. In the 1990s, at least, experiences appear to be converging. Texier and Jaehnig (Chapter 7) illustrate the extent to which news-papers and publics in both Western Europe and North America share the struggle to redefine their relationships to each other in the face of significant changes in the political economy of the press. The assump-tion of the 1980s that these changes by themselves would reconstitute those relationships can no longer be held to be true. The era of economic liberalization, with its faith in 'the customer as king', has no more de-livered press 'answerability' than did the period of social democracy which preceded it.

In the US a new partnership of citizens and journalists, formed under the identity of 'public' or 'civic' journalism, is seen by many as offering the best way of ensuring the accountability of the press. As Jaehnig points out, many feel this is no more than a ruse to prolong the life of the print media at a time when the 'information super-highway' threatens to obliterate them. The conviction that such electronically delivered communications are inherently interactive, more accessible and less subject to professional editorial control, it is argued, will make them more accountable and help them supersede the press. Alternatively, the traditional media have already begun to colonize the Internet, if only to protect a £3.5bn-a-year UK newspaper industry: in 1995 it was estimated that more than 300 European newspapers were on the worldwide web, and most of the major British press conglomerates have a presence there (Tumber and Bromley 1997: 13). Digitalization is as unlikely as liberalization has been to render the press accountable.

Death of a princess

All these issues were given added importance with the death of Diana, Princess of Wales in a car accident in Paris in August 1997 while being pursued by paparazzi on motorcycles, apparently intent on getting photographs of her with her friend Dodi Al Fayed. There followed an unprecedented outpouring of public grief and anger, much of it aimed at the press. Blame was laid on the methods of the mainly non-British paparazzi and on the newspaper and magazine editors and proprietors who bought their photographs (Culf 1997). A few former tabloid newspaper editors admitted publicly to feelings of culpability, and the editor of *The Guardian* said interest in the relationship between the princess and Mr Al Fayed had served to send the press 'hurtling out of control' (BBC 1997); but the press's most articulated defence was that editorial judgement was driven solely by market considerations. News and photographs of the princess raised circulations; the trade in them would stop only if the public appetite abated, Max Hastings, editor of the *London Evening Standard*, argued, and the chairman of the PCC's code of practice committee, Sir David English, believed the public's reaction betrayed its own sense of 'guilt' (BBC 1997). Furthermore, commenting on photographs of the princess and Mr Al Fayed taken prior to their deaths by a paparazzo who supposedly made $3 million from them, Peter Preston (1997), pointed out that the culture of business competitiveness, which was lauded almost everywhere, encouraged paparazzi methods. Moreover, the princess had herself profited from this activity, having courted publicity to establish and maintain her public role, making what sometimes appeared 'a Faustian bargain . . . with the media' (Robertson 1997).

This tragic case re-focused attention on debates over privacy, press intrusion, harassment by photographers and journalists, and the editorial values of newspapers. It placed added pressure on the system of voluntary self-regulation operated by the PCC, and led to renewed calls for legislation. The extent of the spontaneous mass public mourning which followed the accident suggested a potential for a far wider active citizen participation in making the press answerable for its actions and philosophy in covering public figures. Whether, ultimately, this potential would be realised remained an open question.

Notes

1 Based on Audit Bureau of Circulation figures for January 1997. Readership of daily papers includes figures for the *Daily Record*, Glasgow; that for Sunday papers excludes figures for the *Sunday Sport*.
2 This figure was supplied by the Newspaper Society in January 1997.

References

BBC (1997) *Today*, Radio 4, Sept. 3.

Boyce, G. (1978) 'The Fourth Estate: the reappraisal of a concept', in Boyce, G., Curran, J. and Wingate, P. (eds) *Newspaper History: From the 17th Century to the Present*, Constable, London, 19–40.

Bromley, M. (1995) *The Press in Twentieth-Century Britain*, University of Huddersfield, Huddersfield.

Christmas, L. (1997) 'Jolly reads', *The Journalist's Handbook* 49 April: 16–19.

Church, J. (ed.) (1997) *Social Trends* 27, The Stationery Office, London.

Culf, A., (1997) 'Press chances it on Privacy', *The Guardian* Sept. 3: 6.

Curran, J. and Seaton, J. (1991) *Power without Responsibility: The Press and Broadcasting in Britain*, 4th edn, Routledge, London.

Cutts, P. (1997) 'Magazine data', *Magazine News* 40 March: 22–3.

Dahlgren, P. (1992) 'Introduction', in Dahlgren, P. and Sparks, C. (eds) *Journalism and Popular Culture*, Sage, London.

Engel, M. (1996) *Tickle the Public: One Hundred Years of the Popular Press*, Victor Gollancz, London.

Harris, B. (1996) *Politics and the Rise of the Press: Britain and France, 1620–1800*, Routledge, London.

Hetherington, A. (1989) 'The mass media', in Kavanagh, D. and Seldon, A. (eds) *The Thatcher Effect: A Decade of Change*, Oxford University Press, London, 290–304.

Jaynes, M. and Smallman, A (1997) 'Consumer magazine ABCs', *Press Gazette* 21 Feb: 11–13.

McNair, B. (1996) *News and Journalism in the UK*, 2nd edn, Routledge, London.

Preston, P., (1997) 'Science Friction', *The Guardian Weekend* Aug. 16: 5.

Robertson, G. (1997) 'Press for a legal right to inquire – but not to intrude', *The Guardian* Sept. 2: 18.

Tumber, H. and Bromley, M. (1997) 'Political communication in cyberspace', paper delivered to the International Conference on Media and Politics, Brussels, Catholic University, 28 Feb.

Tunstall, J. (1996) *Newspaper Power: The New National Press in Britain*, Clarendon Press, Oxford.

Weymouth, T. (1996) 'The media in Britain', in Weymouth, T. and Lamizet, B. (eds) *Markets and Myths: Forces for Change in the European Media*, Longman, London, 37–75.

Whittam Smith, A. (1989) 'A new "golden age"?', *British Journalism Review* 1 (1): 19–21.

PART I

The press and its discontents

CHAPTER 1

Tickle the public: Consumerism rules

Hugh Stephenson

Private Members' Bills are a curious feature of the British parliamentary system. They almost never turn into legislation and the rare exceptions only do so because the government of the day decides for some reason to take a particular Bill under its protective wing. But every now and then a head of steam builds up behind a particular Private Member's Bill to a point where the administration, though still having no intention of accepting the legislation initiated by a backbencher, concludes that it must at least seem to respond.

Such was the situation in the summer of 1989 with two Private Members' Bills introduced by the MPs who had won first and second place in the ballot for the 1988/89 parliamentary session. John Browne, the Conservative Member of Parliament for Winchester, had introduced a Bill on the protection of privacy. His own financial and marital affairs had been extensively raked over by the newspapers and he was subsequently deselected as a candidate by his constituency association before the 1992 general election. And Tony Worthington, the Clydebank Labour Member of Parliament, had introduced a Bill to establish a statutory right of reply for those finding their names in the media. Both Bills received substantial cross-party support in the House of Commons. The Home Office did not like either Bill as drafted, but it became clear when the Browne Bill reached its Report stage (having had its first and second readings and having been through committee) that it would require whipped votes to stop it going to its third and final reading. Mrs Thatcher's Cabinet did not like the prospect of having to use the Whips Office to kill a measure introduced by one of its own backbenchers and having wide support across the political spectrum. It, therefore, reached for the time-honoured compromise. It offered the House a committee of enquiry. In return John Browne agreed to withdraw his Bill and the Worthington Bill similarly fell.

Thus came into being the Last Chance Saloon. In order to comfort John Browne's many supporters in the House, to put the frighteners on the national press and to give the enquiry a clear sense of direction, David Mellor, then a junior minister in the Home Office, produced his now celebrated soundbite. The press, he said, was drinking in the Last Chance Saloon. If it did not get its self-regulatory act together this time, with the help of what became known as the Calcutt Committee, nameless things (by implication statutory controls) would be visited upon it. For several months uncertainty reigned, because the Home Office had not prepared the ground for its proposed enquiry. Another Royal Commission was out of the question, because Mrs Thatcher had closed this route on the grounds that Royal Commissions were cumbersome substitutes for the smack of firm government. However, neither the exact form of the enquiry nor its chairperson had been agreed. In the interests of saving public expenditure, private pressure was put on the press to fund the proposed enquiry itself. But these overtures were firmly resisted. In the event the Home Office settled on a conventional departmental committee of enquiry, with the barrister, David Calcutt QC, as chairman.[1] Its terms of reference were:

> In the light of the recent public concern about intrusions into the private lives of individuals by certain sections of the press, to consider what measures (whether legislative or otherwise) are needed to give further protection to individual privacy from the activities of the press and improve recourse against the press for the individual citizen, taking account of existing remedies, including the law on defamation and breach of confidence; and to make recommendations. (Calcutt 1990:1)

Without question, during the six years or so from 1988 there was an air of continual crisis in the three-way relationship between the press (particularly the national tabloid press), the general public and the government. The sense of crisis continued until the summer of 1995, with the Lord Chancellor's Department and the House of Commons National Heritage Committee, under its Labour chairman Gerald Kaufman, being in favour of introducing a new civil wrong of infringement of privacy and Calcutt (by now Sir David) in his personal review (Calcutt 1993) of things since his first Report in 1990 being strongly in favour of the Press Complaints Commission being replaced by a statutory Press Complaints Tribunal.

As time wore on it became clear that there were divisions within the government over how to proceed. A government White Paper expected in the summer of 1993, though drafted, did not emerge from the Cabinet sub-committee dealing with it. There was considerable confusion between the Home Office (and after its creation the Department of National Heritage) on the one hand and the Lord Chancellor's Department on the other. Sensing these divisions, the Association of British Editors, the Guild of Editors and the International Press Institute mounted a lobby and published an 'Alternative White Paper' at the start of 1994, analysing the weaknesses of the various proposals for change that had been put forward (Stephenson 1994). By the end of 1994, with the next general election increasingly casting its shadow before it and with the national media continuing successfully to rattle John Major's govenment with exposures of sexual peccadillos and financial sleaze, it became clear that substantial legislation to change the status of the press was no longer imminent. The whole issue was finally kicked into touch in July 1995 when the new Secretary of State for National Heritage, Virginia Bottomley, published the government's reply to the National Heritage Select Committee's 1993 recommendations. This reply contained a remarkably robust defence of the *status quo*, perhaps the most robust in any published government document in modern times. It asserted: 'The right to receive and impart ideas and information, in other words, to freedom of expression, is one of the cornerstones of a democratic society.' It referred to the protection of freedom of expression enshrined in Article 19 of the International Covenant of Civil and Political Rights and Article 10 of the European Convention on Human Rights, to both of which the United Kingdom is a signatory. In rejecting the recommendations of the Select Committee and from Sir David Calcutt, it went on to say:

> A free press is vital to a free country. Many would think the imposition of statutory control on newspapers invidious because it might open the way for regulating content, thereby laying the Government open to charges of press censorship. Furthermore, the Government does not believe that it would be right in this field to delegate decisions about when a statutory remedy should be granted to a regulator such as a tribunal. (National Heritage 1995)

For the time being the issue of press self-regulation had been removed from the political agenda.

Nevertheless, for five years or more until that moment it had been widely accepted wisdom that the offending sections of the press were becoming ever more sensational and ever less responsible. Public support for this view was reflected in a series of high six-figure jury awards and out-of-court settlements in libel cases involving public figures. The size of some of the libel settlements during this period clearly implied that they were intended to be more as a punishment of 'irresponsible' newspapers than as a measure of the 'wronged' person's personal hurt. Those arguing that the press was incapable of effective self-regulation and that some kind of statutory intervention, akin to the controls on the content of broadcasting, were necessary and inevitable became confident that public opinion and the political tide were with them.

The authority of the Press Council, the print media's voluntary self-regulation system set up in 1953 in belated response to the criticisms of the 1949 Royal Commission on the Press, had been coming under increasing criticism during the 1980s. The most coherent single attack on it came in the form of a report written by the barrister Geoffrey Robertson on the basis of an enquiry into its workings by a group of individuals.[2] Robertson's report reviewed the way in which major national newspaper figures flouted or mocked Press Council adjudications (Robertson 1983: 4). In one case, Robertson noted, Sir John Junor, the editor of the *Sunday Express*, criticized for writing an offensive racial slur, had repeated it and counter-attacked the 'po-faced, pompous, pin-striped, humourless twits who sit on the Press Council' (*Sunday Express*, 3 September 1978). Another adjudication in October 1982 condemned *The*

Sun for publishing a 'sensationalized, distorted and racially emotive account of a demonstration by black people'. *The Sun* responded (8 October 1982) under the headline 'Paper They Can't Gag' by repeating the original charges, attacking those who had brought the complaint to the Press Council and boasting that '*The Sun* is flattered to be singled out as the target for complaint'.

Geoffrey Robertson also drew attention to the general flouting in 1983 of the Press Council's declaration of principle on cheque-book journalism in the case of Peter Sutcliffe, the 'Yorkshire Ripper'. The Press Council conducted a thorough investigation of the conduct of newspapers in reporting the case and in buying up the stories of members of Sutcliffe's family and other witnesses (Press Council 1983). Its criticisms were particularly severe of the *Daily Mail* and of its editor, Sir David English. It found that it had been hampered in its consideration of complaints against the paper 'by the behaviour of the *Daily Mail* which failed to disclose to the Council material clearly germane to the inquiry'. It regretted 'a persistent refusal by the editor of the *Daily Mail* to attend an oral inquiry and answer the complaints committee's questions in the presence of the complainant'. It found that, in the matter of cheque-book journalism, 'the explanation offered by the newspaper amounts to a confession that the *Daily Mail* was guilty of gross misconduct' (Press Council 1983: 148–54). The response to the Press Council's report by Sir David English in his own newspaper (under the headline 'Decision that Shackles Freedom') was to describe it as 'short-term, short-sighted and smug' and as proof 'yet again that the Press Council still does not truly understand the concept of a Free Press'.

Beyond this striking evidence about the unwillingness of such prominent national journalists and tabloid newspapers to accept the authority of the very self-regulatory body that they were supposedly supporting, Geoffrey Robertson also came to a further critical general conclusion of the Press Council's performance:

> Attention is drawn to the council's capacity for delay at every stage, the obstacles placed in the path of complainants, its lack of powers to ensure compliance with its rulings, and its failure to develop coherent standards, amongst other debilitating features of its operations. The evidence makes a powerful case for reform, if not for outright replacement, of the council by a new body empowered by law to enforce its rulings. (Robertson 1983: 134)

Given this background, it is not easy to explain why it was not until the end of the decade that the national press found itself in a state of crisis *vis-à-vis* parliament and public opinion. In many ways things were palpably better by 1990 than they had been at other times in the previous twenty years. In a concerted move, responding to the mood of the moment, all national daily and Sunday newspapers (with the single exception of the *Financial Times*, which in any case was somewhat outside the general debate about press ethics) had appointed their own 'readers' representative' or 'Ombudsman' with the aim of ensuring a better deal (or the appearance of a better deal) for readers who complained about some aspect of a paper's behaviour. The Press Council had undertaken a fundamental review of its own proceedings and had published for the first time a code of practice. Previously it had only based its adjudications on cumulative 'case law'.

Indeed a strong case could be made for the view that the popular press in the late 1980s was behaving no worse (and perhaps even a bit better) than it had done for a century and longer. Matthew Engel's recently published study of the last hundred years of the popular press in Britain, entitled *Tickle the Public*, is replete with headlines and articles that, with little or no change, might be found in today's *Sun, News of the World*, or *Mirror* (Engel 1996). The title of his book is taken from an anonymous nineteenth-century verse about Fleet Street which ran thus:

> Tickle the public, make 'em grin, The more you tickle, the more you'll win; Teach the public, you'll never get rich, You'll live like a beggar and die in a ditch. (Engel 1996: 17)

With the Sunday popular press the position has been even clearer for even longer. Engel quotes lines from a contemporary poet about the launch of the *Sunday Monitor* in about 1779, more than a decade before the founding of the *Observer* in 1791. 'So moral essays on his front appear/But all is carnal business in his rear.' Engel comments: 'And in essence nothing has changed in more than two centuries: carnal business and secret sins remain the business of the popular Sunday press, and though the veil of morality has become almost wholly moth-eaten over the years it has never entirely been tossed away' (Engel 1996: 26).

Further convincing evidence to support the case that the recent furore against an irresponsible press is more largely based on fashion rather than fact is to be found buried in the first official history of the National Union of Journalists (NUJ), *Gentlemen, the Press!* (Mansfield 1943). The author, F.J. Mansfield, had been president of the NUJ at the end of the First World War. He was a journalist on *The Times* from 1914 to 1934 and taught for ten years on the pioneer university course in journalism run at London University between the wars. His account of the developing debates within the union from 1908 onwards about the need for higher ethical standards in the face of commercial pressures for more sensationalism and for intrusion into privacy and grief, leading eventually to the adoption of the NUJ's first 'Code of Professional Conduct' in 1936, has an entirely contemporary feel to it. The following extracts illustrate the point.

> Within the last few years the methods of sensational journalism have become invested with a sinister significance.

> Really the problem has always been with us ever since the first crude sheets, replete with horrors and marvels, were published. Why then has it aroused such widespread interest, and such profound public indignation, at this time of day? It may well be that it is the result of an ascending scale of taste and judgement applied to the Press, with a keener edge of social ethics, though of course those who exploit sensation defend their malpractices with the brazen

assertion that they are really 'giving the public what they want'. The question has become so acute in recent times that newspaper organizations have been compelled to give it serious consideration, on grounds of safety as well as morality. (Mansfield 1943: 524)

Mansfield's history of the first half of this century is full of concern about such developments as the employment by newspapers of convicted murderers and criminals as sources of information; reporters and photographers being required to use methods which 'were distressing to the people to whom they were applied, and often repugnant to the sense of decency of those who used them'; and appeals to 'proprietors, editors and managers to endeavour to come to a common understanding as to the limits of licence which should be allowed to, or imposed upon, their staffs'. He tells of one murder case (the 'notorious Exmoor mystery') where the conduct of some journalists was 'reprehensible in the highest degree'; of 'methods which might bring immediate benefit to the papers which took advantage of them' but which 'tended to weaken public confidence in the reliability, judgement, good sense and good taste of the Press'; of letters to *The Times* from 'prominent public persons who had suffered [by such methods]'; of Lady Ellerman, newly the widow of the shipping tycoon Sir John Ellerman, complaining to the Newspaper Society about the behaviour of photographers on her return from the continent and at her husband's actual funeral, behaviour condemned publicly by the Newspaper Society as 'an unusual and unfortunate example of a tendency created by severe competition between popular newspapers'; of the Newspaper Society pointing out that Lady Ellerman's complaints were not made against provincial newspapers, but against Fleet Street; of the Chief Constable of Blackburn giving his view that the then current wave of suicides was being 'fed by gruesome stories in the papers'; and of the 'possible danger of curtailment of the liberty of the reporter to print all that was said at inquests, unless due heed were given to the distinction between liberty and licence'.

All this sensationalism by sections of the national press in the late 1930s was presented in the context of a wider marketing policy of 'frantic and costly efforts to get readers by canvassing and gifts'. Writing in 1943, the NUJ's official historian was able to derive some comfort from a statement (in May that year) by the chairman of the *Daily Mirror*, John Cowley. Common sense, Cowley said, had returned to the industry and 'the old follies of gift schemes, canvassing, and free insurance have disappeared into newspaper history, and I hope that history will not repeat itself'. The outbreak of common sense which the *Daily Mirror* chairman welcomed in fact owed more to newsprint rationing than to rational management and the history of popular papers spending millions in order to buy readers has repeated itself continually ever since the end of the Second World War. Indeed, in recent times, with News International's declaration of its cover price 'war' aimed at dramatically increasing the circulation of *The Times*, the 'frantic and costly efforts' have spilled over from the popular to the broadsheet press.

The account provided by Mansfield of events during 1937 could (with just the dates changed) have been grist to the mill of Calcutt, or the House Commons National Heritage Select Committee in 1990.

> During 1937 the storm continued in full blast ... [The NUJ President] said that Fleet Street was chiefly guilty of putting human souls on the rack, for the provinces mainly observed the cannons of good taste ... [Liverpool journalists] deprecated the conduct of representatives of the national papers in London 'in the intrusion on private grief and muck-raking at the conclusion of Court cases' ... A member of the Union told [in the NUJ's own newspaper, the *Journalist*] how, when his brother was prostrated with grief at a fatal accident to his wife, 'a ghoulish minority of the Press visited his house with requests for pictures and interviews ... Telephone calls, hammering at the door, peals of the bell at the house of death – and then the bloodthirsty horde pursued their inquiries to the graveside at Hull. (Mansfield 1943: 524–8)

Apart from the slightly old-fashioned tone of the prose, the story that Mansfield is telling for the late 1930s could have been translated in its entirety fifty years into the late 1980s. We are left with the strong feeling that, if war had not supervened, a junior minister in the Home Office in 1938 might easily have thought it time to warn Fleet Street that it was drinking in the Last Chance Saloon; that the Lord Chancellor of the day might have contemplated a draft Bill for the protection of personal privacy; but that in the run-up to a general election in 1939 or 1940 Neville Chamberlain, not entirely sharing the view of his predecessor, Stanley Baldwin, that all newspaper proprietors wanted was 'power without responsibility – the prerogative of the harlot throughout the ages', would have persuaded his Cabinet that statutory control of the press, while tempting, would be full of difficulties and that, instead, the press should be told that it was being put on probation and given one further opportunity to regulate itself properly.

Thus, the argument seems to be strong that the journalistic values of today's popular press – and the reaction of politicians and the 'chattering classes' to them – are part of an historical continuum. Sex, lies, and the invasion of the privacy of individuals have certainly been an important part of the staple diet of popular British newspapers since popular British newspapers have existed. However, in certain respects something new also seems to have been happening. The remainder of this chapter will look at respects in which new factors have been at work in today's popular journalism.

The first obvious change in recent years is the extent to which all newspapers, but particularly the popular tabloids, have dropped the 'public service' aspect of their publishing and are now run as conventional businesses whose primary aim is to maximize revenue and minimize cost. Unlike broadcasting organizations, newspapers have not had formal public service obligations placed on them by statute or charter. However, daily national newspapers pitched at whatever readership market have, until the last decade or so, regarded their primary *raison d'être* as being the communication of and comment on news and current affairs.

The point should not be exaggerated. Even the most high-minded broadsheets have always made concessions to the need to 'tickle their public'. For example, the *Sunday Express* first started to carry a regular crossword puzzle for its readers in 1924. Among the heavyweight daily papers, the *Daily Telegraph* followed suit in 1924, the *Manchester Guardian* in 1929 and *The Times* in 1930. However, the situation where the content of all newspapers is decided more on marketing grounds than on the basis of some abstract idea of 'what is news' is a condition of the last two decades. It has been reinforced by more and more stringent control of editorial costs, reflecting the fact that the managements (and in particular the financial directors) in the newspaper industry now have much more nearly the authority and status of their equivalents in normal businesses.

The change is most striking in the popular tabloids, but it is also clear across the whole of the national newspaper industry. Since market research and editorial instinct both combine in coming to the conclusion that tabloid newspaper readerships are only marginally interested in hard news, have no interest in foreign news, but will always read human interest stories and are obsessed by show business and the royal family, the contents of the popular tabloids have been adjusted accordingly. The expensive parts of the editorial budget, like the coverage of foreign news, have been ruthlessly pruned.

It had always been the case that popular British Sunday newspapers thrived on this fare. Engel notes this phenomenon from the very start of regular Sunday journalism at the end of the eighteenth century:

> the Sunday *Morning Herald* loftily dismissed its rivals as weekly papers rather than dailies and said that it would provide the same service as a daily newspaper. It failed. Thus the American tradition, that a Sunday newspaper was a bigger, fatter version of the same paper that came through the door six days a week, never had a chance. In Britain Sundays were to be different. (Engel 1996: 26)

The transfer of popular Sunday newspaper values, epitomized for more than a century by the *News of the World*, to the popular daily market dates from 1969 when Rupert Murdoch bought the moribund *Sun* from IPC. As his biographer notes,

> Murdoch needed no market research to tell him what *The Sun* should be: a daily version of the *News of the World*. He considered the *Mirror* the prime example of the 'gentrification of the press'. [Hugh] Cudlipp had tried to take it upmarket and it now offered serious, investigative sections on contemporary political issues which Murdoch saw as pretentious. He thought readers wanted more fun in their tabloid, and that they hated being preached at. The *Mirror* was the soft underbelly of the tabloid market. (Shawcross 1992: 152)

Although the stylized Page Three nude did not become an established feature of *The Sun* for a further six years, sex became the basis of the formula that transformed it into a publishing phenomenon. By 1978 the paper's circulation had risen from just over 1 million to almost 4 million, at which point the rising *Sun*'s sales graph crossed that of the falling *Mirror*.

By that time the *Mirror* had lost its editorial nerve and sense of direction, as had the *Daily Star*, the *Express*'s Manchester-based tabloid sister paper, and the *Daily Sketch* had given up the struggle and merged itself with the *Daily Mail*. During the rest of the 1970s, the *Mirror* without conviction or flair followed in the wake of *The Sun* in developing the new formula for modern tabloid journalism, a process only accelerated when IPC sold the *Mirror* to Robert Maxwell in 1984. By then the *Sun/Mirror* duopoly dominating popular daily tabloid journalism in the United Kingdom was fully established.

Rupert Murdoch made a second major contribution in the switch from 'editorial' to 'marketing' as the driving force in national journalism, when he took on and defeated the Fleet Street print unions and moved the four News International titles (the *Sunday Times*, *The Times*, the *News of the World* and *The Sun*) to new technology production at Wapping in 1986. Paradoxically, the stranglehold that the London branches of the print unions had been allowed by weak and incompetent managements to establish over the operations of national newspapers meant that normal commercial considerations scarcely applied to these businesses. Since the print unions had managed to impose hugely inflated production costs on the industry and had established a position where they could effectively block innovation and expansion, national newspapers were substantially owned and run in the four decades after the war for motives other than direct profit maximization. Most newspaper proprietors in this period were in effect 'vanity publishers', who derived their satisfaction in other ways than making profit. For some it was social cachet and political influence. For some it was the hope that national newspaper ownership would produce commercial advantages in other areas. Rupert Murdoch's vision was to see that, if British newspapers could be run on these lines at a modest loss, run properly they could generate huge profits.

The initial reaction to the Wapping revolution was that it would allow a hundred new flowers to bloom. Indeed, in anticipation of Wapping, new national daily titles had already appeared, produced outside the restraints placed by the unions on existing titles and using the new computerized technology. *The Independent* was launched by three former *Telegraph* journalists in 1986 and Eddy Shah founded *Today* in the same year. The belief that this revolution would revive the market for 'serious' daily journalism, free from 'tabloid values' was symbolized by *The Independent*'s decision not to be drawn into the general obsession with stories about the royal family. For example, when the Duchess of York gave birth to her first child on 8 August 1988, the story was on every front page except *The Independent*'s, which the following day only carried a short, single paragraph news-in-brief item at the foot of a column on its second page (Glover 1993: 144).

This commitment by *The Independent* to austere news values did not survive the financial crises which rapidly engulfed the paper. On a wider plane the realization quickly dawned that the financial and managerial freedom regained by newspaper managements as a result of the breaking of print-union power by Wapping could be used to great effect by existing and established titles to market themselves aggressively and to expand in previously blocked directions. The result has been an explosion, not of 'serious' journalism, which if anything has been further reduced in terms of space and resources, but in terms of sections of papers designed to appeal to the leisure interests of readers and to advertisers. A symbolic example of this is the way in which broadsheet newspapers, like *The Times*, now devote pages of ostensibly sports news space to columns of 'fantasy football' lists and results.

Most significant, perhaps, of all the changes in the last two decades has been a legacy of Mrs Thatcher's long period of government. The return to neo-classical economics and the rejection of concepts of social cohesion and public responsibility embodied by that Thatcherism helped to reinforce the view that newspapers are just a business like any other. This was not the view that informed, for example, the three post-war Royal Commissions on the Press. To paraphrase the words employed by Virginia Bottomley in 1995, those Royal Commissions based their investigations and reports on the real belief that a 'free press is one of the cornerstones of a democratic society'. They also worked on the assumption that a democratic society required a plural and healthy press, free from the dangers of oligopoly. The 1962 Royal Commission, chaired by Lord Shawcross, was particularly critical about the failure of the Press Council to analyse the factors leading to an unhealthy concentration in newspaper ownership and to give publicity to the public interest considerations involved (Royal Commission 1962: paras 323–4). The 1962 Royal Commission's main recommendation was that the government should establish a new Press Amalgamations Court, with the power to prevent future newspaper mergers above a certain circulation threshold (300 000 copies) unless it were satisfied that the merger would positively serve the public interest in the accurate presentation of news and the free expression of opinion. Unless those seeking a merger could persuade the new court that freedom and variety of opinion were not likely to be reduced, the presumption should be that it would be against the public interest and should not be allowed to proceed.

The Wilson Labour Government elected in 1964 did not accept the idea of a wholly new court, but it enacted the Shawcross recommendations in a watered-down form. Now incorporated in the Fair Trading Act 1973 (Sections 57 to 61) the new provisions laid down that any acquisition of a newspaper with a circulation of over 30 000 by a group which already had titles whose total circulation was over 500 000 required the consent of the relevant Secretary of State, who must not give such consent until the proposals have been examined by the Monopolies Commission to see whether they are in the public interest. This remains the law to this day.

The sale in 1966 by the Astor family of *The Times* to the Thomson Organization (which at the time owned the *Sunday Times*, over 30 other newspapers, over 60 magazines and two television companies) was referred to the Monopolies Commission. It gave its approval after obtaining certain formal assurances, in particular about the Thomson family's financial commitment to the continuation of *The Times*.

Subsequent national newspaper mergers involving Rupert Murdoch's publishing empire were never referred to the Monopolies Commission at all. In three cases the Secretary of State concerned made use of a loophole in the Fair Trading Act which allows for the possibility of a merger receiving his blessing without a Monopolies Commission enquiry, if the case is 'one of urgency' and where he is satisfied that 'the newspaper concerned is not economic as a going concern and as a separate newspaper'.

This provision was invoked without controversy in 1969 when Murdoch bought *The Sun*. There was general agreement, including among the trade unions involved, that, if anyone was foolish enough to think that they could make a go of *The Sun*, they were welcome to have it. However, it was invoked again with major controversy in 1981 when Mrs Thatcher's Government allowed Murdoch to buy the *Sunday Times* and *The Times* without a monopoly reference. The unhappy Secretary of State, John Biffen, was required in effect to declare to the House of Commons that white was black. He asserted, in defiance of known facts, that both titles were not economic as going concerns and that the matter was too urgent for it to be sent to the Monopolies Commission. The urgency derived solely from the fact that the Thomson Organization had chosen to announce that the titles would be closed if they were not sold together to Murdoch by a given date.

Two final cases indicated the Thatcher government's readiness to accept financial *force majeure* instead of insisting on the letter and spirit of the law designed to protect plurality in the media. The first was the take-over by News International of the loss-making *Today* titles from Lonrho without a monopolies reference in 1987, after Murdoch and the Lonrho chairman, 'Tiny' Rowland, had given the Secretary of State for Trade and Industry, Lord Young, a 24-hour ultimatum to approve the deal. The second was the take-over in 1990 by Murdoch's Sky TV of the British Satellite Broadcasting (BSB) to form BSkyB without the necessary consent of the broadcasting regulators, a take-over subsequently sanctioned by the government as a *fait accompli*.

Coming on top of all the rest of the rhetoric of Thatcherism, it is not too much to say that national newspapers have themselves been caught up in a spirit of the times which says that profit-making is the only real measure of socially worthwhile performance. Where the provision of hard news and comment can be packaged in a commercially successful way, so be it. But if tabloidization is the better way to increasing revenue, so be that as well. Consumerism rules!

Notes

1 The other members of the Committee were Sheila Black, John Cartwright MP, David Eady QC, Simon Jenkins, Professor John Last and J.R. Spencer.
2 The inquiry was initiated by the Campaign for Press Freedom. The other members of the group were Sarah Boston, Geoffrey Drain, Jacob Ecclestone, Geoffrey Goodman, Richard Hoggart, John Monks,

Russell Profitt, Muriel Turner, Phillip Whitehead and Katherine Whitehorn.

References

Calcutt, David (1990) *Report of the Committee on Privacy and Related Matters*, chairman, David Calcutt QC, Cmnd 1102, HMSO, London.

Calcutt, David (1993) *Review of Press Self-Regulation*, Cmnd 2135, HMSO, London.

Engel, Matthew (1996) *Tickle the Public: One Hundred Years of the Popular Press*, Victor Gollancz, London.

Glover, Stephen (1993) *Paper Dreams*, Jonathan Cape, London.

Mansfield, F.J. (1943) *Gentlemen, the Press!*, W.H. Allen, London.

National Heritage (1995) *Privacy and Media Intrusion: the Government's Response*, Cmnd 2918, HMSO, London.

Press Council (1983) *Press Conduct in the Sutcliffe Case*, Press Council Booklet No. 7, London.

Robertson, Geoffrey (1983) *People Against the Press*, Quartet, London.

Royal Commission on the Press (1962) *Report*, Cmnd 1811, HMSO, London.

Shawcross, William (1992) *Rupert Murdoch*, Chatto & Windus, London.

Stephenson, Hugh (1994) *Media Freedom and Media Regulation*, Association of British Editors, London.

CHAPTER 2

The 'tabloiding' of Britain: 'Quality' newspapers in the 1990s

Michael Bromley

Introduction

> Newspapers have long enough estranged themselves in a manner totally from the elegancies of literature, and dealt only in malice, or at least in the prattle of the day. On this head, however, newspapers are not much more to blame than their patrons, the public – *Morning Post*, 1788. (quoted Williams 1961: 195)

In the introspective world of the press – and especially newspaper journalism – the 1990s have been characterized by a growing obsession with what has been seen as a decline in standards in the perhaps ironically named 'quality' titles. This debate has been conducted, usually without reference to analytical frameworks, chiefly in the trade press and specialist media sections of the broadsheet newspapers themselves (Greenslade 1996b). Perhaps the most widely accepted explanation is Engel's (1996a) thesis that the publication of the *Daily Mail* in 1896 began a process, which has already lasted for about a hundred years, in which a succession of newspapers have enjoyed periods of dominance of the 'mass' readership by pursuing editorial policies of increasing populism and trivialization. Engel specifically identified those papers as the *Mail*, the *Daily Express*, the *Daily Mirror*, the *News of the World*, and *The Sun*: the *Daily Star*'s foray into 'bonk' journalism in 1987, he argued, began a cautious and partial retreat as the papers apparently finally touched 'rock bottom', causing readers and, more importantly, advertisers to recoil (1996a: 291ff). By the 1980s, all these papers were tabloid in format and, to varying degrees, in style. This seemed to deflect attention away from any similar tendencies in the broadsheet press. Events such as the 'White Swan affair', in which a number of senior journalists at *The Times* wrote to the paper's editor in 1970 raising concerns about a lowering of standards, 'vulgarization', and what was perceived to be an attempt to move the title downmarket under the ownership of Lord Thomson, were soon forgotten (Grigg 1993: 142–53).

Anxieties over the spread of tabloid values to the broadsheet press –

and, incidentally, television news and current affairs as well – were built on a set of specific perceptions. Newspaper proprietors were accused of treating their titles as business properties without 'a social purpose' (Greenslade 1996c), and the 'spin from big media barons' was thus felt to be indistinguishable from that emanating from government or other normally adversarial sources of social and economic power (Sweeney 1995). Editors were expected to act as entrepreneurs on behalf of the corporation (Tunstall 1996: 116–35), or as mere brand managers in an editorial function subsumed, with circulation and advertising sales, into an overall marketing effort (Griffith 1995). Journalism risked becoming a 'market-led' commodity (McManus 1994), with company executives, working from the results of market research, deciding what was news. A newspaper, in the view of one provincial editor, was a fast-moving consumer good – just like a Mars Bar – and ought to be sold like one (Fowler 1994).

The consequence, in the view of many journalists, was a catalogue of horrors: 'the lowest standards of journalism' (Hetherington 1989: 294); 'a play-it-safe recipe of abysmal blandness' (Hitchens 1995); a diet of 'soft porn, gossip and cheap fantasy' (Pilger 1997); an addiction to trivia (Christmas 1996); 'greed and to hell with the readers' (Harold Evans, quoted in Slattery 1996). While the news traditionally had to compete (often on unequal terms) with 'magazine stories, money-spinning games and promotions and quality sports writing' in the tabloid papers (Greenslade 1996e), the permeation of such attitudes into the 'serious' press appeared new (Farndon 1996). Fifty Members of Parliament signed an early day motion in June 1996 deploring 'the steep decline in serious reporting and analysis of politics and current affairs . . . [noting] that this decline has gathered pace in recent times, with increasing emphasis on personalities rather than politics, and on trivia rather than substance' (Peak and Fisher 1996: 44). The comments which carried most gravitas within journalism were possibly those of Anthony Sampson, the author and a member of the Scott Trust which owns *The Guardian*, who asserted that 'the frontier between qualities and popular papers has virtually disappeared' (1996: 44). Sampson noted the demotion of foreign news, parliamentary reporting and investigative journalism in the broadsheet press, and the substitution of personal columns devoted to inconsequential trivia. In 1995 the editor of *The Guardian* invented the word 'broadloid' to describe a broadsheet newspaper with a tabloid editorial approach (Peak and Fisher 1995: 30–1).

It will be argued in this chapter that there has indeed been a convergence of news values among the tabloid and broadsheet press, counteracting a tendency which prevailed for most of the twentieth century (Sparks 1992: 38–9). In that respect, the trend identified by Engel did not reach a climax with the excesses of the *Daily Star*: in fact, at precisely the moment when the polarization of the press seemed most attenuated, tabloid and broadsheet news agendas were actually coming together (Sparks 1991: 66). In market terms, 'quality' and 'popular' newspapers began to overlap, and to compete directly, in the 'middle market' which once seemed to lie like a chasm between them. Although this is often presented as a disjunction, it was more properly part of the continuing development of the press in the twentieth century.

The newspaper 'revolution' of the 1890s, attributed to Northcliffe, was founded on advertising and addressing readers primarily as consumers (Williams 1961: 203–4). As the twentieth century progressed, this press touched deeper and deeper into private life, elevating its 'entertainment' function over its more 'public' educative and informative functions. Information increasingly became a commodity to be managed rather than a requisite of democratic debate (Webster 1995: 217–18). By itself this is not evidence of a 'dumbing down' of either newspapers or the public. The primary basis for such an argument is a highly dubious supposition that 'tabloid' newspapers indoctrinate and brainwash their audiences (McGuigan 1992: 174–5), and that readers are somehow 'stupid' (O'Hagan 1996). In fact, 'popular' journalism may facilitate resistance to, even the transformation of, political, economic and social subordination by empowering its audiences, not as actors in the public sphere but as consumers (McGuigan 1992: 183–5). The exercise of the franchise was mediated, in ways that W.T. Stead (1886) perhaps failed to understand completely, through, as he said, spending a penny on a newspaper. In so far as it was quintessentially a 'serious' occupation, journalism was forced, as a consequence, to retreat to the fastness of the minority 'quality' press (Sparks 1991: 64). Some time, probably in the 1980s, the politics of consumption extended itself to fully incorporate the readers of this press, too.

The spread of tabloid news values

The tabloidization of the 'serious' press, as it is identified here, probably began in the provincial newspaper sector, and reflected perceptions held by proprietors and managers that the nature of the public it was addressing was changing. This, it was proposed, lay behind the steep decline experienced by the provincial press from the 1970s so that by the 1990s it could be regarded as a 'dying business'. A great deal of effort was expended in 'second guessing the readers' (Elenio 1995: 6). At the same time, conglomeration and monopolization resulted in exploitation; 'rationalization, redundancies and [the] cutting [of] costs', particularly among journalists (le Duc 1997; Greenslade 1996d). A provincial newspaper chairman warned that 'news-ignorant' management was giving rise to 'poor quality' editorial content consisting of 'soft news, white space, and yesterday's left-overs' (Slattery 1992). Surveying his local evening paper, the Brighton *Evening Argus*, which had lost 50 per cent of its circulation in twenty years, Roy Greenslade (1996d) argued: 'There is airy talk of increasing readership . . . and brand loyalty and the synergy with its give-away paper . . . [But] by all reasonable journalistic standards, the *Argus* stinks.'

This was seen as an outcome of the attempts by provincial press owners to respond to changing readerships, and to tailor editorial content accordingly (Elenio 1995: 9–12): shopping was now defined as news, as the 'traditional approach to news' was abandoned (Thomson Regional Newspapers (no date); Elenio 1995: 17). While a general 'changing media environment' could be identified, traditional local press values – the use of letters' pages for reader feedback; 'focus on the local community', including in-depth coverage of events; campaigning on local issues, and so on – were still most likely to attract readers (Henley Centre n.d.: 41–3). Nevertheless, provincial newspapers began to adjust their news schedules to reflect new marketable qualities (Morgan 1992b), and space devoted to 'lifestyle' features became inviolable, irrespective of the importance of news stories (Morgan 1992a). All the same, there was little consensus about precisely what content would attract and keep readers. The outgoing deputy chief executive of one of the largest provincial newspaper groups observed:

> We purport to know better than ever what they [the readers] want, but our evening newspapers, at least, do not seem to know how to give it to them. They want more bite; we are still too bland. They crave more detail; we incline to offer them less. (Herbert 1995)

Papers, it was felt somewhat vaguely, ought at least to be 'bright' and 'cheery' (Pritchard *et al*. 1993: 11).

In the national press, too, it was widely believed that readerships had changed, becoming more prone to 'inconsistency and unpredictability' (McCrystal 1995). A 'natural' broadsheet constituency . . . [of] serious-minded men' was no longer interested exclusively in politics and economics (Greenslade 1997b). Moreover, 'a generalized hypocrisy . . . of a public which refuses to grow up' placed a premium on 'titillating tales', particularly of sexual activities (Greenslade 1997a). Broadsheet newspapers deliberately – and successfully – pursued younger readers interested in such stories, winning them away from the tabloids (MacArthur 1997c). The new readers came from:

> the three-minute culture, the 'dumbing down' of the young generation who don't read, aren't interested in politics or foreign affairs and don't like heavyweight articles on 'Whither NATO' . . . this post-modern, post-serious, post-literate generation. (MacArthur 1997a)

The received wisdom was that television had initiated the vicious circle in the 1950s, supplanting traditional newspaper reporting with superficial, suspect 'soundbite' journalism, driven ultimately by the need for pictures and to entertain (Young 1990; Fisk 1992). Others felt that television was no more immune from the 'dumbing down' process, reflected in the failure of the project for TV to pursue 'a mission to explain' proposed by John Birt and Peter Jay in the 1970s. A decline in the numbers of 'discriminating viewers', and the financial interests of independent television companies were among the contributing factors (Woffinden 1996). For example, in response to the need to maintain its ratings, and to reduce its charges to the ITV companies it served in the face of potential competition, Independent Television News spent less, and demoted foreign and political stories in favour of a more 'tabloid' news agenda (Victor 1994; Hellen 1995). One of the UK's most respected TV journalists complained that putting 'quality profit before product quality' had resulted in 'reduction and trivialization' and 'a world of flash infotainment' (Snow 1997). Tabloid news values were imported into television most transparently by the cable operator Live TV, whose news from 1996 featured the 'news bunny', introduced by the former editor of *The Sun*, Kelvin MacKenzie (Brown 1996a; Coles 1996a).

Magazines, too, and especially those appealing principally to women, began to pursue an editorial mix of sex, celebrity and sleaze in a far more aggressive way. Titles such as *Hello!*, *OK!* and *Here!* were described as tabloids in all but name (Marks 1996). The most downmarket of these, *Here!*, launched in June 1996, was in many respects almost indistinguishable from a tabloid Sunday newspaper (Brown 1996c). Interestingly, the magazine published by the Sunday *People*, which spent many months publicizing the activities of the American actress Pamela Anderson in the manner of *OK!*, the self-styled 'home of the stars', adopted the trend begun by *Hello!* in 1988, and took the title *Yes!* (Brown 1996b; Coles 1996b). It might have seemed difficult to distinguish who was imitating whom, except that most observers gave credit for first tapping into the preoccupation of a newly emerging youth culture with celebrity, particularly that associated with television, and sex to *The Sun* (Pilger 1997). The playwright Dennis Potter (1993: 23) went so far as to proclaim that

> an avid wet-mouthed downmarket slide . . . began its giddiest descent on the day marauding Rupert Murdoch first left his paw-marks on our shores in acquiring *The Sun* and dragged so many others towards the sewers.

Others believed that opening up editorial agendas and addressing previously taboo subjects made the press more relevant and more accessible.

News about 'sex, murder and pop stars' had not driven everything else off the broadsheet pages: the 'quality' press carried as much home and foreign news as it had thirty or forty years earlier, and much of it was of better quality. The individual items tended to be shorter, and photographs bigger, although the papers were able to carry more of both because they had grown in size: this constituted a deliberate appeal to the 'soundbite generation', intended to stimulate its interest in 'serious' news rather than pandering to its ignorance. The editor of *The Times* told an international conference that 'quality newspapers must beware allowing dullness to masquerade as seriousness and must address modern readers in modern ways' (MacArthur 1997a, 1997b). The cause of 'popularization', rather than populism, was advanced more in television than the press: news, it was argued, could be presented in much the same way as more popular TV programmes like the consumer show *Watchdog*, or the children's magazine *Blue Peter* (Methven 1996, 1997; Datar 1997).

Since at least the emergence of the 'new journalism' in the 1880s journalists have sought to deflect criticisms of their methods as sensationalist. Stead (1886: 670–2) defended sensationalism as a natural phenomenon: 'the presentation of facts with such vividness and graphic force as to make a distinct even although temporary impact upon the mind'. He distinguished this from 'journalism that can fairly be called exaggerated or untrue:

> Mere froth-whipping or piling up the agony, solely for the purposes of harrowing the feelings of the reader, and nothing more, may be defended ... but I have nothing to say for that kind of work. That is not the sensationalism which I am prepared to defend. The sensationalism which is indispensable is sensationalism which is justifiable. Sensationalism in journalism is justifiable up to the point that it is necessary to arrest the eye of the public and compel them to admit the necessity of action.

Sensationalism is solely a me ins to an end. It is never an end in itself.

Marking the centenary of the *Daily Mail* in 1996, the chairman of its parent company invoked the spirit of Northcliffe, the paper's founder, as the initiator of campaigning and exposé journalism (and also of promotions, competitions and exhibitions), who had laid down the dictum: 'Explain! Simplify! Clarify!' (English 1996: 7, 10). In the later twentieth century sensationalism became associated almost exclusively with the 'popular' tabloid, rather than the 'quality' press. For three decades perhaps its most celebrated exponent was the *Daily Mirror*, which vigorously tackled in print hitherto unaddressed subjects, such as the incidence of venereal disease among troops during the Second World War. The *Mirror*'s postwar editor observed:

> The *Mirror* is a sensational paper. We make no apology for that. We believe in the sensational presentation of news and views, especially important news and views, as a necessary and valuable public service in these days of mass readership and democratic responsibility.
>
> Sensationalism does not mean distorting the truth. It means vivid and dramatic presentation of events so as to give them a forceful impact on the mind of the reader. It means big headlines, vigorous writing, simplification into everyday language, and the wide use of illustration by cartoon and photograph.
>
> Today the needs for sensational journalism are even more apparent. Every great problem facing us ... will only be understood by the ordinary man busy with his daily tasks if he is hit hard and hit often with the facts.
>
> Sensational treatment is the answer, whatever the sober and 'superior' readers of some other journals may prefer. (quoted Cudlipp 1953: 250–1)

Such an approach provoked complaints of falling standards, as they had done regularly for the previous 160 years or more. The *Mirror*'s coverage of 'serious' news fell markedly, and in the postwar period the 'popular' press as a whole significantly 'downgraded' such news (Curran and Seaton 1991: 67, 113–17). Not only 'popular' newspapers, but also television and radio – and, as the 'White Swan affair' illustrated, even as 'serious' a paper as *The Times* – were subjected to criticism, including that articulated by two Royal Commissions, for thereby lowering both standards and the expectations of audiences (Curran and Seaton 1991: 322–3; Carey 1992: 6–10; Negrine 1994: 46–7; Bromley 1995: 87–8; Maddox, 1996; Tunstall 1996: 394–6).

Such critics argued that standards in the 'popular' press reached a new nadir as *The Sun* competed with, and then overtook, the *Mirror* as the best-selling national daily newspaper in the 1970s and 1980s (Tunstall 1996: 404). The paper became 'a byword for the erosion of journalistic standards' (McGuigan 1992: 177). In fact, initially, following its acquisition by Murdoch, the paper set out to closely mimic the *Mirror* as it was thought to have been in the 1940s and 1950s. To that extent, *The Sun* was in all senses a traditional tabloid newspaper – 'less shrill, less harsh' than it was to become after 1981 under the editorship of MacKenzie (Leapman 1992: 61–3). Within about five years, however, the paper began to exert a pervasive influence over much of the rest of the press. In 1986, both the paper's raucous chauvinism and unapologetic political incorrectness were finally set, and the move to Wapping gave it temporary but critical commercial, and perhaps psychological, advantages (Leapman 1992: 64–5; 161–2). Eventually, the tables were turned completely, and the *Mirror* took to imitating *The Sun* (Leapman 1996). The considerable impact of *The Sun* on the provincial press in the later 1980s was traced by Engel (1993). He found these papers consumed by 'Panic, Scare, Horror, Shock, Anger' – 'the drip, drip, drip of years of distortion'. The provincial and local press seemed to have succumbed to *Sun*-type cliché and hyperbole (Bromley 1995: 95–6). A secondary factor was the linking of *The Sun* to the *Sunday Times* through Murdoch's ownership from 1981. The *Sunday Times* shared in – perhaps even gained more from – the advantages of the move to Wapping; but, more significantly, it abandoned the pluralist, radical journalism for which it established a reputation under the editorship of Harry Evans in the 1960s and 1970s, notably after Andrew Neil was appointed editor in 1983 (Seymour-Ure 1991: 244–5; Leapman 1992: 76, 161–2). The paper came to be widely lampooned inside the industry as a tabloid in all but name and size.

The tabloid press's pursuit of the story of the royal family more than any other – 'the biggest story of the past ten years' – in which the *Sunday Times* played a significant role, and various high-profile cases of invasions of privacy, which drew the attention of parliament and the government, themselves became newsworthy. At first, the 'quality' press ignored the substantive issues of tabloid news; then decried them. These papers – and television and radio – subsequently began reporting and commenting on the behaviour of the tabloid press, which led to the vicarious reporting of the issues themselves. Finally, the broadsheet newspapers, too, carried the same news items, ending the 'gentle conceit' that it eschewed the values of the 'grubby end of the business' (Engel 1996b). This did not necessarily itself signal the conversion of the 'quality' press, however:

it can be dated as happening somewhere between 1963, when *The Guardian* belatedly sent a reporter to explain to its readers something about the baffling social phenomenon known as The Beatles, and 1996, when Charles Moore, editor of the *Daily Telegraph*, berated his staff for failing to put the Oasis concert at Knebworth on page one. One can be slightly more specific than that. It definitely pre-dated 1995 when the four broadsheet dailies devoted a total of 1752 column inches to Hugh Grant's dalliance with a Los Angeles prostitute.

Michael Leapman, then *The Times* man in New York, dates the change in the quality press precisely to the takeover [of the paper by Murdoch in 1981]. In 1977, when Elvis Presley died, Leapman's suggestion that he fly to Memphis was greeted with the reaction: 'Sorry. Not a *Times* story.' Two months after Murdoch moved in, when Bob Marley died, not only was Leapman ordered to Jamaica to the funeral, he found another *Times* writer there. (Engel 1996b)

A watershed in the debate

Engel's article, published on Thursday, 3 October 1996 as the cover story of *The Guardian*'s second (tabloid) section, represented some kind of watershed in the debate over 'the tabloidization of the broadsheets' (Engel 1996b). It made reference and responded to Sampson's article, mentioned above, and in turn it stimulated the editor of the influential trade weekly *Press Gazette* to reply with a long article of his own paper (Farndon 1996). An international seminar, called to consider the future of the 'quality' press, also considered the matter (Christmas 1997: 16–17). The issue, it seemed, had finally broken surface.

The Engel contribution consisted of about 3000 words of copy on how 'the broadsheet newspapers have changed beyond recognition in the past ten years'. Given that the paper recognized that the story had been around for a decade, it was perhaps remarkable that it had taken it so long to address it. On the other hand, it was suggested that Sampson's position as a member of the Scott Trust had contributed to 'internal pressures' to do so (Farndon 1996).

Adopting the approach he took in his well-received book published earlier in 1996 to mark the centenary of the *Daily Mail* (1996a: 20–47), Engel began by ridiculing the 'quality' press's potential anachronism.

On the Saturday before Christmas 1984 the following introductory paragraph appeared in the lead article on the features pages of *The Guardian*: 'Everybody knows that by 1400 the Christ child in Western painting had shed the Byzantine garb to appear more or less naked.' . . . In the 1930s it was the custom of *The Times* to print pages from time to time in Ancient Greek, safe in the knowledge that many readers would be able to crack the code. In the 1950s, when Elizabeth Taylor arrived at Heathrow after an illness and told reporters: 'I'm feeling like a million dollars', the *Daily Telegraph*'s ponderous and pedantic rules insisted that it add afterwards: (£357 000).

The 'quality' press, Engel argued, had mainly been by-standers as the tabloids 'pushed the boundaries of acceptable taste further and further downward in the layers between the gutter and the sewer'. The situation had changed with unprecedented rapidity, however. He identified three principal causes for this. First, the price 'war' initiated by the Murdoch press in 1993 had brought the same kind of competition for circulation to the broadsheet press as had characterized the tabloid sector in the 1970s and 1980s. Referring to *The Times*, Engel wrote: 'What was traditionally Britain's premium paper has turned itself into something close to a freesheet, selling on Mondays at 10p, less than the paper cost in 1976 and only four times as much as in 1797.' Second, the arrival of *The Independent* in 1986 disturbed the equilibrium which had existed among the broadsheets since perhaps the nineteenth century, and promoted purchasing promiscuity among broadsheet readers. Third, in interviews the editors of both the *Daily Telegraph* and *The Independent* acknowledged the influence of the *Daily Mail*, particularly in addressing women readers. True, a 'generation . . . conditioned to staring at television and computer screens but not to the discipline of reading in depth' meant audiences had changed but, above all, the editorial tactics for selling tabloid newspapers had been imported into the previously 'Cosy Corner' occupied by the broadsheet press.

Engel concluded that this represented a challenge primarily to journalism:

> Bigger newspapers mean that, whether or not there is as much great journalism, there is certainly far more inconsequential journalism. The standards of presentation have improved; the standards of literacy have not. Up to ten years ago *The Guardian* used to get some words all wrong because the production system could not cope. One fears that in the future it will get them wrong because the journalists will not care enough to ensure they are right.

> Under pressure, the papers have also become blander . . . too often the broadsheets let the tabloids set the pace, and slavishly follow. One can imagine a situation in which the quality papers look and sound more or less identical . . . The truth is that the quality papers are giving the readers what they want in a way that never used to happen. The logical end of that must be the disappearance of the frontier, as Sampson says. But it has not happened yet . . . if we can address our own business honestly, assessing ourselves and our rivals fairly, as well as trumpeting our triumphs and rubbishing the opposition, all is not yet lost.

The albeit severely muted furore of the Sampson–Engel–Farndon exchanges compared to a previously almost total silence on the issue. For example, a souvenir booklet marking the twentieth anniversary of the then *UK Press Gazette*, despite highlighting 'turmoil and change' in the media, made no mention of the tendency for tabloid and 'quality' news values to merge (Wintour 1985). Ten years later, in the same paper's thirtieth anniversary supplement, the issue was passed over in one paragraph (Williams 1995: 16). Was the realization genuinely slow in coming? The testimony of Alan Rusbridger, the editor of *The Guardian*, suggested not:

This is not C.P. Snow-land, where there's high culture and low culture, and you're interested in one or the other. Most of our readers have the capacity to think more broadly than that. They want to know about the single currency, and they would be cheated if *The Guardian* didn't give that. But they also want to know about Liam Gallagher and Patsy Kensit.

They can be broad enough to want to know Martin Woollacott's line on Burundi and Rwanda. But it doesn't mean they don't want to know about Fergie and Di. It's very dangerous if you get into the mind-set that there are broadsheet subjects and tabloid subjects. (Quoted Engel 1996b)

Conclusion

A notable aspect of a debate so far conducted largely within the closed community of the press has been its almost exclusive focus on the implications of tabloidization for journalism. Evidence from the US suggests there are correlations between the levels of morale among journalists, their evaluations of the performance of the media in promoting the public interest, the incidence of market-led editorial values, and the quality and size of editorial staffs: smaller, less experienced and younger newsrooms, resulting from cost-cutting measures linked to short-term managerial desires to meet supposed market demands, are seen as leading to a decline in public interest journalism, which reduces job satisfaction (Weaver and Wilhoit 1992: 10–11; Kurtz 1995). Editorial staffs in Britain have clearly been getting younger and smaller, less experienced and less well paid (National Union of Journalists 1994: 3; Delano and Henningham 1996: 4, 16; Kennedy 1996), and have been subjected to cost-cutting, most notably at the Mirror Group newspapers, *The Independent*, *Independent on Sunday* and the *Mirror*, and in the provincial press (Pritchard *et al.* 1993: 19; Greenslade 1996a; Cohen 1997). Nevertheless, overall morale appears not to have fallen as much as in the USA. A far higher proportion of British news journalists still believe the media are serving the public interest, although nearly half also think that standards have fallen (Delano and Henningham 1996: 18). The feeling of 'spiritual self-doubt' which is said to infect American journalists (Kurtz 1995) appears to be absent from British journalism. That may derive from the division of British journalism into distinct, and increasingly discrete, tabloid and broadsheet cultures with quite different expectations (Delano and Henningham 1996: 17–18). Only some unreconstructed broadsheet journalists, it might be said, condemn contemporary journalism as wholly routinized, 'a treadmill' stripped of its public interest dimension 'doing evil and traducing the good ... with scant regard for truth' (Toynbee 1996). They compare unfavourably the journalism of the *Sunday Times* and its Insight team in the 1970s, and of Mirrorscope in the 1960s, with the 'advertorial' policies of the 1990s under which *The Times* sold its entire print run to Microsoft, and the *Daily Mirror* turned itself blue in a deal with Pepsi-Cola.

This concern with the relative autonomy of journalists as practitioners fuses with the issue of content. The confusion of 'broadsheet subjects and tabloid subjects' has led to fears that broadsheet journalism and tabloid journalism will become indistinguishable – the 'dumbing down' effect. Without doubt, the broadsheet press in the 1990s has shared many of the news values of the tabloids, and has paid almost as much attention to the presentation of this material (Sparks 1991: 70–1). Its explanatory strategies remained distinctive, however: the broadsheet press, unlike the tabloids, still eschewed the personal as the defining prism through which to view the world; its discourse remained fundamentally different (Sparks 1992: 39–41). Surely this is what the editor of *The Guardian* was referring to when, in defending the 'tabloidization' of news agendas, he argued that in the broadsheet press 'there has to be . . . a unity of tone, and that's how you define broadsheet values' (quoted in Engel 1996b). The news may appear to be the same in subject matter and may actually look the same, but it does not always read the same or bear the same meanings.

References

Bromley, M. (1995) *Media Studies: An Introduction to Journalism*, Hodder & Stoughton, London.

Brown, M. (1996a) 'Bunny, I shrunk the news', *The Guardian* 2, 4 Mar.: 11.

Brown, M. (1996b) 'Woman of the *People*', *The Guardian* 2, 11 Mar.: 16–17.

Brown, M. (1996c) 'Cuckoo in *Hello*'s nest', *The Guardian* 2, 9 Sep.: 13.

Carey, J. (1992) *The Intellectuals and the Masses: Pride and Prejudice among the Literary Intelligensia, 1880–1939*, Faber & Faber, London.

Christmas, L. (1996) 'Readers are being deprived of real political issues', *Press Gazette*, 20 Dec.

Christmas, L. (1997) 'Jolly reads', *The Journalist's Handbook* **49**, April: 16–19.

Cohen, N. (1997) 'Press gang', *Red Pepper*, Mar.: 18–19.

Coles, J. (1996a) 'Kelvin: still rabbiting on', *The Guardian* 2, 15 Jan.: 10–11.

Coles, J. (1996b) 'Imimacy rules, *OK!*', *The Guardian* 2, 4 Mar.: 15.

Cudlipp, H. (1953) *Publish and Be Damned! The Astonishing Story of the 'Daily Mirror'*, Andrew Dakers, London.

Curran, J. and Seaton, J. (1991) *Power Without Responsibility: The Press and Broadcasting in Britain*, 4th edn, Routledge, London.

Datar, R. (1997) 'They have news for you', *The Guardian Media* 10 Feb.: 5.

Delano, A. and Henningham, J (1996) *The News Breed: British Journalists in the 1990s*, The London Institute, London.

le Duc, F. (1997) 'The press barons who are proud to be provincial', *The Times*, 20 Jan.: 43.

Elenio, P. (1995) *Capturing Readers: The Battle to Keep and Attract Consumers of Newspapers*, Reuter Foundation Paper 27, Green College, Oxford.

Engel, M. (1993) 'The tears of a clone', *The Guardian* 2, 22 Mar.: 12.

Engel, M. (1996a) *Tickle the Public: One Hundred Years of the Popular Press*, Gollancz, London.

Engel, M. (1996b) 'Papering over the cracks', *The Guardian* 2, 3 Oct.: 2–4.

English, D. (1996) 'Legend of "The Chief"', *British Journalism Review* **7**, (2), 6–14.

Farndon, R. (1996) 'Why the broadsheets have changed', *Press Gazette*, 25 Oct.: 11.

Fisk, R. (1992) 'Challenge the might of the sound-bite', *The Independent*, 8 Jan.: 13.

Fowler, N. (1994) 'What makes an award winning regional paper?', *Headlines*, Apr./May: 3.

Greenslade, R. (1996a) 'Last in the sack race', *The Guardian* 2, 4 Mar.: 13.

Greenslade, R. (1996b) 'Soundbites, not criticism', *The Guardian* 2, 20 May: 17.

Greenslade, R. (1996c) 'The vice of the people', *The Guardian* 2, 27 May: 13.

Greenslade, R. (1996d) 'Regions of despair', *The Guardian* 2, 1 July: 14–15.

Greenslade, R. (1996e) 'The telling selling game', *The Guardian* 2, 12 Aug.: 17.

Greenslade, R. (1997a) 'Amoral maze', *The Guardian* 2, 6 Jan.: 17.

Greenslade, R. (1997b) '*The Telegraph*, it is a-changin' ', *The Guardian Media*, 3 Feb.: 5.

Griffith, J. (1995) 'The glorified brand manager', *UK Press Gazette*, 16 Oct.: 16.

Grigg, J. (1993) *The History of 'The Times'*, vol. vi, *The Thomson Years, 1966–1981*, Times Books, London.

Hellen, R. (1995) 'ITV cuts budget for *News at Ten*', *The Sunday Times*, 16 July: 15.

Henley Centre (n.d.) *Media Futures: Regional Press Report*, Henley Centre/Newspaper Society, London.

Herbert, N. (1995) 'Face forward', *UK Press Gazette*, 16 Jan.: 16.

Hetherington, A. (1989) 'The mass media', Kavanagh, D. and Seldon, A. (eds) *The Thatcher Effect: A Decade of Change*, Oxford University Press, London, 290–304.

Hitchens, C. (1995) 'All aboard the bland wagon', *The Observer Review*, 19 Nov.: 4.

Kennedy, D. (1996) 'The rise of the brat hacks', *The Times*, 28 Aug.: 19.

Kurtz, H. (1995) 'Frightening news for papers', *International Herald Tribune*, 1 Nov.: 13, 17.

Leapman, M. (1992) *Treacherous Estate: The Press after Fleet Street*, Hodder & Stoughton, London.

Leapman, M. (1996) 'The *Mirror* that reflects the *Sun*', *The Guardian* 2, 29 Jan.: 14–15.

MacArthur, B. (1997a) 'New readers, new times', *The Times*, 5 Feb.: 21.

MacArthur, B. (1997b) 'When crisis strikes the quality shines through', *The Times*, 12 Feb.

MacArthur, B. (1997c) 'Not such a dumb idea', *The Times*, 12 Mar.

McCrystal, C. (1995) 'The dream that died', *Observer Review*, 19 Nov.: 1–2.

McGuigan, J. (1992) *Cultural Populism*, Routledge, London.

McManus, J.H. (1994) *Market-Driven Journalism: Let the Citizen Beware?* Sage & Thousand Oaks, California.

Maddox, B. (1996) 'Auntie's class acts and sacred cows', *The Times*, 7 Aug.: 20.

Marks, N. (1996) 'Inside *Hello!*', *Press Gazette*, 25 Oct.: 17.

Methven, N. (1996) 'The popularising of *Panorama*', *Press Gazette*, 27 Sep.: 17.

Methven, N. (1997) 'Colouring the way we watch the news', *Press Gazette*, 17 Jan.: 9.

Morgan, J. (1992a) 'Halting the decline by raising their game', *UK Press Gazette*, 12 Oct.: 24.

Morgan, J. (1992b) 'No dreaming among the spires', *UK Press Gazette*, 16 Nov.: 2.

National Union of Journalists (1994) *NUJ Membership Survey: Report of Main Findings*, Trade Union Research Unit, Oxford.

Negrine, R. (1994) *Politics and the Mass Media in Britain*, 2nd edn, Routledge, London.

O'Hagan, A. (1996) 'Fame games', *The Guardian* 2, 12 Aug.: 2–3.

Peak, S. and Fisher, P. (eds) (1995) *The Media Guide 1996*, Fourth Estate, London.

Peak, S and Fisher, P. (1996) *The Media Guide 1997*, Fourth Estate, London.

Pilger, J. (1997) 'Breaking the *Mirror*: The Murdoch Effect', *Network First*, dir. Munro, D., Central Television, 18 Feb., Birmingham.

Potter, D. (1993) 'A malediction on Murdoch – and his imitators', *British Journalism Review* **4** (2): 21–6.

Pritchard, C., Kelly, G. and Ward, M. (1993) *The Changing Vision*, University of Central Lancashire, Preston.

Sampson, A. (1996) 'The crisis at the heart of our media', *British Journalism Review* **7**(3): 42–51.

Seymour-Ure, C. (1991) *The British Press and Broadcasting since 1945*, Blackwell, Oxford.

Slattery, J. (1992) 'Storey warns of profit-before-news priorities', *UK Press Gazette*, 23 Nov.: 5.

Slattery, J. (1996) 'Harold Evans tells editors to stop news "mutating into trivia"', *Press Gazette*, 1 Nov.: 10.

Snow, J. (1997) 'Is TV news telling the whole story?', *The Guardian Media*, 27 Jan.: 3.

Sparks, C. (1991) 'Goodbye, Hildy Johnson: the vanishing "serious" press', in Dahlgren, P. and Sparks, C. (eds) *Communication and Citizenship: Journalism and the Public Sphere*, Routledge, London, 58–74.

Sparks, C. (1992) 'Popular journalism: theories and practices', in Dahlgren, P. and Sparks, C. (eds) *Journalism and Popular Culture*, Sage, London, 24–44.

Stead, W.T. (1886) 'Government by journalism', *The Contemporary Review*, 653–74.

Sweeney, J. (1995) 'Get out of my light', *The Guardian* 2, 11 Sep.: 12–13.

Thomson Regional Newspapers (no date) *The Key*, editions 1–4.

Toynbee, P. (1996) 'Why not to be a journalist', *The Big Issue*, 4 Sep.: 4.

Tunstall, J. (1996) *Newspaper Power: The New National Press in Britain*, Clarendon Press, Oxford.

Victor, P. (1994) '*News at Ten* takes a turn towards the tabloids', *Independent on Sunday*, 22 May.

Weaver, D. and Wilhoit, G.C. (1992) *The American Journalist in the 1990s*, The Freedom Forum, Arlington, Virginia.
Williams, G. (1995) 'Riding the roller coaster', *UK Press Gazette* supplement, 17 Nov.: 16–17.
Williams, R. (1961) *The Long Revolution*, Chatto & Windus, London.
Wintour, C. (1985) 'A world of turmoil and change', *UK Press Gazette* souvenir, 26 Nov.–3 June: 9–12.
Woffinden, B. (1996) 'Fast and loose', *The Guardian* 2, 12 Aug.: 13.
Young, H. (1990) 'Can television tell the truth?', *British Journalism Review*, **2**(1): 11–16.

CHAPTER 3

Demographics and values: What the British public reads and what it thinks about its newspapers

Robert M. Worcester

Introduction

Readership of the national tabloid press has fallen dramatically over the past quarter of a century. Many more people in the UK read no national daily newspaper regularly, and the demographic structure of readership has changed. This chapter looks at these changes in the British public's national newspaper reading habits compared with twenty-five years ago, drawing on data from MORI's founding year, 1969, and comparing readership then to 1993 aggregate data of over 30 000 respondents. It also examines the attitudes of the British public to its newspapers, their role in society and public support for restrictions on the press, showing that while the public still buys the tabloids in the millions and approves of breaches of individuals' privacy to uncover criminal conduct or personal hypocrisy, it does not approve of press intrusion into the royal family.

MORI was founded in 1969. From the outset I was conscious of the role of the press in the diffusion of information about my clients' activities and especially its effect on their corporate images. One of the earliest surveys MORI conducted was the first in a series of 'corporate image' studies, carried out on a cooperative basis: that is, with the core data shared by a number of participating clients. Such a study maximizes the value of the survey, ensuring that a large sample (c 2000 respondents) is available to a number of companies which share the cost of basic demographic, behavioural (for example, readership) and some attitudinal (for example, attitudes to large companies) questions of interest to them all, while allowing each client to 'hitch-hike' on their own specific questions of interest only to themselves and not shared with the other clients (at extra cost). This first corporate image study was conducted among a national probability sample of 1930 respondents throughout the UK in October–November 1969, and included a basic regular readership question in it: 'Which of these national daily newspapers do you read regularly – by regularly, I mean three out of

Table 3.1 National newspaper readership 1969–1993

	1969	1993	Change
Dailies	%	%	%
Daily Express	25	7	−18
Daily Mirror	36	14	−22
Daily Sketch	6	n/a	−6
Daily Mail	11	10	−1
The Sun	6	17	+11
The Times	3	2	−1
Daily Telegraph	8	6	−2
The Guardian	2	4	+2
Financial Times	1	1	0
The Independent	n/a	3	+3
Sundays			
Sunday Express	23	8	−15
Sunday Mirror	31	12	−19
People	32	8	−24
News of the World	33	21	−12
Sunday Telegraph	4	3	−1
Sunday Times	9	6	−3
Observer	5	4	−1
Independent/Sun	n/a	3	+3

Source: MORI.

every four issues, on average?' Comparisons then (and later) with the National Readership Survey (NRS) showed the data were comparable to the more complex questioning done by the NRS, each newspaper's readership being within sampling tolerance levels (at least 95 per cent, most at 99 per cent).

The availability of national newspapers has undergone a significant change over time. There is now no Daily Sketch; The Sun has been transformed; The Express and the Daily Mail moved from broadsheet to tabloid, and Today, the Daily Star and The Independent were launched (and, in the case of Today, subsequently closed). The first thing to note about the data comparing regular readership over twenty-five years, in 1969 and 1993 (see Table 3.1), is how many fewer readers there are in 1993 as a percentage of the adult population, and the massive falls in the penetration of readership among the popular newspapers, especially the Sundays. The readership of the Express and the Mirror[1] fell massively, and although the penetration of readership of The Sun nearly tripled under Murdoch ownership (and MacKenzie's editorship), it did not make up the difference. In 1969 'average issue readership' was 98 per cent of the adult population; in 1993 it was 70 per cent (adding together the percentages of daily newspapers' 'regular' readers, thus taking into account the decline in multiple newspaper readership).

Overlap readership – people reading more than one newspaper daily – fell, with more than 20 per cent overlap between dailies in 1993 most unusual (except among *Financial Times* readers), although 30 per cent of *Star* readers read *The Sun*, and 22 per cent of *Star* readers also read the *Mirror*. Four in five adults in Britain read at least one national newspaper daily in 1993, but fewer than two-thirds (63 per cent) read a national newspaper regularly, and of those who did, almost exactly half read either *The Sun* or the *Daily Mirror*. Two out of three adults (65 per cent) read a Sunday newspaper regularly, and of those who did, almost exactly half read either the *News of the World* or the *People*. Only one person in six (15 per cent) in 1993 read a 'quality' national daily newspaper regularly (three out of every four issues, on average); *The Times* 2 per cent (before the price reduction), *The Guardian* 4 per cent, *The Independent* 3 per cent, the *Daily Telegraph* 6 per cent, and the *Financial Times* 1 per cent. Some people read more than one.

Over the decade of the 1980s the percentage of the public who read **any** national daily newspaper fell by 6 per cent, and the percentage of the public who read a Sunday newspaper regularly fell by 5 per cent. A review of the decline in readership of the Sunday papers over two decades, going back to readership levels in 1969 shows a 20 per cent decline in sales of the *News of the World* and the *Sunday Times*; 23 per cent for the *Sunday Mirror*; 52 per cent for the *People*, and 60 per cent for the *Sunday Express*. Whereas on a Sunday in 1969 some 23 million papers were sold every weekend, at the beginning of the 1990s, despite extra pages, colour magazines, routine run-of-paper colour and a range of editorial treatments from newsbites to 10 000-word features, book serials and cartoon supplements, a little over 16 million were sold.

In total, 51 per cent of the public in 1993 read a 'popular' daily newspaper regularly, while 15 per cent read a national 'quality' title. Hardly anything so divides the British by class as does their newspaper reading habits. While the class divide is now roughly four in ten middle-class and six in ten working-class, in 1993 of the middle-class households eight in ten (79 per cent) read the so-called 'quality' papers and only one in five (21 per cent) working-class adults did; at the same time, the 'popular' papers were read by only one-third (32 per cent) of middle-class people, while two-thirds of their readers were working-class. It is fair to say that newspaper readership is a surrogate for the class composition of the population, reflecting as it does such a clear division across the middle-class/working-class division that exists in this country, as shown by the class profile of the various newspapers' readers (see Table 3.2).

Other demographic classificiations are not so telling, and those such as trade-union membership, home ownership and even region of residence are class-based rather than independent variables, ranging from 88 per cent owner-occupiers among *Telegraph* readers to 60 per cent for *Star* readers. Having said that, it is interesting to note that while 24 per cent of *Mirror* readers in 1993 were trade-union members, 32 per cent of *Guardian* readers were members of trade unions.

Henry's analysis (1993) showed that the combined circulations of the national daily newspapers in 1992 was a 'bare 14.2 million', having tumbled from 15.6 million in 1988, but this is misleading, for longer term trends over several decades show that since 1970 the combined

Table 3.2 Social class of national newspaper readerships, 1992

	AB (%)	C₁ (%)	C₂ (%)	DE (%)
All	18	23	28	31
Dailies				
Financial Times	57	28	9	5
The Times	55	27	9	9
Daily Telegraph	47	31	13	10
The Independent	45	32	13	10
The Guardian	39	33	13	15
Daily Mail	23	32	24	21
Daily Express	22	31	24	21
Today	15	27	31	27
Daily Mirror	7	16	37	40
The Sun	6	15	38	41
Daily Star	4	15	39	43
Sundays				
Sunday Express	26	32	24	17
Mail on Sunday	26	34	26	15
Sunday Mirror	8	18	37	38
News of the World	6	15	37	42
People	7	17	37	40
Sunday Telegraph	44	33	15	8
Independent/Sun	44	32	14	10
Observer	48	28	13	11
Sunday Times	50	31	12	8

Source: MORI.

circulations of the national dailies behaved rather like a snake in a tunnel, the boundaries of which were 15.9 million and 14.1 million; that while circulations were down to 14.7 million in 1971 and again in 1976, they peaked in 1984 at just under 16 million. His conclusion was that the 'worst recession for four decades should have affected the sale of newspapers – as of other consumer goods – is hardly surprising'. His collorary was that over the period there was an increase in the price of newspapers in real terms of 53 per cent, far outstripping inflation, so that it is hardly surprising that this had an effect on circulations (and on profits of the more successful of the national daily newspapers).

Sunday newspapers have fared less well. Between 1970 and 1979 their prices, indexed, rose by 34 per cent, while circulations fell by 'only' 22 per cent; between 1979 and 1989 prices rose nearly as fast (30 per cent) but circulations held – the decline until the recession of the late 1980s and early 1990s was a 'bare' 2 per cent. Segmenting the market, between 1978 and 1992 the national daily upmarket papers began the run with 2.1 million circulations and ended in 1992 with 2.4 million, up 14 per cent. The mid-market papers moved from 4.4 million to 3.8 million, down 14 per cent; and the downmarket papers fell from 8.5 million

Table 3.3 Circulations of national newspapers (millions), 1978–1993

	1978	1979	1980	1981	1982	1983	1984	1985	1986	1987	1988	1989	1990	1991	1992	1993
Dailies																
Upmarket	2.1	2.2	2.3	2.2	2.2	2.2	2.3	2.4	2.6	2.6	2.6	2.6	2.5	2.5	2.4	2.4
Mid-market	4.4	4.3	4.2	4.1	3.9	3.8	3.8	3.7	3.8	3.8	3.9	3.9	3.8	3.7	3.8	3.6
Downmarket	8.5	9.1	9.2	9.5	9.5	9.6	9.8	9.4	9.3	9.1	9.1	8.9	8.7	8.2	7.9	6.9
Total	15	15.6	15.7	15.8	15.6	15.6	15.9	15.5	15.7	15.5	15.6	15.4	15	14.4	14.1	12.9
Sundays																
Upmarket	2.9	2.5	3.4	3.2	2.9	2.8	2.8	2.7	2.6	2.7	2.8	2.7	2.8	2.7	2.7	2.7
Mid-market	3.3	3.2	3.1	3	3.6	4.1	4.2	4.1	4.1	4.1	4	3.8	3.6	3.6	3.7	3.5
Downmarket	12.8	12.5	12	11.4	11.4	11	11.3	11.1	11	11.6	11.4	11.4	11	10.3	9.8	9.3
Total	19	18.2	18.5	17.6	17.9	17.9	18.3	17.9	17.7	18.4	18.2	17.9	17.4	16.6	16.2	15.5

Source: Audit Bureau of Circulation.

to 7.9 million, a fall of 7 per cent. Over the same period the upmarket Sundays dropped from 2.9 million to 2.7 million (down 7 per cent), while the mid-market Sunday papers increased their circulations by 12 per cent from 3.3 million to 3.7 million. The downmarket Sundays, however, and this is where the big numbers are, plummeted from 12.8 million to 9.8 million, a decline of 23 per cent, or 3 million copies (see Table 3.3).

What the British public thinks about its newspapers

In the Independent Broadcasting Authority's (now Independent Television Commission's) tracking of which source is most preferred for world news, newspapers as the first mentioned source fell from 27 per cent in 1982 and 28 per cent in 1983 to 18 per cent in 1990. Attacks on the press are frequent. In a MORI poll at the end of February 1990 some 36 per cent of the British public said they were dissatisfied with the way national newspapers handled the Gulf War, and about four in ten were dissatisfied with the coverage on BBC-TV news (40 per cent) and Independent Television News (ITN) (37 per cent). Of those who had relatives serving in the Gulf, 48 per cent said they were dissatisfied with newspapers and proportionately more than the average with the BBC and Independent Television (ITV). A survey published in 1990 reported that when asked how satisfied or dissatisfied they were with national newspapers, four in ten adults said they were dissatisfied, double the number saying they were dissatisfied with the BBC or ITV. Dissatisfaction with national newspapers was more or less equally held across gender and age, although 10 per cent more of ABC[1]s were dissatisfied with the way the BBC was performing its role in society (Jacobs and Worcester 1990).

NOP for *The Independent* and BBC's *Newsnight* found that while 69 per cent of the public said they had a great deal or at least a fair amount of trust in the BBC to tell the truth about what was happening in the Gulf War and 67 per cent said they trusted ITV, only one person in three said they had faith in their own daily newspaper to tell the truth. In fact, over one-third of *Sun* and *Daily Star* readers, and nearly one-third of *Today* and *Daily Mirror* readers, said they had 'no trust at all' in their own paper's war reporting. Another NOP poll for Ayer Advertising reported a different perception. In Britain, 57 per cent of adults claimed to have been viewing more ITV, while one-third said they had listened to less radio, and one-quarter said they had read fewer papers. The survey found only 13 per cent of the British who believed the British press was free of bias and according to a report in *Campaign* (1 March 1991) 'we also rate feebly on comprehension and clarity' (compared with the rating of the national newspapers in other European countries as viewed by their readers). When asked, 'If you could only get the news from one source, which one would it be? By that, I mean a TV programme, or a newspaper, or a radio station', half chose some BBC programme, with 15 per cent each choosing the *Nine O'Clock News* or the *Six O'Clock News*; 9 per cent choosing BBC Radio 4; 8 per cent ITN's *News at Ten*; and 4 per cent each choosing the BBC's *One O'Clock News*, BBC *Breakfast Time*, and the *Daily Telegraph* – the only newspaper to make it into the top ten chosen.

At the time of the Calcutt inquiry into the conduct and role of the press, the *News of the World* approached MORI to conduct a major survey into the British nation's views of the press.[2] The paper placed no restrictions on us, but allowed us complete freedom to ask any question we believed relevant to the issue. The study was conducted among a representative quota sample of 813 adults nationwide, between 28 and 30 November 1989. It was subsequently reported, first in the *News of the World*, then in various other media. The full tabulations were provided to Simon Jenkins, a member of the Calcutt commission, at his request and were examined by the members and staff of the commission. Subsequently, during the course of other studies, we updated questions incorporated in the *News of the World* questionnaire for comparison purposes, specifically in a survey for *The Times* in August 1992. When asked to agree or disagree with the statement, 'The press generally behaves responsibly in Britain', in 1990 there was a bare plurality against, with 49 per cent of the British public in disagreement, while 46 per cent agreed. Two years, and many column inches about the young royals later, especially in the popular papers, a majority (51 per cent) disagreed, while support for the proposition fell five points to 41 per cent. *The Times*/MORI survey found a significant discrepancy between the various types of newspapers, with eight in ten of the public in agreement that the local and regional newspapers behaved responsibly; two-thirds saying that the broadsheets did, too; but two-thirds (68 per cent) believing that the tabloids did not.

In 1990 close to a majority (48 per cent) felt that there was too little control of the activities of the newspapers in Britain: two years later the 'culprits' were broken out. Against the generalized finding of 1990, 40 per cent said that there was too little control generally; but 53 per cent felt that the tabloid newspapers were under too little control, while 31 per cent said there was the 'right amount', and 8 per cent too much.

Public figures and the royal family were thought by nearly two-thirds in 1992 to receive too much intrusive reporting by the nation's newspapers, compared to about one-quarter who thought it about right; but politicians were thought to be fairer – much fairer – game. Politicians, 41 per cent thought, got too much intrusion; but 39 per cent thought it was the right amount, while 16 per cent actually thought it was too little. By contrast, only one person in twenty thought the intrusion of the press into the lives of public figures and the royal family was too little. Nearly everyone in Britain, which is renowned for its love of animals, thought newspapers should report on ordinary people involved in cruelty to animals, and the same (94 per cent) in child abuse; more than nine in ten (92 per cent) thought that acts of vandalism should cause ordinary people to be reported on. Adultery, on the other hand, was thought worthy of newspaper exposure by one-quarter of the adult British population.

Table 3.4 Public attitudes to invasions of privacy, 1990–1992

Q: *For which of these groups of people, if any, do you think it is justifiable for the press to invade their privacy in pursuit of a story?*

	1990 (%)	1992 (%)	Change
Politicians	33	40	+7
Magistrates/judges	29	39	+10
Police officers	29	36	+7
Royalty	17	33	+16
Clergy	20	28	+8
Lawyers	20	26	+6
TV stars	18	26	+8
Civil servants	18	25	+7
Journalists	18	25	+7
Businessmen	15	23	+8
Teachers	14	22	+8
Sports personalities	14	21	+7

Source: MORI.

The groups of people whom the public felt should be invaded seemed to have hardened across the board between 1990 and 1992 (see Table 3.4). On average, this feeling was about eight points up in each case, and for royalty double that.

Finally, over the years we have measured support for a Freedom of Information Act. In the study for the *News of the World* the British public was asked: 'Would you approve of the introduction of a Freedom of Information Act which would allow newspapers and the general public the right of access to official documents which Whitehall departments and the local authorities currently keep?' Once again, a majority (52 per cent on this occasion) said they would approve, and fewer than four in ten (37 per cent) disapproved.

A personal postscript

As MORI looked forward to its twenty-fifth anniversary year, we also looked back at some of the interesting polls that we have done; some very serious indeed (for instance, our tracking panel study on the British public's reaction to the Falklands War for *The Economist* and *Panorama*), some just for fun (where kids want to go on holiday, for Thomas Cook), and some both great fun and with a serious undertone, such as our 1983 survey for the *Sunday Times* on who the public believes tells them the truth. This has gone down in many people's mind as the most memorable poll finding we ever produced. Frequently referred to by politicians and journalists alike, it was the poll that in shorthand we called 'Veracity' (see Table 3.5).

Predictably, we found most people in the UK felt they could gener-

Table 3.5 Who would you trust to tell the truth?

Q: Would you tell me whether you generally trust them to tell the truth or not.

| | Tell the truth | | Not tell the truth | | Net change |
| | 1983 | 1993 | 1983 | 1993 | 1983–93 |
	%	%	%	%	%
Teachers	79	84	14	9	10
Doctors	82	84	14	11	5
Clergy/priests	85	80	11	13	–7
TV news readers	63	79	25	18	23
Professors	n/a	70	n/a	12	n/a
Judges	77	68	18	21	–12
Ordinary people	57	64	27	21	13
The police	61	63	32	26	8
Pollsters	n/a	52	n/a	28	n/a
Civil servants	25	37	63	53	22
Trade union officials	18	32	71	54	31
Business leaders	25	32	65	57	15
Politicians generally	18	14	75	79	–8
Government ministers	16	11	74	81	–12
Journalists	19	10	73	84	–20

Source: MORI/*The Times*.

ally trust doctors and clergymen to tell the truth, and not very many people felt they could trust politicians, trade-union leaders and journalists. That a majority said they felt they could trust TV newsreaders to tell the truth, but not journalists prompted Sir Alistair Burnett to write me a note to say: 'I wonder who they think writes what the newsreaders read?' I also got a call from the late head of the Central Statistical Agency, Sir John Boreham, who invited me in to talk about the low veracity score for civil servants, worried that people might not believe government statistics. More surprisingly, we learned that only just a majority of the ordinary man or woman in the street thought their fellow ordinary man or woman in the street could be trusted to tell the truth. Over one-quarter thought they could not. Only one-quarter believed business leaders, and nearly two-thirds did not.

Journalists (19 per cent) took heart from the fact that they were not bottom of this poll. In fact, politicians generally (18 per cent) weren't either; lowest of all were government ministers – only 16 per cent thought they could be trusted to tell the truth, and a whopping 74 per cent thought they could not. I proposed to *The Times* that we repeat our 'Veracity' questions, asking ten years on about the groups of people we had measured in 1983 to see how, if at all, they fared on the truthfulness test, adding pollsters (and professors, just for fun) to the list. Much to my astonishment, and no doubt to other people's, there were five times as many people who believe they can trust pollsters to tell the truth as have confidence in the veracity of journalists or government ministers.

Northerners, except the Scots, are the most sceptical about the veracity of pollsters, but even in the north 47 per cent said they believed that pollsters tell the truth (against the quarter [27 per cent] who said they do not). Older people were slightly more sceptical – as were, for some reason, Liberal Democrats (perhaps because they have done their own polls in by-elections for so long) – while Conservative and Labour supporters were more or less equally trusting of pollsters, 56 per cent of each group saying they could be trusted. There was nothing in it between middle-class and working-class respondents.

There was good news in the poll for civil servants, for while in 1983 only one-quarter of the public said they could be trusted, a decade later over one-third (37 per cent) said they could be. And the biggest jump of all was among television newsreaders, from 63 per cent a decade earlier to 79 per cent in 1993. This is especially surprising in light of the fact that the 19 per cent score for journalists in 1983 plummeted to just 10 per cent ten years later, taking the wooden spoon, and dropping below government ministers who themselves fell from their lowly 16 per cent to an even lowlier 11 per cent. There was also good news for trade-union leaders, who nearly doubled their veracity score from 18 per cent in 1983 (as bad as politicians) to 32 per cent – two-and-a-half times better than politicians. Judges (down nine points) took a knock, but the police did better. In 1983, 32 per cent said they could not trust the police to tell the truth: that fell to 26 per cent. Professors and teachers got very high marks.

The overall scores also tell an interesting story: we are constantly told that things are getting worse; confidence in institutions is falling; there is moral decay and degradation of the spirit. Not in these figures which were up 5 per cent collectively over the decade. As Abraham Lincoln said: 'Trust the people.'

Notes

1 The names of these two papers were changed after 1993 from the *Daily Express* and the *Daily Mirror* to *The Express* and the *Mirror*.
2 I am grateful to the *News of the World* for freedom to use the data.

References

Henry, H. (1993) 'Twenty years in the life of the nationals', *Admap* (May).
Jacobs, E. and Worcester, R.M. (1990) *We British*, Weidenfeld & Nicolson, London.

Further reading

McLaughlin, C. and Gunter, B. (1991) 'Attitudes to television in 1990', ITC Research Paper, ITC, London.
Worcester, R.M. (1992) 'Who buys what – for why?', *British Journalism Review* 2 (4).

CHAPTER 4

An overview of the current debate on press regulation in France

Christophe Texier

Introduction

As well as undergoing a financial and readership crisis, the French press is currently suffering from an enormous lack of credibility. This is mainly because of the recent fall in its standards recorded since the late 1980s, and is illustrated by many cases of misconduct perpetrated by the press. Recent affairs have triggered violent criticism both from the public and the political establishment in France, and have reignited the age-old debate about the regulation of the press.

The French press is currently regulated by a complex and rather intense body of legislation whose roots lie in the law of 29 July 1881. This defines the limits of the fundamental right to freedom of expression while setting out sanctions for the most common offences. In addition to this, as early as 1918 the National Union of Journalists (Syndicat National des Journalistes) adopted a code of conduct which clearly laid out the profession's governing principles. Both of these regulatory texts have been regularly updated and amended by legislators in attempts to maintain public order, while guaranteeing individual freedoms, and also by newspaper professionals whose concern has been to maintain their legitimacy in the eyes of the public.

However, it does seem that both forms of regulation – legislation and a code of conduct – are currently unable to curb the French press's excesses, and reduce them to a socially acceptable level. Hence the calls for more amendments, more changes and more control over the press by both the public and politicians. Introducing such reform seems a particularly complex task at the moment, largely because of the radical transformations which the French press has undergone since the 1960s. Up until now, none of the suggestions put forward by any of the parties involved in this debate – representatives of the press, the public and the State – seems to offer a solution likely to please everyone.

After a brief summary of the origins and contents of the rules that constitute the regulatory apparatus of the French press, I shall examine the main grievances levelled at the press in France and look at a few telling examples. Finally, an examination of the various proposals advanced to solve some of the problems posed by the evolution of journalistic practice will enable me to emphasize their weaknesses.

The tools of regulation

French legislators adopted measures relating specifically to the press very early on. Most of these rules were introduced in order to ensure economic and political transparency in accordance with the press's status as a public interest body, while, at the same time protecting citizens against the potential abuses of its position. Contrary to the situation in the UK, in France there is no authority which determines the journalist's rights, obligations and practices. However, a number of texts, codes or charters set out the basic tenets of the profession through clear and concise guidelines.

The French press on parole

The judicial regime governing the French press was largely established by a law passed on 29 July 1881. This law is itself directly based on Article XI of the Declaration of the Rights of Man and the Citizen of 1789 according to which 'Any citizen can exercise his right to write, speak and publish freely, except when doing so constitutes an abuse of this right as determined by the Law'.[1] The law of 1881, while it was modified several times as well as amended by numerous – generally more restrictive – clauses,[2] still governs the activity of the French press today, with the exception of the audiovisual sector which, because it did not exist at that time, has since been the object of a particular body of legislation.

Apart from reinforcing the principle of the freedom of expression, the 1881 law sets out the obligations to which publications are subjected with respect to their content, and defines the offences which might be likely to give rise to judicial action were the rules not respected. The role of this text (Bilger and Lebedel 1991) is, first and foremost, to impress on the press respect for certain social values such as a minimum amount of discretion and reliability, as well as an understanding of the responsibility it bears. As such, the dissemination of certain information is prohibited, such as, for example, anything concerning national defence or any information subject to judicial secrecy. The circulation of false information, affronts to public decency, as well as incitements to crime, are also severely condemned.

To these limits imposed in the name of moral values we must add those designed to protect particular individuals or public institutions, such as the judicial system, the Army and the State treasury, as well as the representatives of foreign governments. With respect to the protection of individuals, the 1881 law also institutes a right of reply: that is, the right of any individual to respond to any article in which they are cited or designated. Finally, since 1972, French law punishes incitements to racial hatred as well as slander and racial insults.

A code of conduct established early on

The 1881 law deals with press offences: that is, what is prohibited. With respect to its duties, as it has become increasingly organized and complex, the profession has adopted instruments which, although they have been unable to ensure effective exhaustive regulation from a legal point of view, have nevertheless remained a professional point of reference. For example, French journalists often refer to a code of conduct adopted in July 1918 – and subsequently revised and completed in January 1938 – by the National Union of Journalists (Charte des devoirs professionnels des journalistes Français) (Bilger and Lebedel, 1991: 115–16). This charter, which is the equivalent of the British Press Complaints Commission's code of conduct, constitutes a very real code of ethics, a moral reference for journalists, which clearly indicates the type of conduct they are to abide by and uphold. This first text already made much of the duty of dignity, honesty and professional responsibility. A more recent and more complex version of the same text (*Déclaration des Devoirs et Droits du Journaliste*) (Bilger and Lebedel 1991: 117ff) was compiled in Munich in 1971 by representatives of the European Community's federation of journalists and was adopted by the French National Union of Journalists.

The degradation of journalistic standards

Examples of violations of the laws and ethics of journalism committed by the French press since the beginning of the 1990s abound, and it would be impossible to compile an exhaustive list of them here. I shall simply list a few of the most-often cited examples, therefore, before giving a rudimentary typology of the more frequently committed forms of misconduct.

A proliferation of faux pas

Among the cases of misconduct committed in the last few years, one of the most frequently cited examples is the undue haste with which, in November 1992, journalists revealed the existence of a mass grave in Timisoara, Romania (Castex 1990). The mass grave was immediately interpreted as evidence of genocide perpetrated by a demented Ceauşescu regime then in its final days. Investigations later revealed that the mass grave was nothing but that, and was located in a banal cemetery where the bodies had been hurriedly buried in a pit, for lack of time and space. Along the same lines, in May 1990, the desecration of a Jewish cemetery in Carpentras in the south of France gave rise to another *faux pas*, as journalists promptly attributed the regrettable incident to a surge in antisemitism in France. The latter was seen in turn to be the result of the racial intolerance promoted by parties of the extreme right at the time. A few days later, in fact, the French police arrested a gang of local delinquents, who confessed to the crime but also admitted that they had not desecrated the cemetery in the name of antisemitism but simply out of boredom. French media coverage of the Gulf War in 1990–91 marks the apogee of irresponsible journalistic practices. The manner in which the French press covered the Iraqi invasion and then the liberation of Kuwait by the allied troops is a perfect example of the manner in which French journalists increasingly substituted entertainment for information, and therefore failed to verify information at the risk of reporting erroneous 'facts' and thus playing into the hands of official propaganda machines.

Criticism of the press raged from every possible source: public opinion and media researchers both condemned the role of the press in the conflict, but things worsened when the suicide of the former French Prime Minister, Pierre Bérégovoy, was attributed to the press's unjustified and unrelenting persecution of a man whom everyone held in high esteem. Both friends and political enemies of Mr Bérégovoy agreed that only the attitude of the press towards him and its relentless attacks on his honour could have pushed so seasoned a politician to commit such an act. At the time of his death the press was accusing Mr Bérégovoy of not being able to justify the compensation granted to a French industrialist who had once done him a personal financial favour when he was leader of the government. The hesitant attitude of the former Prime Minister did not, in the eyes of French public opinion, justify throwing 'a man's honour, and ultimately his life, to the hounds' as President Mitterrand said in the speech he delivered at Bérégovoy's funeral.[3] François Mitterrand himself suffered from the press's seemingly uncontrollable lack of discretion and scruples when in November 1994 pictures of his illegitimate daughter were published without his consent (*Paris Match*, 10 Nov. 1994).[4]

The case against the press

In an attempt to wade through the endless accusations levelled at the French press, the French sociologist Jean-Marie Charon (1993a: 280) classifies the current journalistic misconduct in three distinct categories. In the first of these categories he classes what he calls 'little inaccuracies' ('les petites inexactitudes') or approximations, such as using one name instead of another, or a lack or verification of figures or dates; little things that are the result of a lack of rigour and which are insufficiently exposed by the press itself.

The second category, which contains more serious errors whose consequences are more far reaching, includes a deliberate disregard for privacy laws and for the judicial process (le 'non respect délibéré des règles visant au respect de la vie privé ou des procédures juridiques en cours') (Charon 1993a: 281). The Villemin case, which was launched by the press as the result of the – apparently motiveless and culpritless –

murder of a four-year-old child (Grégory Villemin) in 1984, is without a doubt the case that best symbolizes the generalization of these practices in the French press. In a minutely documented investigation published in 1993, Laurence Lacour (1993) reveals the behind-the-scenes behaviour of the media throughout the Villemin case (often referred to as 'l'Affaire Grégory'), or how the written press, in particular, adopted a *modus operandi* which had nothing to do with the objectivity, impartiality, prudence and honesty required in such tragic circumstances.

According to Charon, the third category of wrongdoings includes the French press's current tolerance towards violence or the spectacular, and its relentless search for 'emotional impact' at whatever cost. During one of the many debates on the topic of ethics and information which are currently being organized in France, Robert Ménard, the director of the association Reporters sans Frontières, lamented the French press's tendency to privilege a sensationalist and reductionist approach to information, at the expense of the complexity of the reality it evokes.[5] He noted that despite the number of reports published on topics such as the level and nature of the violence in the former Yugoslavia, or in Rwanda, the public's understanding of these crises does not seem to have increased. The moral indignation triggered by this type of report paradoxically seems to go against the best interests of the victims by eclipsing the essentially political dimension of these conflicts.

This is not the first wave of criticism to which the French press has been subjected. Throughout its history it has been the object of severe criticisms, and André Fouillé, a French philosopher, gave rise to an emotional debate on the role of the press as early as 1897–98, when he accused it of being 'out of control' ('dechaînée') and of 'daily fanning the flames of vengeance, jealousy and wrath' (quoted Ferenczi 1993: 213ff).[6] This accusatory attitude towards the press was the result of the real antagonism which then characterized the relationship between writers and journalists, the former never missing an opportunity to sling mud in the face of those who might have written negative or disrespectful literary reviews.[7] Throughout the twentieth century French journalists have often been called to task by the State and by public opinion, following behaviour which was deemed unacceptable. What distinguishes the current situation from those of the past is the apparent incapacity of governmental or professional institutions to introduce measures which might halt the decline of press standards and journalistic practice.

Regulation at a deadlock

The examples which we have just listed can in fact be seen as failures of the existing system of press regulation in France. Neither do the legal sanctions which are applicable nor the existing code of ethics seem capable of dissuading the press from adopting reprehensible methods. Given this state of affairs, the French authorities' reaction has been to call for a reinforcement of the existing legal framework as well as harsher sanctions in the cases of infringements of the law. Newspaper professionals, as well as legal experts and victims of the press, on the other hand, maintain that such measures would not be effective in the face of the mounting offences and appeals to journalists' sense of ethics and to an increased sense of responsibility.

The obstacles to repression

A repressive political attitude cannot possibly be the solution to the current problem. The introduction of a new Bill by the centre-right MP Alain Marsaud is the most recent example of a failed attempt to toughen legal sanctions against the press. This Bill was first voted in by French MPs on 21 November 1994, but in view of the protests to which it gave rise, it was rejected by the Senate shortly after (*Libération*, 8 Dec. 1994: 21). This amendment's primary effect would have been to throw a shroud of silence over all the trials in which politicians and business people found themselves implicated at the time, by denying the press access to the trials in order to avoid prejudicing the proceedings. The adoption of the Marsaud amendment had triggered the anger of professional press associations and organizations, all of which described it as a serious infringement of the principle of freedom of information. Its explicitly repressive nature also created great confusion in French political circles. The latter were clearly reluctant to start a guerrilla war against the press, given their dependency on it – not to mention the danger of the prospect of coming across as an adversary of basic rights and freedoms during an electoral campaign.

To these obstacles of a political nature we can add those of a more technical nature. In an article published by the French daily *Libération*, Maitre Henri Leclerc, a lawyer and vice-president of the Ligue Française des droits de l'homme, underlined that cases of abuse of the freedom of the press can only be punished by judges once the law has classed them as such (Leclerc 1992).[8] For example, this is the case with respect to slander or the violation of privacy. But according to Leclerc the law will never be able to regulate every possible offence committed by the press. Furthermore, legal experts highlight the fact that in the case of major offences, penalties already exist (right of reply, fines, etc.) and these do not seem to have any effect on the behaviour of journalists.

From the victims' viewpoint, this type of approach suffers from two major disadvantages: first and foremost, the victims emphasize that so far they have not had a significant dissuasive effect; second, and more important, the victims emphasize the *post facto* nature of legal sanctions, which come into play only once the damage has already been done.

The shortcomings of a code of ethics

Given the many obstacles to the reinforcement of legal sanctions, proposals of a different nature have emerged, calling for an increase in the development of the means of self-regulation by the press. The most often called-for solution proposes the adoption of a new charter of journalistic ethics – since the existing ones seem obsolete – as well as the creation of a press council (Conseil Supérieur de la Presse) which would enforce certain standards of professional ethics. These proposals might seem a bit naïve in the eyes of some foreign observers well acquainted with the difficulties encountered, for example, by the Press Complaints Commission in the UK – difficulties which reveal that it is no longer enough to enunciate principles in order to guarantee they be respected. Moreover, at a time when most French institutions suffer from a lack of credibility and legitimacy, it is hard to believe that a new body entrusted with upholding the ideals of self-regulation could wield enough moral authority over the press and the public to be effective. We need only glance at the unconvincing results obtained by the Conseil Supérieur de l'Audiovisuel (Superior Council for the Audiovisual Media) to see the limits of such a project.

With respect to a possible reformulation and restatement of the principles set out in the 'Charte des devoirs professionnels des journalistes Français' of 1918, many professionals, such Franz-Olivier Gisbert, the editor-in-chief of *Le Figaro*, admit that this would in no way alter the current situation and that the principles set out in the 1918 text have a surprisingly modern ring (cited in Salord 1994: 15). On closer inspection it is true that, save for a few terminological alterations, any shortcomings in this text are above all the result of the current conditions in which most journalistic practice takes place: conditions which do little to encourage its application.

Journalism and corporate culture

Most recent scholarship on the press in France (Mathien 1992; Charon 1993a) brings to light the existence of a real gap between the principles which govern the journalistic profession and its daily practice. The diversification of contemporary means of communication seems to be working toward the gradual extinction of traditional French journalism whose references are slowly being eclipsed. These studies also reveal that the pre-eminence of economic objectives and managerial practices over editorial considerations contribute to an often regrettable modification of the content of today's newspapers.

The fragmentation of the profession

Historically, as emphasized by Charon (1993b: 23), the French press has always been dominated by journalism of a political variety. It is around this élitist and independent form of journalism that most of the profession's ethics and rules of competence were elaborated. For a long time the great figures of French journalism drew their inspiration from these sources. For example, people like Hubert Beuve-Mery of *Le Monde* always insisted on individual expertise and competence and aimed to create a relation of trust between the readers and their newspaper. Today this type of journalism is without a doubt on the wane in the written press. First, the written daily press has become quantitatively marginal, because of the dwindling circulation which has affected all large French daily newspapers for the past twenty years, and it is now slowly being replaced in its role as the main source of information by the audiovisual media.

To this trend we must also add the increasing number of specialized publications which started invading the news-stands in France as of the mid-1980s, a sector which has attracted young inexperienced journalists. The body in charge of the annual allocation of press cards to French journalists[9] thus issued 26 600 cards in 1990, as against 21 300 in 1985, 13 600 in 1975 and 9900 in 1965 (Mathien 1992: 238). In 1991 the commission registered 2300 newcomers. Yet, as emphasized by Daniel Junqua, then the director of one of France's most prestigious schools of journalism,[10] officially recognized French schools of journalism had only produced 300 graduates that year (Junqua 1993: 39ff). Although Junqua admits that the situation is alarming, he nevertheless refuses the – albeit logical – hypothesis put forward by some critics according to which the decline in journalism standards might be because of journalism's young recruits' lack of awareness of the ethics of their chosen profession. Junqua's claim is that whatever ethics we choose to live by, our values are based on principles acquired as a child. He is quick to emphasize that French society itself seems to be exhibiting some difficulty in upholding the kinds of moral principles it so urgently and relentlessly requires of its journalists: 'the primacy of money, the lacklustre nature of any debate on ideas, the discrediting of the political, the cult of individualism and craving for celebrity, the decline of morals, both secular and religious, which used to serve as points of reference, that is the context in which most young people live'.[11]

Concluding, he adds 'the teaching and imparting of a code of ethics is one thing, its application is another',[12] and he further notes that in his view, it is the current context in which journalism is practised which 'does not create conditions favourable to the observance of a code of ethics' (Junqua 1993: 39–40).[13]

Business logic

The economic difficulties which have plagued many French newspapers, and particularly the daily press since the 1970s, as well as the intense competition from the audiovisual media, have prompted editors to radically transform the functioning of the newspaper trade. For the French press, the 1970s and 1980s thus bear the stamp of what Charon (1993a: 184ff) terms 'an aggressive business logic characterized by an increase in marketing techniques' and a 'rationalization' of the profession's methods of operation.

This phenomenon is most concretely translated into the introduction of a commercial dynamic in the press sector, this resulting in turn in a drastic disruption of its senior managers' hierarchy of preoccupations and objectives. Journalists and editorial boards saw themselves abruptly edged out of the decision-making processes and excluded from strategic decisions concerning the paper's orientation. The status of the editorial board and that of the journalist were gradually reduced to simply carrying out higher level decisions, in which they participated less and less.

The offensive of Robert Hersant, a manager who makes no bones about the fact that he dislikes journalists, in the French daily market at the end of the 1970s and his take-over of *Le Figaro* in 1975, *France Soir* in 1976 and *L'Aurore* in 1979, are, according to Charon, the tell-tale signs of the end of what he calls 'journalists' newspapers'[14] in France (Charon 1993a: 188). From this moment on, it seems that 'the press no longer holds the informing citizens as its main goal' (Mathien 1989: 216), but rather aims at maximizing profits; the quality of its performance becomes secondary. The acceleration in the pace and rhythm of producing information, the increasingly short, market-driven deadlines to which all editorial teams are subjected may have, as their side-effect, the abundance of superficial work and an increase in the risk of the abuses, inaccuracies and major or minor offences we are witnessing.

This is how a journalistic tradition steeped in the principles of privacy, which had hitherto disapproved of discourteous investigative tactics and which refrained from using the entrapment of its sources as a means to a story, found itself shaken to its very foundations by the new imperatives governing the profession. Economic reasoning often supersedes the duty to tell the truth which lies at the basis of professional ethics; the editorial content is subordinate to the market-oriented endeavour of the modern press. The increasing reliance on freelance journalists, on temporary workers, on young trainees or occasional contributors, and the simultaneous reduction of permanent, full-time staff to a minimum, have resulted in extremely precarious employment conditions in the press. Furthermore, even in cases in which a journalist is offered a full-time job, the decision-making structure now in place in most papers does not allow them to contribute to most of the decisions, nor does it allow them a say in the overall editorial project, if such a project exists. Finally, the need for a guaranteed source of income may also drive many journalists into accepting work with little regard for whether it might pose ethical problems.

The most recent studies on the workings of the French press indicate that the economic strategy of the modern press, and the conditions in which most journalists practise their profession are two factors which most certainly impact on the process of the production of information and on its general contents. It is impossible not to take these into account, therefore, when we contemplate disciplining the press.

Conclusion

Although the French press – just like its British counterpart – is today undeniably guilty of many offences with respect to the principles which are supposed to govern its actions, it would seem that the complex problems which such offences bring to the fore cannot possibly be solved by simple solutions. Ethical principles are not simply up against reluctant or immoral journalists, but rather they are continuously put to the test by the harsh realities of a French press whose frame of reference has become a commercial one. The studies effected in this area of research highlight the fact that the margin for the application of a code of ethics has been reduced to its narrowest expression by the economic guidelines to which it is subordinated.

Systematically reinforcing or 'renovating' existing measures for the control of the press consequently appears to be a pointless exercise, and might even prove dangerous in terms of the protection of fundamental rights. Before speculating on such matters, it might be profitable to speculate on the underlying causes of the degradation of modern journalistic practices. To avoid further misinterpretation and oversimplification it would also be profitable, at a time of a growing internationalization of all means of communication, to adopt a comparative and cross-national approach to the problems caused today by the modern press.

From our point of view, although the British press is still, in terms of readership as well as in its configuration, in a different situation from its French counterpart, there are some obvious similarities between the problems observed in these two countries. On the one hand, the criticisms that the British press is currently undergoing sound largely familiar across the Channel. Journalists in France are generally being blamed for similar reasons: that is, for their lack of social responsibility and ignorance of the rules set out to protect individuals. On the other hand, the British press has also recently been subjected to deep transformations in its mode of production as well as in its basic ideals, following the introduction of what Michael Leapman (1992: 62) described as a 'new journalistic mix', more tightly based on market-driven methods and commercial motives. Some British analysts, such as Geoffrey Goodman, also consider the fact that the 'concentration of media power in the hands of a few individuals who recognize no other discipline than the one of the market' is becoming more and more problematic in the sense that it seems to fundamentally undermine the basis of journalistic ethics (Goodman 1994: 3).

A new approach to these questions of regulation is consequently urgently needed both in France and in the UK before it is too late to stop the censorial threats looming over the press. The actual paralysis that is affecting this debate is symptomatic of the lack of comprehension of the mechanisms that underpin the functioning of the modern press. A deeper socioeconomic analysis of the recent transformation of the media industry would certainly lead us towards a better understanding of the motives and reasons that lie behind the decline of press standards and methods today.

Notes

1 All translations into English are my own.
2 For example, the edict of 26 August 1944, in turn reinforced by the

law of August 1986, both of which founded the current status of the press in France as underpinned by an obligation of transparency of ownership whose aim is to uphold and guarantee the pluralism of the French press.

3 'qu'on ait pu livrer aux chiens l'honneur d'un homme et, finalement, sa vie': quoted in Plenel 1994: 44.

4 The pictures were published after a well-known journalist, Philippe Alexandre, revealed the existence of the girl in a book.

5 'privilégier une approche sensationnelle et réductrice de l'information aux dépens de la complexité de la réalité qu'elle évoque': quoted in *Midi Média. La mémoire d'Hourtin* (1994) **93** Nov.: 22.

6 'de ne faire que l'apologie journalière de la vengeance, de la jalousie et de la colère'.

7 C'est ainsi que certains mots sont passés à la postérité: 'Si la presse n'existant pas, it ne faudrait sourtout pas l'inventer' (Balzac); 'Je ne comprends pas qu'une main pure puisse toucher un journal sans une convulsion de dégoût' (Baudelaire).

8 'les abus de la liberté de la presse ne peuvent être réprimés par les juges que lorsque la loi les a caractérisé'.

9 La Commission de la carte d'identité de journalistes professionnels.

10 Ecole Supérieure de Journalisme de Lille.

11 'le primat de l'argent, la pauvreté des débats d'idées, le discrédit de la politique, le culte de l'individualisme et la recherche de la notoriété, le recul des morales tant laïques que religieuses qui fournissaient des repères et des critères'.

12 'l'enseignement de la déontologie est une chose, sa mise en oeuvre en est une autre'.

13 'conditions favorables a l'observation d'une déontologie'.

14 'journaux des journalistes'.

References

Bilger, P. and Lebedel, P. (1991) *Abrégé du droit de la presse*, CFPJ, Paris.

Castex, M. (1990) *Un mensonge gros comme le siècle, Roumanie, histoire d'une manipulation*, Albin Michel, Paris.

Charon, J.-M. (1993a) *Cartes de presse, enquête sur les journalistes*, Stock, Paris.

Charon, J.-M. (1993b) 'Face a un journalisme éclaté', *Après-domain* **353** (4) Apr.–May.

Ferenczi, T. (1993) *L'invention du journalisme en France*, Plon, Paris.

Goodman, G. (1994) 'The power to say no', *British Journalism Review* **5** (4): 3.

Junqua, D. (1993) 'Formation au journalisme et déontologie', *Après-domain* **353**(4) April.

Lacour, L. (1993) *Le bûcher des innocents*, Plon, Paris.

Leapman, M. (1992) *Treacherous Estate: The Press After Wapping*, Hodder & Stoughton, London.

Leclerc, H. (1992) 'Faut-il discipliner la presse?', *Libération*, 24 Nov.

Mathien, M. (1989) *Le system médiatique, le journal dans son environement*, Hachette, Paris.
Mathien, M. (1992) *Les journalistes et le systeme médiatique*, Hachette, Paris.
Plenel, E. (1994) *Un temps de chien*, Stock, Paris.
Salord, H. (1994) Interview with Franz-Olivier Gisbert, *Label France* 14 Jan., Ministry of Foreign Affairs, Paris.

PART II

Press regulation and accountability

CHAPTER 5

Managing the press in a medium-sized European power

John Tulloch

Twice a year, Britain's Central Office of Information – the unobtrusive machinery behind the State's public relations and propaganda operations – produces a directory of information and press officers in government departments and public corporations. In June 1996 249 organizations were listed, ranging from the Advisory, Conciliation and Arbitration Service, sometimes pressed into action to resolve industrial disputes, to the Women's National Commission, by way of the BBC, the Ministry of Defence, Her Majesty's Treasury, the Prime Minister's Office and the UK Ecolabelling Board. A number of the organizations listed would be very indignant indeed to be regarded as part of the State – particularly the BBC, which has long had a problem defining the precise nature of its relationship to Leviathan. But the BBC World Service remains directly funded by a Foreign Office grant. Even the Trades Union Congress, which in eighteen years of Conservative government has been snubbed and ignored rather than treated to beer and sandwiches, still hankers (April 1997) after a consultative role now that a Labour government has been elected. It is an interesting tribute to the continuing corporate bias of the British State that this stalwart of the consensus politics of the 1950s and 1960s is still included in the directory, along with its confrère, the Confederation of British Industry.

A simple count of the press and public relations officers and support staff listed gives a total of 1772. If a tighter definition of the State is taken as simply constituting ministries, the police and operators of statutory systems – for example, the British Radio Authority – but excluding cultural and artistic organizations such as the British Film Institute, the British Library, etc. – the total is about 1200. This gives some indication of the scale of the machine but can only be a fraction of the *real* total – excluding, for example, local authority press operations, the use by the State of the private PR sector and a whole range of organizations that have power over our lives.

But what is the British State? Although British politics since the Second World War has been dominated by a debate about the role of the State, it remains a term with which British politicians are uncomfortable unless they are claiming that it is over-mighty or that they have slimmed it down. The leading British politician of the 1980s loudly waged a one-woman war against it and vowed to cut the numbers of civil servants. But it is now clear that, in Britain, 'instead of a steady withdrawal, the State has taken new forms' (Dynes and Walker 1995). Some familiar institutions have disappeared but the network of institutions through which power is exercised in the public sphere has expanded to create a bewildering array of new bodies, many of them barely known to the public. In particular the 'peripheral' State of non-departmental public bodies – also known as Quangos – embraces according to official estimates at least 650 bodies with over 36 000 appointees. A wider official definition admitted to a total of nearly 1400 organizations in 1993. Some non-official estimates have been much higher: one from the Charter 88 Trust claimed there are more than 5000 (Dynes and Walker 1995). And in a 1993 investigation headed 'Rise and Rise of the Quangocrats' *The Guardian* claimed that by 1996, 7700 public bodies controlled by government-appointed 'placemen' would be responsible for one-third of all public expenditure: about £54 billion (*The Guardian*, 19 Nov. 1993).

Traditionally, journalism in Britain has related to the State in three ways. The State provides the framework within which law and regulation operate. Through laws on defamation, contempt, official secrets and confidence, for example, the State sets various limits to the professional activity of journalists (Robertson and Nicol 1992). Through economic regulation it has a role – to an increasingly limited extent – in shaping the ownership and economic environment of media organizations. And through a large official machinery for news-making and news management it functions as a major – still perhaps the major – information source for British journalism. For, whatever the appearances, journalism in Britain has long had a close and problematic relationship with official sources (Leigh, 1980; Cockerell *et al.* 1984; Tulloch, 1993; Franklin, 1994).

All these features might be said to belong to other EU States but there are intriguing aspects of British press-State relations that make them of more than parochial interest. As any European visitor to London can testify, Britain has a press which combines some good quality, even worldclass newspapers, with some of the worst in Europe. Few British journalists today would sincerely mount a defence of newspapers like *The Sun*, the *Mirror* and *The Express*, but when they do they use three arguments: that the price of a free press is to have some bad newspapers; that, although the ethics of their newsgathering or their regard for privacy are indefensible, they are extremely well-produced; and that élite journalists are snobs who take themselves too seriously and fail to realize the entertainment value of popular newspapers. For example, in an interview the aging *enfant terrible* Julie Burchill dismissed criticisms of *The Sun* as attacks on the working class (*The Guardian*, July 1995).

Everyone also agrees about the vigour of the British press market. This is a press environment that continues to attract a number of overseas players, that sustains a large number of diverse titles, and in which if newspapers die, they are also reborn. Despite an overall downward trend in national newspaper daily circulation, from 15.6 million in the early 1980s to around 13.8 million today, and a three-year price war which has killed off one daily title and may soon finish another, more newspaper pages circulate than ever before, with the market-leading *Sunday Times* selling eleven forest-levelling sections every week (see *The Guardian* Media, 15 July 1996: 25). But, to an extraordinary extent, these robustly commercial newspapers, braving market forces like noisy middle-aged swimmers in winter, who proclaim commercialism as a guarantee of their 'freedom', have a history of quietly conniving at remarkable levels of censorship and informal news management. Rather than being doughty adversaries of the State, Britain's newspapers have been some of its most willing collaborators, with a long record of 'sleeping with the enemy' and not just in wartime. According to Robert Harris:

> The instinctive secrecy of the military and the Civil Service; the prostitution and hysteria of sections of the press; the lies, the misinformation, the manipulation of public opinion by the authorities; the political intimidation of broadcasters; the ready connivance of the media at their own distortion ... all these occur as much in peacetime Britain as in war. (Harris 1983: 151)

Dancing with dogma, sleeping with the enemy

The chief ways in which relations between the State and the British press are problematic lie in their secrecy and in the scope they offer for a mutual game of manipulation, one of whose aims is to keep the public in the dark. Britain, like France, has a set of cultural and legal traditions inherited from its former role as a highly centralized, imperial power which means that the management of the State is regarded by its practitioners as a private affair. Managing the State entails managing the media. Managing the media, in Britain, has always involved creating a tribe of 'insiders'. Equally media 'insiders' have a strong interest in maintaining good relationships with the State to protect their economic interests, their sources of information and an unimpeded and enormous flow of comparatively cheap information.

Thus, relations between the British State and the press are like an intricate and complex dance in which the audience has at the most only a dim understanding of the 'rules' observed by the dancers and the motives of their performance. What they see is a complex performance: an interaction between formal codes for public consumption and informal mechanisms for managing relations negotiated by senior journalists, proprietors and elements of the State apparatus. This does not mean that, for example, the relationship between the press and particular political actors or parties can be characterized as simple dominance. As Bob Franklin points out, the mutual work done by press and politicians in 'packaging' politics:

does not necessarily imply that politicians dominate media in any direct or conspiratorial way, although it does not preclude such a possibility. Sustained media criticism of John Major, despite the wealth of communication resources a Prime Minister possesses, scotches any such simplistic notion. Media do criticize and challenge politicians; on occasion they test them to destruction. (Franklin 1994: 13)

Large sections of the British press have had an adversarial relationship to recent UK governments. But governments, like politicians, are a relatively small and temporary part of the picture. The State, on the other hand, is a very large and in places a very old picture indeed. Apart from the legal blunderbuss of official secrecy, defamation and contempt, in Britain there have been three mechanisms that have evolved for handling the press – or perhaps allowing the press and the State to mutually handle each other under the bedclothes. Two of them are relatively old and fairly shadowy, and one is young and keen on publicity. The first is the lobby system, which evolved in the nineteenth century. The second is a large State machine for handling press information, government public relations and media relations, which began to arise in the early 1900s, a generation after the lobby. The third is the machinery that developed, under State patronage and the threat of legal restrictions, for press 'self-regulation' from the early 1950s.

Lobbies: establishing the rules of the club

Observing the political coverage of the British press during the American Civil War the US ambassador grudgingly admired:

> many instances of the uses made of the press, from certain points and high sources in order to affect public opinion . . . it almost takes the character of ubiquity. One effect of it is to render it rather hard for persons not in the secret to distinguish the genuine from the spurious article. (*History of the Times* 1939)

Victorian politicians were adept at creating press cronies who knew their place. The Victorian press was politically managed by a combination of proprietorial influence – many local politicians were on the boards of newspapers and had financial stakes in the London-based press (Lee 1976) – bribery and discreet briefing. But as the century wore on the disadvantage of an informal system of confidential briefings, tips and leaks became more marked. Such a system was difficult to control and coordinate. Too much information might be leaked, different ministers might float contradictory stories. The increase in the circulation of the press and its development away from direct Party control aggravated the problem. The centre of political reporting was the House of Commons. Here in the lobby outside the debating chamber journalists were able to accost ministers and MPs. Parliamentary reporters used such opportunities to supplement the verbatim reporting of the debates by shorthand and the writing of parliamentary 'sketches': a lightweight form of political reporting increasingly used by the new London evening newspapers and the popular press. In a bid to control leaks reporters were banned from the lobby in 1871. But that was in nobody's interests, and ten years later journalists were readmitted. In 1884 a 'lobby list' was created of a few correspondents mainly from the London morning and evening newspapers. All other journalists were excluded. Membership of the lobby was rigidly policed by the journalists themselves who agreed a set of 'lobby rules' enshrined in a secret rule book. By 1910 the lobby consisted of no more than thirty correspondents, often writing for half-a-dozen different newspapers. The monopoly was jealously guarded. Provincial newspaper correspondents were only admitted in 1950 and Sunday newspapers in 1961.

Officially the lobby did not, and does not, exist and the cardinal lobby rule is the requirement that members keep its activities secret. According to one of its longest-serving members, James Margach, the lobby's purpose 'was to create a new group of insiders and exclude the public and the mass of writers' (Margach 1979). Lobby business was mainly done by a system of unattributable 'briefings' by government ministers and senior officials. The effect of this was to control the flow of information to the press, allowing governments to set an agenda for coverage by planting stories or suggesting interpretations of policy without taking any responsibility for the end product.

But the sheer informality with which important government business was conducted before the First World War militated against systematic news management. British Cabinets functioned more like the governing bodies of exclusive gentlemen's clubs than organs for collective decision-taking. Until 1916 no formal records or minutes were taken at Cabinet meetings and ministers were discouraged from taking private notes. In public, ministers were assumed to be on their honour as gentlemen to observe the absolute secrecy of Cabinet proceedings. In private, ministers routinely leaked often contradictory stories to favoured journalists. But such casual, manipulative amateurism could not long survive the blast of war.

Creating the State news machine

The State news machine in Britain arose in response to total war and involved the quiet incorporation of a large part of the British media within the State's propaganda effort. A machinery for disseminating official information and undertaking censorship was set up in 1914, at first in an *ad hoc* way but then organized into a Ministry of Information by 1917–18. Similar measures were undertaken in 1939, when a 'shadow' Ministry of Information, planned since 1936, was rolled into action. A number of ministries had created their press departments during the interwar period to handle their information needs. These had a difficult relationship with the Ministry of Information but came out on top and substantially increased the scale of their own operations (Cockett 1994).

At the same time, steps were taken to incorporate the media into the State machinery in a formal and informal way. Most obviously, Britain's war correspondents were put into uniform. Former journalists were appointed as censors or co-opted from news organizations to act in censorship and propaganda roles. Most notoriously, press proprietors were given key roles in managing the machinery. In the First World War, Beaverbrook, Northcliffe and Rothermere were all given senior roles in running the propaganda effort. In the Second World War, after an uncertain series of appointments, Churchill put his old crony Brendan Bracken, the proprietor of the *Financial Times*, into the job of Minister of Information. At a lower level, many information functionaries were recruited from Fleet Street. Attlee's first press officer in 1945 was Francis Williams, the former editor of the *Daily Herald*. His second was Philip Jordan, a respected foreign correspondent for the *News Chronicle*. Such appointments remained controversial within Whitehall and a long battle was fought within the State machinery to have ex-journalists accepted as suitable candidates for these posts rather than civil servants. Sir Bernard Ingham, Margaret Thatcher's burly press secretary, was a former *Guardian* journalist. In contrast. John Major's press secretaries all had an impeccable civil service background.

Many of the staff who had begun to make careers in the postwar information machine found the climate less promising in the late 1940s as government cutbacks reduced opportunities. As the economy revived the postwar British PR industry was in part based on people who had acquired their skills in the State machine and left as it was run down. (For example, Lex Hornsby, the director of PR at the Ministry of Labour, became director of Notley advertising agency's PR service.)

But in many respects the machinery was only partly dismantled after 1945. Even after the First World War the skills and lessons that had been learned frequently still operated in the service of the State. The Foreign Office News Department was expanded to incorporate some of the Ministry of Information personnel. The Post Office imbibed some of the techniques of mass persuasion for its innocent-seeming propaganda, with its corporatist and nation-building messages. And some key practitioners of propaganda techniques simply migrated – notably to the Conservative Party. Propaganda in the Conservative Party after the First World War was developed by a number of people who had served their time at Beaverbrook's Ministry of Information or at Northcliffe's rival directorship of propaganda in enemy countries at Crewe House and in some cases in MI5 (Middlemas 1979; Cockett 1994). By the late 1920s, Conservative Central Office was operating a sophisticated mix of propaganda services.

> The Lobby press service provided 230 weekly and daily provincial papers with a regular diet of political news. Every day, each editor received a leading article and up to six 'notes' supplied free of charge. A guarantee was given to every editor that the service would not go to any other paper in the area of his circulation, so as to avoid any obvious duplication. (Cockett 1994)

So, although the Ministry of Information was dismantled in 1919, press offices had been set up in many departments by 1939, and a shadow ministry was established in 1936 to prepare for the Second World War. By 1945, the total State information staff in ministries and overseas was around 10 000 people (Ministry of Information: 2900 in the UK plus at least 3600 overseas; ministry press officers at least 1700; and many information workers in semi-official organizations). By 1948 there were still at least 4000 information workers on the State payroll according to some estimates (Tulloch 1993). The incoming Labour Government saw huge advantages in maintaining a large State information machine as it embarked on a process of social reform, despite the inevitable political flak from the Beaverbrook, Harmsworth and Kemsley press. Labour's economic information campaign of the late 1940s cost more than any wartime campaign.

Journalists and editors might complain bitterly about the size of the peacetime machinery, but many welcomed the new arrangements. There were clear advantages in terms of creating new media jobs. For example, in 1946 a report on the expansion of public relations by the Institute of Journalists forecast that PR jobs in government departments, politics, local authorities and private industry would employ more than 1000 journalists over the next fifteen years (*World's Press News*, 18 April 1946). This was to prove a huge underestimate. Both the IoJ and the Overseas Empire Correspondents' Association attacked the *lack* of journalists in the new government information service. The latter was 'convinced by our war-time experience that a government information service not directly influenced by journalists is a hindrance rather than a help. It neither appreciates the needs and problems of journalists nor fulfils the purpose for which it was established. Furthermore it fails to impress on Ministers and Civil Servants the essential difference between news and propaganda' (*The Times*, 16 March 1946). Although Fleet Street on the whole was hostile to the large State machine, it was seen by many local newspaper editors as doing something to correct the bias of the prewar informal arrangements towards London-based papers. Some editors also regarded it as a index of modernity and a new style of citizenship. The *Yorkshire Post* editor W.L. Andrews declared that he wanted more army press officers – in fact one with every unit:

> I have known a general of long ago reply to a reporter politely requesting some information 'What the hell has it got to do with you?' The public press has a very great deal to do with a citizen army. Today the press is warmly welcomed by the Army and given good facilities . . . if an Army PRO gets an idea for a story he invites the papers that are likely to be interested to send reporters and photographers to such and such an army camp or depot. If a news editor gets an idea he rings up or writes to the Army PRO. These contacts are valuable and work well. But I would like to see the relations between the Army and the Press made much more intimate. (*World's Press News*, 3 July 1947)

Less formal and covert mechanisms for incorporating media organizations in the news-management operation were pioneered, alongside these mechanisms. For example, during the First World War the Foreign Office subsidized coverage by Reuters of official messages that Reuters would not have sent commercially. Again in 1939–40 the agency was secretly subsidized by the Ministry of Information – although when this was revealed, the chairman Roderick Jones was forced out by the Reuters board. But the Government continued to secretly finance certain services (Lawrenson and Barber 1986; Read 1992).

Both Labour and Conservative Governments found a large information machine tremendously useful, not only in the day to-day business of putting the official line across but in pursuing the totally mundane requirements of a medium-size European power – ensuring people paid their taxes on time, got their children inoculated and took taxis home from the pub. Although the 1945–51 information machine was repeatedly attacked by the Conservatives, and some leading figures publicly committed themselves to abolishing the CoI and sending the tribe of Whitehall PR men packing, when they were returned to power in 1951 the proposals were largely dropped after a half-hearted review. Leading Conservatives conceded that the machinery was really very useful (author's interview with Lord Boyd Carpenter, May 1995). This has remained the case, and a comparison of information-officer staffings over a fifty-year period shows some considerable increases, with the exception of the CoI itself. Under Margaret Thatcher, this was severely slimmed and is now approximately half the size it was in the 1960s and 1970s. As I write, another round of redundancies is about to strike. But the picture is now an extremely confusing one. Attacking Labour's information services in 1948, the Beaverbrook's *Evening Standard* claimed that 'Every Board, every Authority, every Commission set up the Socialists to run a nationalized industry makes haste to establish a large and expensive public relations staff' (*Evening Standard*, 3 March 1948).

This has been doubly true during the Conservative offensive against Whitehall. We might claim that every agency, every office and every partnership set up by the Conservatives has also hastened to employ a PR team, no doubt on highly insecure contracts.

Table 5.1 Estimates of Home information staff – selected departments 1938, 1947, 1996

	1938	1947	1996
Education	5.25	8.5	84
Agriculture	64	9	41
Treasury	0	27	15
Home Office	6	8	44
Foreign Office	n/a	10	–
Health	26	40	73
PM's Office	1	3	10

Sources: Based on PRO INF 12/298 and 1996 *IPO Directory*, HMSO, June 1996.

From Press Council to Press Complaints Commission

One mechanism available to the British State for overseeing the press is the Royal Commission: a cumbersome device that has been pressed into service three times by British governments since 1945. The Commissions demonstrate rather cruelly a Habsburgian tendency in the British State to worry about problems without producing solutions. The key issues have been how journalistic conduct can be restrained and reformed, how newspaper culture can be improved and how the range of publications can be protected or widened. All discussion tends to be stymied by the equation of the free press with the free market. But what passes for a debate about the role and conduct of the press for forty years from 1945 has been reflected in their findings and recommendations.

A British Press Council was first proposed by the National Union of Journalists in 1945, in the context of a public row about the concentration of press ownership, the power of press proprietors (and their mainly Conservative affiliations) and their ability to control and distort news after the 1945 general election (Robertson 1983). The row resulted in the setting up of the first British official enquiry into the press, the Royal Commission of 1947, in a move that was interpreted by the Conservative-supporting press as a political attack. In the event, the Commission proved quite a political embarrassment to the Labour Government, as it turned its attention to the operations of the State's own information services. So its 1949 report not only warned against the excessive development of the official information machine, but recommended that the press be overseen by a 'General Council' with a lay chairman, 20 per cent lay members and representatives of proprietors, editors and journalists. The Commission considered whether this council should be a governing body established by law – like the General Medical Council which was created to oversee doctors and had the power to stop a doctor practising if they breached its professional code. But although some members believed that no council would be effective unless it was given legal powers, they all preferred a voluntary organization. What perhaps held the Commission's worthies back was the sense that, unlike medicine, journalism was not quite a profession in the same sense, but still the refuge of the gifted amateur, the well-connected youngster, and craftsmen of fairly dubious origins – that is, citizens or rather (as this was a *Royal* Commission) subjects, exercising their right to free expression.

The Commission saw the job of the council as 'censuring undesirable types of journalistic conduct' and expected it to build up a code of conduct 'in accordance with the highest professional standards'. It was also to encourage training and keep an eye on any changes in the industry likely to restrict the flow of information. One thing it suggested the council should keep its eye on was the relationship between the press and government information officers and 'developments affecting the sources and supply of information of public interest' (Royal Commission on the Press 1947: para. 654).

71

These pious hopes came to nothing in the short term. The industry was extremely reluctant to set up any body until it was forced to act when a private member's Bill, proposing to set up a statutory body, was introduced into parliament by a Tory MP in 1953. The industry set up its own Press Council the same year. From the outset, therefore, the Press Council was designed as a public relations tool to protect the press from a media law that might, for example, create a right of reply or define personal privacy (Robertson 1983: 1) Twenty-five journalists and proprietors sat on the council with the chair elected from within the membership. No lay members were included, a derisory budget was allocated, and the council restricted its investigation of press mergers to a summary of events in its annual report. No code was developed and no serious investigation of press developments was undertaken.

The next Royal Commission on the Press in 1962 strongly criticized the council and said that the government should set up a statutory body if the industry did not reform it. The Commission called for the council to comply with the 1949 recommendations and have a lay chairman and 20 per cent lay membership. 'If the press is not willing to invest the council with the necessary authority and to contribute the necessary finance the case for a statutory body ... is a clear one.' Under this threat, the industry increased the funding, appointed a senior retired judge as chairman, selected five lay members and changed the constitution so that 20 per cent of members were drawn from outside the media. The 1972 Younger Commission on Privacy recommended that there should be equality between press and lay members. The Press Council refused to accept this but did agree to double the number of lay members to ten and agreed that the council's complaints committee – which heard complaints from the public and reported to the council with adjudi-ca-tions – should have an equal number of press and lay members. At this point the method of selection was changed from what the former direc-tor of the council (author's personal interview with Ken Morgan) de-scribed as a 'rather incestuous' method of selection to the setting-up of an appointments committee of up to five members who would not be members but would select new public members from a list put for-ward by the council.

Although the revamped council achieved a higher public profile, the third Royal Commission in 1977 savaged it. 'The Council has so far failed to persuade the knowledgeable public that it deals satisfactorily with complaints against newspapers' (Royal Commission on the Press 1977: chapter 20, para. 15). It detected 'inexcusable intrusions into pri-vacy' and 'flagrant breaches of standards'. Among its recommendations was the demand that the number of lay members on the council be in-creased to 50 per cent. The council duly increased its membership to eighteen press and eighteen lay members, and an independent chair, giving the non-journalists a majority for the first time. The method of appointment was also revised. Instead of the appointments committee making their selection solely on the names put forward by the council, vacancies were advertised and members were invited to serve a three-year term. In the first selection round there were ten seats available and

Table 5.2 Press Council/Press Complaints Commission Memberships, 1953–1996

	Press members	Lay members	Chair
Press Council			
1953	25	0	Press: *The Times* proprietor
1964	20	5	Independent: judge
1973	20	10	Independent: lawyer
1977	18	18	Independent: lawyer
Press Complaints Commission			
1991	9	6	Independent: lawyer/journalist
1996	7	8	Independent: politician

only forty-four candidates. By 1989 there were seven seats available and 1095 candidates.

The appointments committee's general instructions were widened and they were asked to aim at a balanced panel which reflected the social, geographical and educational diversity of modern Britain. Members therefore ranged from the usual great and the good – a Labour peeress, a former clerk to the privy council, etc. – to a nurse from Bristol, a British Steel boilermaker, the vice-chairman of the Mountain Rescue Committee of Scotland and a female undertaker's assistant (Robertson 1983). The council also tried to achieve a balance of gender and locality and also some ethnic representation (author's interview with Ken Morgan). The increase in membership and the attempt to reflect the wider society were all worthy, proto-democratic exercises, animated by the political idea that the more representative the institution was, the more legitimate and authoritative it would seem in the eyes of politicians, journalists and newspaper readers. It did nothing of the kind (see Table 5.2). As Geoffrey Robertson observes, there was a serious problem with the strategy of trying to make the council reflect the social composition of modern Britain. 'There is a danger that members chosen because they are "representative" of certain groups in society will actively seek to represent the interests of these groups in a manner which may detract from the impartial adjudication of individual complaints' (Robertson 1983: 22–3). In one notorious case a Labour councillor from Bristol told a council meeting that she would be using her new position to monitor how the press treated her own council. Thus, although the public profile of the council was higher through the 1980s, it was increasingly treated with contempt by its key constituency, the newspaper industry. According to Robertson and Nicol (1992: 524) it was 'a confidence trick that had ceased to inspire confidence'. Even the *Daily Telegraph* refused to abide by its rule that the race of criminals should not be included in stories. *The Sun* delighted in pillorying people who complained to the council about it. A succession of tabloid sensations, and in particular the treatment of the Hillsborough football stadium disaster in April 1989, alienated and disgusted sections of the public. So in 1989 when an MP introduced a private member's Bill to set up a legal body to enforce a right of reply it attracted support from all parties and was only stopped when the government promised to set up an inquiry to investigate press intrusions into privacy under a lawyer called Calcutt.

Calcutt reported in June 1990. He said that there was a contradiction between the role of the Press Council in defending the press and its job of protecting the public from bad press practices. He wanted a Press Complaints Commission (PCC) to deal with the latter but was sceptical as to whether any voluntary body set up by the press would work, given the dismal record of the Press Council. He drew up plans for a statutory tribunal which would have legal powers to take evidence, order corrections and apologies and award compensation and would be able to stop the publication of anything that breached the code of practice he outlined. Calcutt forced the hand of the press owners: they withdrew funding from the Press Council and set up a new body, the Press Complaints Commission, from January 1991 with a new code of press conduct to administer. The Commission itself was a slimmed-down body with sixteen members, compared to the Press Council's thirty-nine, made up of editors and a small collection of the great and the good, headed by Lord McGregor who had chaired the 1977 Royal Commission on the Press and more recently had run another 'voluntary' body, the Advertising Standards Authority.

Further political pressure was applied by the Minister for National Heritage, David Mellor, who notoriously warned the press that it was 'drinking in the Last Chance Saloon' – meaning that if statutory self-regulation did not work within a short time, the government would be forced to bring in the statutory tribunal suggested by Calcutt. He asked Calcutt to review the working of the Commission after eighteen months. Calcutt's review, published in January 1993, concluded that press self-regulation had not been effective and that the press was unwilling to make the changes needed: 'The PCC is not the truly independent body it should be. The Commission is . . . a body set up by the industry, financed by the industry, dominated by the industry, operating a code of practice devised by the industry and which is over-favourable to the industry.' Calcutt said that the code drafted by the industry had insufficient protection for the individual. Shortly after Calcutt 2 was published the MPs of the National Heritage Committee (1993) presented their own report on *Privacy and Media Intrusion*. This committee said there must be a right to privacy and that even prominent people such as politicians or media stars had a right to what they termed a zone of privacy. It called for a protection of privacy Bill, a strengthening of the PCC and a statutory press ombudsman.

The MPs took evidence from the widows of two soldiers killed in Northern Ireland. One murder happened before the code of practice had been introduced, the other after. They found no improvement in the conduct of the reporters to the families.

Despite the provision in the Code which states that 'in cases involving personal grief or shock, enquiries should be carried out and approaches made with sympathy and discretion', the press started telephoning at 11 o'clock at night and kept the phone going all night. And in what seemed to the committee to be a callous and totally unacceptable breach of the Code, as well as more general canons of decency and compassion, the new widow, having been persuaded to give an interview in order to reduce press pressure, was asked by the accompanying photographer to 'look like a grieving widow'. (National Heritage Committee 1993: para. 31)

But the government refused to pick up the challenge either from Calcutt or the MPs. Despite the fact that sixteen government ministers have been forced out of office since 1992 by newspaper revelations of sexual or financial scandal and a continuing controversy about the privacy of the prominent people, the newspaper industry has so far escaped a tribunal. The PCC got a new chairman – a former government chief whip – and a bevy of new lay members, so that a majority are now technically from outside the media. Parts of the code have been tightened and one of the commissioners has been given special responsibility for privacy. And the PCC has continued to actively promote the code of practice.

At a public level relations between journalists and politicians appear to be as healthily bad as they have ever been. A survey for *The Independent* (11 May 1995: 1) found that politicians put journalists below even opinion pollsters in terms of integrity – 77 per cent of a sample of 167 MPs said they held a low or very low opinion of journalists' honesty and moral standards. Only building contractors came out worse. Relations behind the scenes, however, continue to be as close as ever with little sign that the press will surrender its cosy relationship with the British State. So what is going on? Why do the British refrain from legislating about privacy or creating a press commission with real teeth? Part of the answer may come from considering the peculiar nature of the PCC and how it reflects British State arrangements.

The sinews of the patronage State

Relations between politicians and the media should not be understood as simply adversarial. They may on occasion pursue different goals but this occurs within an agreed framework which offers potential benefit to both groups . . . Politicians' and journalists' mutual reliance prompts a continual adjustment or 'adaptation' of their relationships to ensure continuity despite the conflict and cooperation which characterise them. Politicians and journalists are adversaries but, on occasion, they are just as certainly accomplices in the enterprise of political communication. (Franklin 1994: 18)

The membership of the PCC in July 1996 consisted of five lords, two knights, one professor, a publisher, a dentist, an NHS Trust chair and seven editors from the national, local and magazine press (see Table 5.3). The political intention behind the construction of this group is to

Table 5.3 Composition of the Press Complaints Commission, April 1997

Lord Wakeham (chair)	Conservative politician; Government Chief Whip, 1983–87; 1990–92: Minister responsible for 'co-ordinating development of presentation of government policies' (*Who's Who*, 1996). Education: public school (Charterhouse)
Lady Browne-Wilkinson	Partner, eminent firm of lawyers; married to Lord of Appeal
Lady Elizabeth Cavendish (left PCC early 1997)	Chair, Inner London Juvenile courts, 1983–87; chair, Cancer Research Campaign; Extra Lady-in-Waiting to Princess Margaret; daughter of tenth Duke of Devonshire. Education: private
Sir Brian Cubbon	Retired senior civil servant; permament secretary, Home Office, 1979–88; Northern Ireland Office, 1976–79. Education: Bury Grammar School, Trinity College, Cambridge
Baroness Dean	Former printing trade unionist; general secretary, SOGAT, 1985–91. Education: Stretford High School for Girls
Professor Robert Pinker	Professor of Social Administration, London School of Economics. Education: Holloway County School, LSE
Baroness Smith of Gilmorehill	Chair, Edinburgh Festival Fringe; widow of John Smith, former leader of the Labour Party
Lord Tordoff	Principal deputy chairman of committees, House of Lords; Liberal Democrat Chief Whip in House of Lords, 1988–94. Education: Manchester Grammar School, Manchester University
David Williams	Editor, *Bury Free Press*
Tom Clarke	Editor, *The Sporting Life*
John Witherow	Editor, *The Sunday Times*
Iris Burton	Editor-in-chief, *Woman's Realm* and *Woman's Weekly*; chair, IPC editorial steering group
Sir David English	Editor, *Daily Mail*, 1971–92; editor-in-chief and chairman, Associated Newspapers, 1992–
Jim Cassidy	Editor, *Sunday Mail*
John Griffith	Editor, *Liverpool Echo*
Arzani Bhanji	Dental Surgeon, Director, Royal Hospitals NHS Trust

balance its contacts with the political world and with the press. So, in a very transparent way, it is not a body which in any modern democratic sense 'represents' the public, except as a trustee or guardian might rep resent an infant. But it does, to an intriguing extent, represent certain corporate interests involved in press/State relations. Above all, there are the political interests. Lord Wakeham is an eminent Conservative – once Margaret Thatcher's right-hand man, a key figure in her Cabinet, and a political fixer of the first rank. As chief government whip (1983–7) he had a formidable reputation for being able to manage the parliamentary Conservative Party. Apart from enforcing party discipline in what remains one of the noisiest but most rigorously managed legislatures in Europe, a crucial role for a government whip is to know when a scandal is about to break and be ready to do something about it – either by containing it or exploiting the news to political advantage. Handling the media is part of a whip's job.

As minister responsible 'for co-ordinating the presentation of government policies' before the 1992 general election (*Who's Who*, 1996) Lord Wakeham's key role was to influence Fleet Street's major players. He understands the network of clubs which make British politics work – and described the most important job of the prime minister as 'to appoint the right people to his Cabinet and give them the right jobs to do' (quoted in Hennessy 1995). A frequent lunch partner is the second leading Conservative in the PCC, the chair of the Commission's code of practice committee, Sir David English, the editor-in-chief of Associated Newspapers and once editor of the *Daily Mail*, the quintessential Tory loyalist newspaper and the pre-eminent backer of Margaret Thatcher. Labour's interests are looked after discreetly by Baroness Smith of Gilmorehill, the widow of the former Labour leader, John Smith. She is supported by the sole trade unionist on the commission, Baroness Dean of Thornton-le-Fylde, the former boss of the printing trade union, SOGAT (1985–91), spectacularly defeated in the bitter, year-long dispute created by Rupert Murdoch's move to Wapping. The third main political party is represented by Lord Tordoff, a Liberal and now a Liberal Democrat of long standing and the party's chief whip in the House of Lords (1988–94). Apart from the major political players, the royal family gets a look in as well – the channel here was, until recently, Lady Elizabeth Cavendish, who apart from being chair of the Cancer Research Campaign is the daughter of the tenth Duke of Devonshire and an extra Lady-in-Waiting to Princess Margaret.

What are we to make of this? The old Press Council, in its blundering way, seemed to be moving towards some principle of public representation, with a notion that 'ordinary people' might conceivably have a role in its deliberations in the same way that a jury is drawn from the public. There is no trace of that in the present body, whose pedigree is essentially that great invention of the Conservative 1980s: the Quango. Essentially the PCC has to be seen not as a representative body but a fixer – a pre-democratic body whose interest is in handling complaints and not opening up an agenda for discussion about ownership or accountability. Being realistic about handling complaints means that it has

Table 5.4 Results of complaints dealt with by the PCC, Jan.–Feb. 1993–96

Date	Outside remit	Disallowed delay	No code breach	Third party	Resolved directly	Not pursued	Adjudi- cated	Upheld	Rejected	Total	Total disallowed	% disallowed	% adjudicated	% upheld
Jan.–Feb. 1993	59	17	116	23	25	56	19	4	15	315	215	68.25	6.03	1.27
Jan.–Feb. 1994	103	18	103	22	24	30	17	11	6	317	246	77.6	5.36	3.47
Jan.–Feb. 1995	72	10	79	21	20	25	11	5	6	268	182	67.91	4.1	1.87
Jan.–Mar. 1996*	157	20	126	19	76	**	20	9	11	418	322	77.03	4.78	2.15
TOTALS	391	65	324	85	145	111	67	29	38	1318	865	65.62	5.08	2.2

* PCC provided Jan.–Mar. consolidated total only in 1996.
** Resolved directly and not pursued categories combined for 1996 by PCC.

Source: Press Complaints Commission reports numbers 16, 23, 28 and 33.

to be restricted: it was, for example, only with great reluctance that a hotline was established in 1995.

The PCC's annual report for 1995 (and previous years) makes a virtue of the relatively small number of 'real' complaints received and their speedy resolution (see Table 5.4). For example, in 1995 the PCC received 2508 complaints – an increase of nearly 30 per cent on 1994, which is taken in the annual report as 'a welcome sign of growing public awareness of the PCC and the service it offers'. The rate of complaints works out at ten per working day: roughly one for every 1.96 million daily and Sunday newspapers sold. If local paid for and free newspapers are included (in 1995 about 46.56 million copies a week were paid for and distributed, according to the *Advertising Statistics Yearbook* 1996) the figure is 1 to 2.91 million.

Complaints that raise possible breaches of the code are forwarded to editors – 413 complaints are claimed to have been resolved directly with publications or not pursued in 1995. Eight hundred complaints are describing as falling outside the commission's remit. Just under half of all complaints – about 1230 – were therefore found to present no case that could be pursued under the code of practice. Roughly seven out of 10 (68.9 per cent) of complaints related to inaccurate reporting and the next largest category of complaints related to privacy, with 12.4 per cent falling under this heading.

The PCC sets great store by resolving complaints by getting editor and complainant to agree a solution without recourse to the Commission. And it is striking how small a proportion of complaints actually ends up before it. Only 63 complaints were actually adjudicated by the Commission in 1995 and of these 28 were upheld (44.4 per cent of adjudications but a tiny 1.12 per cent of complaints). One comparison is with the Advertising Standards Authority – another voluntary watchdog, set up by the advertising industry to administer a code of advertising and sales promotion. In 1995 the ASA received 12 804 complaints: 3504 were upheld or 27.37 per cent (ASA 1995). The statutory Broadcasting Complaints Commission received 1095 complaints in the year from April 1995 and upheld 39: about 3.56 per cent.

A very peculiar watchdog

The animating notion behind the PCC is that its public is a body of individual consumers of a product with a particular problem of quality delivery of a service – a consumer who wishes their individual complaint resolved. The model in a sense is that of a customer complaints division – a key element of PR strategies – rather than a regulatory body. The health and general good intentions of the corporate players are taken for granted. This shows a ruthless and breathtaking political realism in terms of working with the grain of established institutions: it is emphatically not a talking-shop or deliberative body.

Like Conan Doyle's watchdog, the PCC's code is interesting for not barking – that is, for what it leaves out; for example, on the quality of sources, relation to pressure, and its blankness about individual integrity and conduct and the larger issues of how that relates to media structures within which journalism happens. Clause 4 of the code, on privacy, effectively rejects critics such as Calcutt or the National Heritage Committee who argued that intrusions into an individual's private life without their consent can only be justified on the narrow grounds of public interest defined as 'detecting or exposing crime, protecting health or safety, or preventing a harmful deception of the public' (National Heritage Committee's proposed code of practice). Although the PCC's code includes all these provisos, it does not exclude a range of other appeals to 'public interest'. Equally the PCC's code on intrusion into grief and shock also rejects Calcutt, who argued that the press should not intrude into grief or shock except to expose crime, protect public health or prevent the public from being misled. The PCC sticks to the formula that enquiries and approaches should be made 'with sympathy and discretion'.

The impression remains that the PCC, constructed out a pact between the great and the good and the newspaper establishment, is most concerned to look after its own. A significant proportion of cases that reach the adjudication stage concern aristocrats, politicians and other prominent people. The PCC appears reluctant to act, however, where more lowly subjects are being bullied. For a chilling reality of the patronage-dominated, secretive and partly privatized State of the late 1990s is that, apart from mugging or burglary, ordinary people also have the attentions of the press to fear.

Case study: On the dangers of standing up for your rights

An unsuccessful complaint to the PCC was made by Val Goulden, a college lecturer in media studies, in June 1995. Ms Goulden's employer, Halton College, decided to monitor her lectures for bias after one of her students alleged that her lectures were anti-male. She took the college to an industrial tribunal. Soon after the case, but before the verdict, *Daily Mail* reporters approached her nextdoor neighbour, her partner's ex-wife and teenage son and asked them if they blamed Ms Goulden for the break-up of her marriage. (Ms Goulden has been divorced since 1977.) *Mail* reporters also telephoned her ex-husband's elderly mother and tried to get her to blame Ms Goulden for the marriage break-up. A *Mail* reporter then confronted her and demanded details about her personal life. She refused to answer. The verdict of the tribunal in June found that the college principal was biased against her. The *Mail* then printed a long article on 5 June 1995 dwelling on her marriage and divorce, and asserted that she became a feminist after a relationship with a fellow lecturer which ended with his death in a climbing accident. The paper claimed that 'almost every aspect of her teaching' had a feminist slant. The next day the *Mail* columnist, Richard Littlejohn, described her as 'a ghastly harridan'. Ms Goulden complained to the PCC on 17 June that the *Mail* had breached clauses 1, 3, 4, and 10 of the code: that the re port was distorted, that comment and fact had not been distinguished, that intrusions had been made into her private life without her consent and that the *Mail* had intruded into her personal grief without sympathy or discretion. The PCC's verdict in September 1995 turned down all her complaints. On the breach of privacy the Commission argued that although the coverage may have been embarrassing, as the industrial tribunal was a public event it did not regard the reporting of personal matters concerning her as an invasion of privacy as defined by the code and that 'the *Daily Mail* was entitled to describe a woman who had taken a matter to an industrial tribunal whose hearings were in public' (Beckett 1996). Ms Goulden's response is that 'if you have the temerity to stand up for yourself you have to accept that they will inquire into any aspect of your past. The PCC? It's there to protect royalty and people like that – not ordinary people.'[1]

Backs to the future?

The Press Complaints Commission exists in a political space between the press and the State which depends on an understanding that, while it may bark like a watchdog, it will not get its teeth into certain existing arrangements including the ownership of the press; the status of journalists; the quality of sources – for example, an overdependence and refusal to question official sources; and political control and bias in reporting. What appears to be an ethical crisis in journalism is frequently blamed on an unremitting climate of competition which drives 'standards' down. But it could equally be laid at the door of those processes which have created a casualized and acutely insecure workforce, many of whose members may have to balance conflicting commitments. A code of practice that is not rooted in some investigation and discussion of the culture of journalism is a set of loopholes bound together with good intentions rather than a framework of values.

What should be the future relationship between the press and the State? And how should press freedom be protected whilst guaranteeing that private citizens are not trampled on by over-mighty newspapers?

It might be immediately conceded that Britain is not a good model for other European States to follow: we exist, at best, as a dreadful warning of what untrammelled commercial forces, and a weak and casualized journalistic workforce can produce in terms of a semi-managed media which tramples on the rights of its citizens while loudly proclaiming itself as their wisest protector. Of course, this is an over-gloomy account for several reasons. First, the media are rightly the site of enormous inquiry, both in terms of their own navel-gazing and in academic work. In this context the fact that more students than ever are taking media studies courses at universities – the occasion of predictable press furore – is a perverse sign of hope. Nothing is more likely to improve journalistic culture than a media-literate population, wise to its scams and unprepared to be bamboozled. Second, there are alternative spaces opening up to criticize and investigate media performance such as web publication. Third, the new British State appears to be a rather fragile and perhaps temporary creation, under threat at a regional level from the component parts of the UK, and at the supranational level from the movement towards European union. All bets on snug little deals between the press and political establishment are off.

For the wrong reasons – the protection of press privileges to trample the rights of ordinary citizens while not posing too great a threat to the powers that be – the UK has avoided any form of official tribunal overseeing newspapers and any system of licensing journalists. The paradox is familiar in Britain: the reasons are wrong but the outcome is right. It is unlikely that a privacy law can coexist with an active investigative press and Britain already has enough legal and official roadblocks in the path of serious investigative journalism. The challenge is to remake the culture of British journalism and make the Commission an effective force. Rather than giving its edicts the force of law, the answer is to devise a democratic and open structure for it, so that rather more than ten people a day feel it is worth making a complaint.

Note

1 I am grateful to Mr Francis Beckett for bringing this case to my attention.

References

Advertising Standards Authority (1995) *Annual Report 1995*, ASA, London.
Advertising Statistics Yearbook (1996) Advertising Association and NTC Publications, London.
Beckett, F. (1996) 'Polly Toynbee is not the only *Mail* victim', *Press Gazette*, 21 June.
Broadcasting Complaints Commission (1996) *Annual Report*, BCC, London.
Cockerell, M., Hennessy, P. and Walker, D. (1984) *Sources Close to the Prime Minister: Inside the Hidden World of the News Manipulators*, Macmillan, London.
Cockett, Richard (1994) 'The party, publicity and the media,' in Seldon, A. and Ball, S. (eds) *Conservative Century*, Oxford University Press, Oxford.
Dynes, M. and Walker, D. (1995) *The 'Times' Guide to the New British State*, Times Books, London.
Franklin, B. (1994) *Packaging Politics*, Edward Arnold, London.
Harris, R. (1983) *Gotcha! The Media, the Government and the Falklands Crisis*, Faber & Faber, London.

Hennessy, P. (1995) *The Hidden Wiring: Unearthing the British Constitution*, Victor Gollancz, London.

History of the Times (1939) Vol. II, Times Newspapers, London.

Lawrenson, J. and Barber, L. (1986) *The Price of Truth. The Story of the Reuters Millions*, revised edn, Sphere Books, London.

Lee, A.J. (1976) *The Origins of the Popular Press, 1855–1914*, Croom Helm, London.

Leigh, D. (1980) *The Frontiers of Secrecy*, Junction Books, London.

Margach, J. (1979) *The Anatomy of Power*, W.H. Allen, London.

Middlemas, K. (1979) *Politics in Industrial Society*, André Deutsch, London.

National Heritage Committee (1993) *Fourth Report: Privacy and Media Intrusion*, Vol. 1, HMSO, London.

Press Complaints Commission (1996) *Annual Report 1995*, PCC, London.

Read, D. (1992) *The Power of News – the History of Reuters*, Oxford University Press, Oxford.

Robertson, G. (1983) *People Against the Press*, Quartet Books, London.

Robertson, G. and Nicol, A. (1992) *Media Law*, 3rd edn, Penguin Books, Harmondsworth.

Tulloch, J. (1993) 'Policing the public sphere – the British machinery of news management', *Media Culture and Society* **15**, 363–84.

Who's Who (1996) A & C Black, London.

CHAPTER 6

Demanding accountability: The press, the Royal Commissions and the pressure for reform, 1945–77

Tom O'Malley

During the 1980s and 1990s the national newspaper press in the UK came under sustained criticism for its sensationalism, inaccuracy and intrusion into privacy. A series of attempts by MPs to achieve a statutory right of reply to factual inaccuracies and protection of privacy failed. These moves prompted the British government to launch two inquiries into the ethics of the press chaired by David Calcutt in 1989 and 1992 and stimulated a bout of internal reform of the industry's system of self-regulation (McNair 1994: 144–9). During this period broadcasting underwent changes (O'Malley 1994) which involved introducing more market forces into the public service system. Political concerns about how to regulate new media, such as satellite and cable TV, in the interests of promoting high standards and forms of redress for aggrieved viewers prompted widespread debate (for example, see Collins and Murroni 1996). In short, questions about the standards and accountability of the old print and newer electronic media were never far from the centre of political and public concerns in the 1980s and 1990s.

This chapter explores the development of ideas about press accountability by examining the origins and nature of the three postwar Royal Commissions on the press in 1947–49, 1961–62 and 1974–77. It argues that the establishment of these bodies paralleled the growth of concerns among political parties, government and a wide range of groups in society about the proper role of the press in the twentieth century. They also represented a *de facto* acknowledgement by politicians that debates about press freedom should move beyond nineteenth century ideas which focused on the relationship between the State and the press to include questions about the nature of press accountability and responsibility to the public. All three Commissions endorsed outdated ideas from the nineteenth century about the press, in particular the notion that State interference in the press was a bad thing.[1] They did, however, provide a platform for public anxieties about the press and can be used to track changes in the nature and scope of these over time.[2]

The first part of the chapter looks at some general trends in the postwar press, and places the Commissions in the context of the proliferation of inquiries into matters directly or indirectly relating to the press. The second part charts the shifts and continuities in the reasons why the Commissions were established. The final part shows how an examination of aspects of the Commissions' Reports charts how they were faced with an increasingly wider set of concerns about press accountability from an expanding range of groups within society.

Press inquiries: A postwar growth industry

> Official newspapers are not the answer. To contemplate in peacetime any extension of Government influence on the press, or any curb except on the grounds of national security or the common law, is to contemplate the death of democracy, the birth of dictatorship and the eclipse of the nation's stability. (Cudlipp 1962: 365)

Hugh Cudlipp was joint managing director of the Mirror Group when he wrote these words in 1962. They were written after concern about concentration of ownership had led to the establishment of the 1961–62 Royal Commission by the Conservative Government led by Harold Macmillan. Cudlipp's comments summarize the view of senior managers and proprietors in the industry after 1945. It was a position they never really abandoned in public battles over the press.

Postwar conflicts over the press sprang from genuine concerns about the state of the industry. Although by 1945 the nature of the links between newspapers and the political process had shifted from the nineteenth century when politicians owned papers and subsidized journalists, newspapers were still intimately linked to the political process, through social networks, mutual dependence and overt political affiliation (Negrine 1994: 39–80). This meant that shifts in the allegiance, ownership or behaviour of the press prompted recurrent bouts of speculation about the future of the industry. Writing at the end of the 1970s about the postwar period, Stephen Koss comments that 'the history of the British press since 1947 has been an unremitting story of crisis, closure and complaint'. The closures of national papers, the increasing costs of production, the trends towards concentration of ownership, poor industrial relations and competition from broadcasting were one side of the coin (Koss 1990: 1080, 1096). On the other were concerns about the power of proprietors, the political bias of national papers, the autonomy of journalists, sensationalism, inaccuracy and privacy (Curran and Seaton 1991).

The fear of direct government intervention into the press, as expressed by Cudlipp, was justified if only because of the numbers of opportunities that occurred in these years for direct intervention. In fact, in the postwar years the Royal Commissions were three among a cluster of private- or State-sponsored inquiries which dealt directly or indirectly with the press. In 1947 the Labour government established the first postwar Royal Commission. One of its proposals was that a General

Council of the Press should be set up to deal with questions of standards, training and ownership. In 1953 a much watered-down version was established, mainly to head-off calls for statutory controls.[3] As television grew in importance, so too did concerns about newspaper companies having interests in commercial TV. For instance, the 1962 Royal Commission took the view that it was 'contrary to the public interest for such companies to be controlled by newspaper undertakings'. In 1965, as a result of recommendations made by the 1961–62 Commission, the Labour government under Harold Wilson legislated to require mergers in the newspaper industry to be referred in certain circumstances to the Monopolies and Mergers Commission (Royal Commission on the Press 1947–1949: para. 352(39);[4] Royal Commission on the Press 1974–1977: para. 1.10).[5]

In the 1960s a number of private Bills were introduced into Parliament to deal with privacy, a topic which had direct implications for the press. Lord Mancroft introduced one in the House of Lords in 1961, Alex Lyon MP in 1967 and Brian Walden MP in 1969. All these Bills failed. In 1970 the British Section of the International Commission of Jurists, Justice, published its report on the matter, *Privacy and the Law*, which put the case for legislation (Wacks 1995: 3, n. 4).

Anxieties about costs and industrial relations in the industry recurred throughout the 1960s. In 1966, a report was commissioned by members of the industry into its problems. The report ran to three volumes and recommended changes in practices within the industry. Similar anxieties prompted two inquiries by the National Board for Prices and Incomes in 1967 and 1969–70, both of which recommended reform of practices within the industry. Concerns continued throughout the 1970s. A spate of government-sponsored inquiries into laws affecting the regulation and behaviour of the press had reported by 1975. A committee on the Official Secrets Act (Cmnd 5104) and one into Privacy (Cmnd 5012) reported in 1972. The committee on Contempt of Court (Cmnd 5794) reported in 1974 and one on Defamation (Cmnd 5909) in 1975 (Economist Intelligence Unit 1966; RCP 1977: paras 1.1, 1.8; National Board for Prices 1967, 1970).

In addition to the three Commissions, the number of private- and government-sponsored initiatives around the press in this period reflected an acknowledgment among politicians that there were issues of public interest in the press and of accountability that involved government intervention in one form or another, if only to promote inquiry, reflection and debate. This was in contrast to the period after the 1860s and up to 1945, when such interventions were, relatively, few. Managers, such as Cudlipp, and proprietors sought to limit the scope of such intervention by raising the spectre of government interference with press freedom. Yet this did not stem the tide of concerns which continued to stimulate debate and inquiry into the press.

Shifting concerns

Concerns about the nature and activities of the press grew in the twentieth century with the spread of a mass circulation press. By the mid-1940s there was pressure both outside and inside the Labour Party for action. This concern must also be seen in the context of a wider set of media-related issues which came before the Labour Cabinet of 1945–51. These included the nature of government information services, the future of broadcasting and the problems of the film industry. Indeed, the 1947–49 Royal Commission was established, in part, because ministers and civil servants considered that the press should, like broadcasting, be subject to periodic public inquiry. Thereafter each of the Royal Commissions on the Press occurred roughly around the same time as the first three major postwar inquiries into broadcasting, although it is not clear whether, with the exception of the 1947–49 Commission, this link was intentional. By 1947 the British Government was acknowledging that it had a role in stimulating debate about the print and electronic media, and this is what happened over the next thirty years (O'Malley 1997).[6]

The 1947–49 Commission was established by a Labour government which was responding to concerns about trends towards monopoly in the national and local press, especially the growth of chain ownership. There were questions about the autonomy of journalists from proprietorial interference, the ethical standards of the press and the wider issues of press freedom. All of these concerns extended beyond the Labour movement and predated the 1940s. The pressure for an inquiry came in large part from within the Labour movement, especially the National Union of Journalists (NUJ). There was also a sense among Labour MPs that the press was hostile to the government. For Michael Foot, then a backbench MP, the initiative paralleled attempts in the USA in the 1940s to inject social responsibility into the press. He and other Labour Party members were concerned about concentration in the film industry and hoped the Commission would lead to some 'intelligent rules about cross-ownership' (O'Malley 1997).[7] The Cabinet wanted to stimulate voluntary reform by the industry and did not want to be vulnerable to charges that it was encouraging State interference with press freedom in the interests of he Labour Party. Herbert Morrison, the Cabinet minister in charge of establishing the Commission, told the House of Commons that: 'The Government certainly did not pack this Royal Commission with critics of the Press ... if anything, we leaned over backwards to get an impartial Commission.'[8] The first Commission was, arguably, designed to steer a middle way between demands for controls on ownership and the fierce opposition to such measures from proprietors. It recommended voluntary self-regulated reform, a view which at the time echoed a widespread consensus on the way forward.

In establishing the second Commission a Conservative Government provided another public platform for debate about the press.This marked the fact that by this period there were concerns about the press that transcended party divisions. The report shifted attention more firmly in the direction of discussion about the efficiency of production methods and industrial relations: a theme which by the end of the 1970s was at the centre of proprietorial and left-of-centre concerns about the press.

The left critiques of ownership which drove the establishment of the 1947–49 Commission found an echo in the reason why the Conservatives set up the second Commission in 1961. Between 1949 and 1961 seventeen daily and Sunday papers in London and the provinces closed, and ownership had become concentrated in fewer hands. This had threatened the idea that a healthy press was a diverse one with a wide spread of ownership – a view endorsed by the 1947–49 Commission. As the Report indicated, 'Public anxiety about the state of the press was brought to a head' by the death of two national papers. One of these, the *News Chronicle*, had a large circulation. The other event that stimulated public anxiety was the acquisition by the Mirror Group of the Odhams Press, publisher of the *Daily Herald* and the *Sunday People* (Royal Commission on the Press 1961–62: paras 2–3).[9] *The Guardian* reflected this anxiety by attacking the take-over, and Cudlipp at the *Mirror* was conscious of the 'anxious public discussion about the future of the Press and Parliamentary questions about the dangers of monopoly' (Cudlipp 1962: 347; Hetherington 1981: 138). Although its focus was on ownership, the second Commission criticized self-regulation of the press. The 1949 Commission had recommended a wide range of powers for the General Council of the Press, including monitoring issues of ownership and control. The 1961–62 Commission insisted that a body such as this be set up voluntarily or, failing that, by statute (RCP 1962: paras 320–26, 352(51)–(53)).

The 1961–62 Commission's recommendations on regulating mergers and on the Press Council were welcomed by the NUJ. The Press Council underwent a period of mild reform and, in 1965, a version of the Commission's recommendations on the monitoring of mergers became law (Anon 1962; Shawcross 1995). But concern about the press continued after 1962 and fed into the decision to set up the 1974–77 Commission.

Concerns were voiced about the effects of concentration on choice. The English lecturer, Graham Martin (1964: 95), writing in 1964, feared more 'mergers, concentration of resources in fewer hands, homogeneity in the product plus marginal differentiation'. Prior to the 1964 general election, Jim Northcott, from the Labour Research Department, in a book devoted to putting the Labour Party's case to voters, condemned some newspapers for 'the sensationalism with which they deal with crime and violence, the hypocrisy with which they treat sex, or the intolerance with which they pursue personal vendettas and intrude into people's private lives'. He considered that the 1961–62 Commission's proposal for a strengthened Press Council would help remedy this. The 'cause for greater concern', he argued, 'is the dangerous trend towards concentration'. The impact of advertising revenue on press finance was leading to the closure of otherwise widely read papers and this flew in the face of the need to 'preserve the widest possible choice in our principal channels of communications'. He floated ideas about differential taxes, subsidy and loans, but put his faith in the 1961–62 Commission's recommendations on mergers (Northcott 1964: 92–6). In the same year the future Conservative MP, Timothy Raison, dealt tangentially with the topic, showing awareness of the problems, but asserting the need for a solution to emerge out of voluntary reform and consumer rights. He welcomed the idea of involving consumers in industry bodies designed to check abuses, and considered that the Press Council was doing this. He advocated 'self-restraint, not imposed restriction' (Raison 1964: 94–6). But, like Northcott, his views represented continuing anxieties about the behaviour, rights and duties of the press that had not been put to rest by the two postwar Commissions.

On the left, within and outside the Labour Party, concern about these issues was strong by the late 1960s. The group of New Left writers who, in 1968, produced the *May Day Manifesto*, articulated concerns about ownership in terms that echoed the inclusive category of consumers invoked by Raison, but framed it in terms of the exclusion of left and minority views from the mass media:

> It is a paradox of the modern means of communication . . . that they are so expensive that their control passes inevitably, unless there is public intervention, into minority hands, which then use them to impose their own views of the world . . . Of course, within a particular consensus, rival opinions, rival styles and rival facts are offered . . . But it is then not only that minorities and emergent opinions find great difficulty in being heard on anything like equal terms. It is, even more crucially, that the continuous description of social reality is in what are clearly minority hands, with no possibility for effective majorities to articulate their own experience in their own terms. (Williams 1968: 40–1)

The New Left position was not that different in its views on ownership from the mainstream Labour movement of the 1940s. But it articulated the problem in broader terms, with less emphasis on party political bias and more on the general forms of exclusion which operated through the structures within the industry. Northcott's notion of the need for the widest possible choice and Raison's emphasis on consumerism signalled, as the range of evidence submitted to the 1974–77 Commission examined below indicates, a broadening of the notion of what kind of accountability should operate in relation to the press.

In 1972 the Home Policy Committee of the Labour Party's ruling body, the National Executive Committee, convened a study group to discuss the media. Labour was in opposition at the time, having lost power in 1970 to the Conservatives. When the Committee reported in 1974, Labour was back in office (1974–79). The Committee's report articulated the notion of the press's failure to be accountable in the broadest sense, not to political parties, or to notions of impartiality, but to the wider public. It proposed reform 'to enable the Press to give more equitable treatment to all its readers and to cater for minority audiences who are not so attractive to advertisers' (Labour Party 1974: 25).[10]

Thus, through the 1960s and early 1970s writers conjured up a view that outside the charmed circle of the State, proprietors and journalists, there was a wider public whose rights in the media should be looked to and taken into account. This was a marked shift from 1947–49 when the debates implied a set of concerns about the proper relationship between the State and the press, and had less of a focus on the notion of the responsibilities of the press to the public at large. This was the context in which the 1974–77 Commission was established.

Although there is a view that the 1974–77 Commission was established to punish Fleet Street for its attacks on the Prime Minister and one of his ministers, the reasons, as has been indicated, ran deeper (Pimlott 1992: 694). The Commission considered that the thirty years after 1945 had witnessed an 'anxiety about the press which has been marked in most democratic countries in Europe' (RCP 1977: para. 1.1). The immediate concerns were economic and these, in a sense, echoed concerns, though different, on the left and the right about economics, ownership, standards and choice. The Prime Minister, Harold Wilson, considered that there were 'long-term', as well as 'more urgent problems' for the Commission to consider. One argument he used was that there was some evidence of 'an appalling lack of confidence in the national Press on the part of the British Public'. Another MP, Ioan Evans, asserted that there was 'a deep anxiety about the concentration of Press ownership in this country'.[11] It was this combination of long-term anxieties about the economic structure of the press and how that impacted on standards, independence and choice that underpinned the move to set up the Commission. It was also part of the wider view, articulated by the New Left and the Labour Party study group, that the press had particular difficulty in fairly representing the range of views in society.

So the three Royal Commissions were established in the context of a series of private and public inquiries into the press after 1945. They were also part of a shifting body of concerns which moved from the 1947–49 and 1961–62 concerns with the relationships between the State, ownership and freedom of expression for the press to the much broader issue of the way the press related to its public. In a sense this was an extension of the notion of accountability, beyond the realm of the traditional press-versus-the-State relationship, to one that drew accountability to the wider public into sharper focus. This shift can be tracked more closely by looking in some detail at aspects of the final Reports of each of the Commissions.

A wider sense of accountability

Examining the terms of reference and the kinds of social groups who offered evidence to each of the Commissions illustrates how these bodies were reflecting a broadening of public concerns about the press and a widening of the types of groups who felt they had a role in commenting on the nature and functions of the press.

The terms of reference of the 1947–49 Commission were as follows:

> furthering the free expression of opinion through the Press and the greatest practicable accuracy in the presentation of news, to inquire into the control, management and ownership of the newspaper and periodical Press and the news agencies, including the financial structure and the monopolistic tendencies in control. (RCP 1949: iii)

The concerns here are with freedom of expression and opinion and accuracy, and how they connected with ownership and monopoly. The issues were not about direct accountability to the State or the public, but how the industry's structure affected the way the press fulfilled its function as a vehicle for the freedom of expression.

By 1961–62, although the focus was economic, the range of concerns was broadened and spelled out more fully:

> examine the economic and financial factors affecting the production and sale of newspapers, magazines and other periodicals in the United Kingdom, including (a) manufacturing, printing, distribution and other costs; (b) efficiency of production; and (c) advertising and other revenue, including any revenue derived from interests in television; to consider whether these factors tend to diminish diversity of ownership and control or the number or variety of such publications, having regard to the importance, in the public interest, of the accurate presentation of news and the free expression of opinion. (RCP 1962: 3)

This Commission considered the issues in economic terms that emphasized questions of efficiency in contrast to the preceding Commission's emphasis on monopolistic tendencies. Both Commissions were concerned with accuracy and freedom of expression. But the 1961–62 Commission was concerned, overtly, with advertising and the link with television. This reflected the postwar realization that it was advertising that impacted most heavily on a newspaper's chances of survival. It also reflected the concerns about television as both a rival to the press and as a possible problem in terms of media concentration. The two Commissions shared an interest in ownership but read off different consequences. The 1961–62 Commission's terms articulated the goals of the press in relation to 'diversity' and the 'public interest'. This registered a widening of concerns from those focused on in 1947–49 by including the need for pluralism and to consider the press more directly in relation, not just to its function as vehicle for freedom of expression, but also its relation to a wider public interest that it was meant to serve.

The terms of the 1974–77 Commission were longer, more complex and reflected a further broadening of the concerns registered in 1961–62:

> to inquire into the factors affecting the maintenance of the independence, diversity and editorial standards of newspapers and periodicals, and the public's freedom of choice of newspapers and periodicals, nationally, regionally and locally, with particular reference to:
>
> (a) the economics of newspaper and periodical publishing and distribution;

(b) the interaction of newspaper and periodical interests held by the companies concerned with their other interests and holdings within and outside the communications industry;

(c) management and labour practices and relations in the newspaper and periodical industry;

(d) conditions and security of employment in the newspaper and periodical industry;

(e) the distribution and concentration of ownership of the newspaper and periodical industry, and the adequacy of existing law in relation thereto;

(f) the responsibilities, constitution and functioning of the Press Council.

(RCP 1977: 1)

The questions of newspaper economics, production practices, and management echoed those in the terms of reference of its immediate predecessor. But the range of concerns broadened considerably. Freedom of expression, which was in the terms of reference of the first two Commissions, was omitted from the third. The problem facing the press was reformulated not as one of freedom but of independence, diversity and editorial standards: a much broader set of issues. By focusing on freedom of choice, the 1974–77 terms placed emphasis on the question of the press's relation to the public in terms of the choice the industry offered, not in terms of the constraints on the industry's ability to practise freedom of expression. Since 1947–49 the key problem identified by the terms of refer- ence had, therefore, shifted. In 1947–49 the problem was one of constraints on the freedom of the press to express opinions. By 1974 this had become the problem of how much choice, diversity and independence was offered by the press to the public.

The question of cross-media ownership had broadened since 1961–62. The press was now seen as being linked to other industries both inside and outside a newly described formation: the 'communications' industry. Thus, underpinning concerns in the 1970s was the sharpened sense of the problems posed by a newspaper industry which was increasingly integrated into the wider industrial structure of society. Between 1947 and 1974, then, the understanding of the press as an industry had shifted as the industry had become more complex.

Running parallel to the postwar initiatives around the press outlined above and to this shift in focus towards the question of the press's accountability to the public was the tendency for employers within the industry to deal with inquiries into their activities collectively, rather than as individual employers. The numbers of individuals and organizations listed as giving oral or written evidence or both to the Commissions increased. In 1947–49 this was about 198, in 1961–62, 169 and in 1974–77, 247. All three Commissions issued general and specific requests for evidence. The overwhelming numbers of respondents to the first two Commissions were newspaper publishing companies, about 100 to the first and 75 to the second. Industry-wide employers' organizations, such as the Newspaper Publishers' Association, the Newspaper Society and the Scottish Daily Newspaper Society, also gave evidence. But by 1974–77 it was these industry-wide organizations that represented the interests of the industry to the Commission. Thirteen advertisers submitted evidence in 1947–49 and some agencies made individual representations to the first and second Commissions.[12] But in 1974–77 it was trade organizations like the Advertising Association and the Incorporated Society of British Advertisers who represented the industry. This development reflected other changes in the nature of lobbying after 1945 and was not caused by the existence of the Commissions. But it meant that at a time when there were increasing demands on the press from outside of the industry, it had equipped itself to lobby in a relatively unified manner.

The evidence in the Reports also reveals an expansion in the numbers of non-industry organizations submitting evidence. In 1945 there were seven such organizations, including the Association of British Science Writers, the British Soviet Society, the British Soviet Society for International Understanding, the Greek News Agency, the National Council for Civil Liberties, the United Kingdom Alliance and the Treasury. In 1961–62 none of these organizations presented evidence, but eleven others did. These included the Church of Scotland; the Communist Party of Great Britain; the Independent Labour Party; the Trades Union Congress; the Young Fabians and the Post Office.

But it was the 1974–77 Commission which witnessed an expansion of the types of groups giving evidence to fifty. Government departments like the Central Office of Information, the Home Office, the Department of Industry, the Department of Prices and Consumer Protection were included. Political parties were represented, including the Labour Party, the Liberals, Plaid Cymru, the Scottish National Party and the Communist Party of Great Britain. Local government was represented by organizations like the Greater London Council, the Inner London Education Authority and the Association of Metropolitan Authorities. A range of pressure groups, covering a wide area of interests, also submitted evidence. These included the Consumers' Association, Release, Aims of Industry, the Confederation of British Industry, and the Campaign for Homosexual Equality. The TUC submitted evidence, as did the local government union the National Association of Local Government Officers. Groups concerned with women's issues who submitted evidence included the Fawcett Society and Women in Media. Educational bodies like the Council for National Academic Awards and professional bodies, including the British Medical Association, the Institute of Public Relations and the Royal Institute of British Architects, submitted evidence.

The numbers of organizations outside the industry presenting evidence in 1974–77 was considerably more than in 1947–49, and represented a much wider range of social constituencies. Thus, the scope of the matters considered as relevant to the debate had widened in those thirty years. The kinds of groups who felt able to comment, and make demands, on the press represented a widening in the notion of what constituted the range of issues involved in press accountability over a thirty-year period.

Finally, all three Commissions recommended the maintenance of the *status quo*, with the minimum of direct State interference in the owner-ship or management of the press. They all recommended strengthening self-regulation. But the 1974–77 Report contained a minority report by the trade-union leader David Basnett and the journalist Geoffrey Good-man. They argued for State intervention to secure a National Printing Corporation and a launch fund to help promote:

> greater flexibility and freedom for newspapers to emerge so that they can better respond to the developing social and cultural impulses of modern society, without having to depend on the all pervasive influences of mass market pressures. (RCP 1977a: paras 22, 27, 35)

These recommendations were taken up more widely within the Labour and trade-union movement, but did not gain the backing of any govern-ment. This minority Report represented a genuine difference of opinion among members of the Com.nission over the issue of State involvement. David Basnett and Geoffrey Goodman were, in a sense, able to make this break with the orthodoxy in the rest of the Report because of the range and depth of postwar public criticism of the inadequacies of the press. The dissenting Report was responding to concerns which were more widely articulated in 1974–77 than had previously been the case.

Conclusion

The problems of the concentration of ownership, lack of accountability and bias arguably intensified after 1977 (Hollingsworth 1986; Williams 1996). The failure of the three Commissions to produce policies which would have checked the tendencies they addressed, or produced a pol-itical consensus for systematic reform, awaits a more detailed study. This would include a consideration of the decision-making process around the selection of commissioners, the conduct of the Commissions, and the political factors shaping British Government decision making.

It is clear, however, that an examination of the circumstances sur-rounding the creation and concerns of these Commissions provides evi-dence of an intensification and broadening of governmental and public concern about the relationship between the press and the public. It is evident that after 1945 it became increasingly commonplace to make de-mands of the press for public responsibility which assumed that public accountability in the press was not the same as State interference with press freedom, in spite of the way in which this threat was energetically deployed by proprietors and press managers. The Commissions, then, are a testimony to a central problem of postwar press policy in the UK. That is the recurrent failure of governments to fully articulate the grow-ing and widespread concerns about the press into workable policies, in spite of the proliferation of private and government-sponsored in-quiries, of which the three Commissions were the most prominent.

Notes

1 The three Royal Commissions have rightly been criticized for the conservatism of their recommendations. See Boyce 1978: 38–40; Curran 1978; Koss 1990: 1078–80; Curran and Seaton 1991: 288, 290–91.
2 The UK's failure to enact legislation stands in marked contrast to countries like Austria, France, Germany, The Netherlands, Norway and Spain, which by the 1990s had laws on privacy and right of reply. See Humphreys 1996: 59.
3 A more detailed discussion of the first Commission is in O'Malley 1997.
4 Hereafter, RCP 1949.
5 Hereafter, RCP 1977.
6 The broadcasting inquiries were the Beveridge, Pilkington and Annan Reports.
7 Author's interview with Michael Foot, November 1996.
8 House of Commons Debates 5s, vol. 467, 28 July 1949, col. 2690.
9 Hereafter, RCP 1962.
10 Concerns about the press treatment of students, another minority that felt misrepresented in these years, were expressed in National Union of Students 1975.
11 House of Commons Debates, 5s, vol. 872, 2 May 1974, cols 1326–1329.
12 The figures in the rest of this section, and the discussion of organizations which gave evidence, is based on the material listed in the appendices of the three Reports: that is RCP 1949: Appendix I; RCP 1962: Appendix I; RCP 1977: Annex II. They are approximate indicators of the levels of interest, and do not fully represent the range of activities, research and contacts of the three Commissions.

References

Anon (1962) 'Press Council plan welcomed by NUJ', *The Times*, 24 Sept.
Boyce, G. (1978) 'The Fourth Estate: the reappraisal of a concept', in Boyce, G., Curran, J. and Wingate, P. (eds) *Newspaper History: From the 17th Century to the Present Day*, Sage/Constable, London.
Collins, R. and Murroni, C. (1996) *New Media New Policies*, Polity Press, Cambridge.
Cudlipp, H. (1962) *At Your Peril*, Weidenfeld & Nicolson, London.
Curran, J. (1978) *British Press: A Manifesto*, Macmillan, London.
Curran, J. and Seaton, J. (1991) *Power Without Responsibility*, 4th edn, Routledge, London.
Economist Intelligence Unit (1966) *The National Newspaper Industry*, 3 vols, EIU, London.
Hetherington, A. (1981) *'Guardian' Years*, Chatto & Windus, London.
Hollingsworth, M. (1986) *The Press and Political Dissent*, Pluto Press, London.
Humphreys, P. (1996) *Mass Media and Media Policy in Western Europe*, Manchester University Press, Manchester.

Koss, S. (1990) *The Rise and Fall of the Political Press in Britain*, Fontana, London.

Labour Party (1974) *The People and the Media*, Labour Party, London.

McNair, B. (1994) *News and Journalism in the UK*, Routledge, London.

Martin, G. (1964) 'The Press', in Thompson, D. (ed.) *Discrimination and Popular Culture*, Penguin Books, Harmondsworth.

National Board For Prices (1967) *Costs and Revenue of National Daily Newspapers*, Cmnd 3535, HMSO, London.

National Board For Prices (1970) *Costs and Revenue of National Daily Newspapers*, Cmnd 4277, HMSO, London.

National Union of Students (1975) *Press and Prejudice*, NUS, London.

Negrine, R. (1994) *Politics and the Mass Media in Britain*, 2nd edn, Routledge, London.

Northcott, J. (1964) *Why Labour?* Penguin Books, Harmondsworth.

O'Malley, T. (1994) *Closedown? The BBC and Government Broadcasting Policy, 1979–1992*, Pluto Press, London.

O'Malley, T. (1997) 'Labour and the 1947–9 Royal Commission on the Press', in Bromley, M. and O'Malley (eds) *A Journalism Reader*, Routledge, London.

Pimlott, B. (1992) *Harold Wilson*, HarperCollins, London.

Raison, T. (1964) *Why Conservative?* Penguin Books, Harmondsworth.

Royal Commission on the Press 1947–1949 (1949) *Report*, Cmnd 7700, HMSO, London.

Royal Commission on the Press 1961–1962 (1962) *Report*, Cmnd 1811, HMSO, London.

Royal Commission on the Press 1974–1977 (1977) *Report*, Cmnd 6810, HMSO, London.

Royal Commission on the Press 1974–1977 (1977a) *Minority Report*, Cmnd 6810, HMSO, London.

Shawcross, H. (1995) *Life Sentence*, Constable, London.

Wacks, R. (1995) *Privacy and Press Freedom*, Blackstone Press, London.

William, G. (1996) *Britain's Media – How They Are Related*, 2nd edn, Campaign for Press and Broadcasting Freedom, London.

Williams, R. (ed.) (1968) *May Day Manifesto*, Penguin Books, Harmondsworth.

CHAPTER 7

Kith and sin: Press accountability in the USA

Walter Jaehnig

Late in 1900, the young Mr Winston Churchill appeared in New York City on a speaking tour promoting his book about his exploits in the Boer War. Many prominent Americans, opposed to British policy in South Africa, refused to serve on his reception committee. It fell to the humorist Mark Twain (Samuel Clemens) to introduce Churchill to a rowdy crowd of 1200 people at New York City's Waldorf Hotel. He did so while castigating both British military activities in Africa and American adventures in the Philippines:

> Yes, as a missionary I have sung this song of praise [for England and her liberal tradition] and still sing it; and yet I think England sinned in getting into a war in South Africa which she could have avoided without loss of credit or dignity – just as I think we have sinned in crowding ourselves into a war in the Philippines on the same terms.

> Mr Churchill . . . [b]y his father he is English, by his mother he is American – to my mind the blend which makes the perfect man. We are now on the friendliest terms with England . . . We have always been kin: kin in blood, kin in religion, kin in representative government, kin in ideals, kin in just and lofty purposes; and now we are kin in sin. (Fatout 1976: 368–9)

Twain's remarks about the temptations of imperialist politics might as well be applied to a comparison of the journalism systems of the two countries. The British and American presses are kith and kin, claiming a common bloodline in the philosophical ideas of the Enlightenment, professing allegiance to their nations' democratic ideals, preaching the virtues of watchdogging governing authorities, and sharing, to a degree at least, an increasingly common language. And, while American journalists might be more likely than their British counterparts to wrap themselves in Twain's 'just and lofty purposes' in moments of self-justification, it should be noted that they are also 'kin in sin' in failing to reconcile their responsibilities to the communities they serve with the demands of the marketplaces in which they function.

Pointing out the obvious kinship between British and American press systems should not obscure the fundamental differences between them. These differences exist at many levels and have unmistakable influences on the journalism that is produced. For the purposes of this chapter, we might consider three which must be kept in mind to comprehend American attempts to develop a conception of press accountability: the predominant localism of the American press, its pre-occupation with objectivity as its basic operating philosophy, and the reflexive separation between State and press in the United States.

In economic and geographical terms, British journalism has long been dominated by the huge circulations and extensive advertising reach of London-based publications – the 'national press' – headquartered in the political, economic and cultural capital, and the BBC. The establishment of regional television entities and local radio may have reduced the national press's influence to some degree, but there is little question that content and style are determined by the London press corps. Because the United States lacks a city commensurate with London's dominating influence, political, economic and cultural power have been dispersed across the nation; accordingly, the economic health and journalistic vitality of the American press have been dependent on the advertising interests of local and regional marketers. 'Localism' is the hallmark of the 1550 daily and 7400 weekly newspapers, and 11 500 radio and 1515 television stations in 211 different broadcasting markets (Dominick 1996: 114, 208, 308). The activities of local people and local events are given priority by these news organizations, with news from even adjoining States, other regions and foreign countries covered on a crisis-by-crisis basis. (Even neighbouring Canada and Mexico rarely get mentioned in American news accounts.) Only relatively recently, with the development of television network news programming financed by national advertisers, the coming of CNN and *USA Today*, and the wider availability of newspapers such as the *New York Times* and *Wall Street Journal* has anything resembling a 'national press' been evident in the United States. Issues concerned with press responsibility until recently have been largely local issues.

This focus on localism has consequences for the operating philosophies of American news organizations. To sell themselves as efficient advertising vehicles to local merchants, they try to obtain the largest possible circulations or audiences. News accounts, accordingly, must be homogenized and distinct from the preferences of special interest groups because the news must appeal to all and cannot offend large segments of the audience. Since the coming of the wire services in the nineteenth century, which sold news as a commodity to newspapers regardless of their political orientation, American journalists have adopted 'objectivity' as their operating standard, though there has never been a consensual definition of the term, or even agreement as to whether truly 'objective' reporting was even possible, and though most American newspapers traditionally endorse Republican presidential candidates (Cirino 1971: 73) and journalists are more likely to vote for Democrats (Lichter *et al.* 1986: 28–39; Graber 1993: 105), American news organizations do not usually identify with specific political parties or ideologies, referring to themselves instead as 'independent' or 'middle-of-the-road.' The European practice of aligning a newspaper with a political party or cause is truly a foreign concept in American journalism. And the British distinction drawn between 'quality' newspapers for upmarket audiences and 'popular' papers with mass appeal means nothing to American news organizations where the existence of social classes is not even acknowledged (Breed 1958: 113).

American journalism also reflects the deep and profound distrust of government found on this side of the Atlantic. The First Amendment to the US Constitution (a written statement adopted in 1791 which, among other things, prohibits Congress – and by extension other federal, State or local governmental units – from enacting laws limiting the freedom of the press) is a talisman for American journalists.[1] Though recent opinion surveys suggest that many Americans would not provide the current press with the same protection, the First Amendment remains the defining element of the relationship between press and government in the United States. Politicians and government officials understand that while many citizens do not trust the news media, they trust the government even less. While they gain political mileage by criticizing the press, they understand there is much to be lost by interfering with the press.[2] And while journalists remain vigilant about government attempts to stem the free flow of information, the free press principle has not been under sustained attack in recent years.[3] It might even be argued that American journalists receive significant forms of assistance from government, both in terms of access to information (as guaranteed by laws requiring open meetings by public bodies, open public records, political candidate financial disclosure, access to judicial procedures, and financial reporting by publicly held corporations, to name only a few) and forms of financial subsidy (such as required legal advertising by public authorities, subsidized postal rates, and the free use of public airwaves by privately owned broadcast corporations). American journalists often wonder how their British colleagues can function effectively when the editorial process is more circumscribed by central authority, such as through strict limitations on the pretrial reporting of criminal cases, punitive libel laws, official secrets legislation, D-notices, and other laws and practices that seem, to American eyes, to narrow the practical meaning of 'freedom of the press'. And the idea of a publicly supported broadcasting corporation, such as the BBC, has never achieved broad support in the United States; American public radio and television has small audiences, is starved of funding and is vulnerable to the shifts in the Washington political winds.

This distrust of government, along with the pronounced localism of the American press and its emphasis on objectivity, leaves questions of responsibility and accountability in the hands of journalists and the local community. But this is not the same as saying that accountability issues are left to the whims of the marketplace. Public debates about the values and ethics of the press have taken place in the United States periodically since the closing decades of the nineteenth century. De Tocqueville noted in the 1830s that Americans loved to form associations and this is still true. Many groups debate the roles and ethics of the press: journalists themselves, their professional associations, their employing organizations, the universities through schools and departments of journalism, advertisers, many public interest groups, as well as members of the reading and viewing audience. While solutions to accountability questions have proved to be elusive, there is little question that the context for the discussions in the past half century was provided by the Hutchins Commission in 1947.

The Hutchins Commission and the responsibility ideal

The Commission on Freedom of the Press, better known by the name of its chairman, Robert M. Hutchins (chancellor of the University of Chicago), was itself an aberration. Americans are not in the habit of appointing the US equivalent of royal commissions to inquire into important public policy matters. But in 1944 Henry L. Luce, head of the *Time* magazine publishing empire, saw the need for a strong statement supporting the value of the free-press system to American society and prevailed upon his friend and fellow Yale University alumnus Hutchins to head such a project. Luce provided $200 000 and Hutchins appointed the commission members and assumed total editorial control.[4] Named to the commission were some of the leading members of the academic community from the fields of philosophy, law, theology, history and the social sciences, such as Harold Lasswell, Reinhold Niebuhr, Arthur M. Schlesinger Sr, Archibald MacLeish and Zechariah Chafee Jr, but no active journalists.[5]

The Hutchins Commission concluded in its 133-page summary report early in 1947 (six supplementary volumes were also published) that freedom of the press in the United States was in danger, for three reasons. First, while the importance of the press in modern societies has increased, the technological revolution and increasing economic concentration of the media industries have greatly reduced the proportion of people who can express their opinions and ideas through the press. Second, the large corporations that control the press have failed to provide the exchange of information, the daily intelligence and the public forum needed by a democratic society. Third, press content is weakened by sensationalism, coloured by ownership bias, and weighted by advertiser influence. American society, the commission wrote, condemns these practices and their continuation could lead to regulation or control of the press because, ultimately, the press must be accountable:

> It must be accountable to society for meeting the public need and for maintaining the rights of citizens and the almost forgotten rights of speakers who have no press. It must know that its faults and errors have ceased to be private vagaries and have become public dangers. The voice of the press, so far

as by a drift toward monopoly it tends to become exclusive in its wisdom and observation, deprives other voices of a hearing and the public of their contribution. Freedom of the press for the coming period can only continue as an accountable freedom. Its moral right will be conditioned on its acceptance of this accountability. Its legal right will stand unaltered as its moral duty is performed. (Commission on Freedom of the Press 1947: 18–19)

Reading the Hutchins report a half century later, one is struck by the prescient nature of the Commission's remarks on economic trends then evident in the media industries. As new communication technologies increase their reach and influence, the commissioners noted, industry concentration also increases. They noted declining levels of competition produced by the increase in single-newspaper cities, the growth of large newspaper chains, the growing concentration of ownership in the magazine, motion picture and book publishing industries, and the powerful influence of four major networks in the radio industry. These trends – all far more advanced in the American media industries of the 1990s – raise important questions, according to the commission. To what extent has concentration reduced the variety of press content? Has it limited the opportunities to reach an audience by those with something to say? Has the struggle for power and profit harmed the public interest? 'Have the units of the press, by becoming big business, lost their representative character and developed a common bias – the bias of the large investor and employer? Can the press in the present crisis rise to its responsibility as an essential instrument for carrying on the political and social life of a nation and a world of nations seeking understanding?' (Commission on the Freedom of the Press 1947: 51).

The Commission proposed solutions to problems of the press's performance, but largely ruled out government intervention or legal solutions: 'In the judgment of the Commission everyone concerned with the freedom of the press and with the future of democracy should put forth every effort to make the press accountable, for, if it does not become so of its own motion, the power of government will be used, as a last resort, to force it to be so' (Commission on the Freedom of the Press 1947: 80). Instead, the Commission tried to clarify the appropriate role in government with relation to mass communication, and called on the public and the press itself to produce the needed reforms. The government, for example, might encourage new communications ventures, maintain competition in the industry through the use of anti-trust laws, and ensure that the public receives the benefits of economic concentration when such concentration is necessary or unavoidable. Radio and motion pictures should receive the same constitutional guarantees of freedom as the newspaper industry. As an alternative to libel, legislation should provide injured parties with a retraction, a restatement of the facts or an opportunity to reply. Laws limiting free speech should be loosened where no clear and present danger of violence is evident. The government should be free to develop and use media of its own when the press fails to inform the public of its policies.

The public and public institutions could also help to develop a better press system, according to the commissioners. They suggested that non-profit institutions, such as universities and libraries, use the new communication technologies to produce news services. The universities should also create academic–professional centres for the advanced study, research and publication in the field of mass communications. Their schools of journalism should provide their students with liberal educations to better prepare them for professional work. A new and independent agency to appraise and report annually on the performance on the press should be developed.

Ultimately, however, the commissioners thought that the press had a primary responsibility to put its own house in order. The key word here is 'responsibility'; the commissioners were convinced that the press owed the public something in return for its constitutional protection. Siebert, Peterson and Schramm (1956) later enlarged the phrase to 'social responsibility' in their *Four Theories of the Press*, but the responsibility concept has been the fundamental idea in American discussions of accountability since the publication of the Hutchins Report.

Responsibility, according to the Commission, was 'largely a question of the way in which the press looks at itself. We suggest that the press look upon itself as performing a public service of a professional kind. There are some things which a truly professional man will not do for money' (Commission on the Freedom of the Press 1947: 92). Among its recommendations was the idea that the press should 'accept the responsibilities of common carriers of information and discussion', operating as public utilities providing news and information to the public. The press should also finance new and experimental ideas in the field; engage in mutual criticism; increase the competence, independence and effectiveness of its staff; and ensure that advertisers do not control content, especially in radio. How can these goals be achieved?

> By a recognition on the part of the press that, while its enterprise is and should remain a private business, its efforts to define and realize its standards are also a community concern and should be systematically associated with corresponding efforts of community, consumers and government ... the main positive energy for the improvement of press achievement must come from the issuers. Although the standards of press performance arise as much from the public situation and need as from the conscious goals of the press, these standards must be administered by the press itself. This means that **the press must now take on the community press objectives as its own objectives**. (Commission on the Freedom of the Press 1947: 126–7; emphasis in original)

Responding to the call for responsibility

Not surprisingly, the press response to the Hutchins Report was defensive and dismissive.[6] Though the politically conservative *Chicago Tribune* headlined its report '"A Free Press" (Hitler Style) Sought for US', most press reaction was more temperate. The composition of the Commission was criticized, especially the absence of journalists, as was its failure to carry out systematic research into the operations of the press. The Commission's broad definition of 'press' – including radio, motion pictures and book publishing – was unacceptable to many journalists, who saw themselves in a different light from their colleagues in these industries. Some critics pointed out that many monopoly or chain-owned newspapers in the United States were excellent, while certain competitive or independently owned newspapers were hardly models of exemplary performance. Others found the Hutchins recommendations to be vague and ill-defined; how could it be determined if the press accepted its responsibilities and what could be done if the press refused to do so? Who should decide when and how the government should intervene in the affairs of the press? Perhaps most important from the standpoint of public discussion of the press-responsibility issue, many newspapers virtually ignored the report's publication, electing not to carry news stories about it or burying the stories on inside pages.

Nonetheless, many in the newspaper industry and academic journalism acknowledged the importance of the Commission's point about the press's responsibilities in a democratic society. In succeeding years, as the postwar generation of journalists assumed positions of influence in the industry, discussion about the proper role of the press acquired a new prominence in industry publications, professional meetings and academic circles. Gradually, Hutchins-style mechanisms and practices were adopted to heighten the professional standing of journalists and address questions of the accountability in the American press.

Ombudsmen

About thirty newspapers and a number of broadcast stations have appointed ombudsmen: staff members assigned the task of monitoring the news media for accuracy and fairness, explaining the news media to the public, and conveying viewpoints of audience members to the media management (Lambeth 1992: 114). Other media have employed media critics or reader advocates in similar capacities in attempting to bridge the gap between the audience and staff journalists.

Ethics codes

Most journalists' professional associations, such as the Society of Professional Journalists, the Associated Press Managing Editors, the American Society of Newspaper Editors, and many newspapers, magazines and broadcast stations have adopted ethical codes and operating standards for their staff members. A 1992 survey found that 46 per cent of American newspapers and television stations had written ethics' codes for their employees (Black et al. 1993: 210). Though these codes vary in their degree of specificity and most do not prescribe sanctions for violation of the code, their main value seems to lie in the process of their construction, when journalists debate the press's roles and responsibilities with their colleagues.

Journals of self-criticism

The American journalism field has spawned a number of magazines that publish informed criticism of the industry itself, such as the *Washington Journalism Review* (circulation 30 000, published by the University of Maryland), the *Columbia Journalism Review* (circulation 37 000, published by Columbia University), *Quill* (published by the Society of Professional Journalists), the *St Louis Journalism Review*, and several other publications. They ensure that the performance of journalists is always under scrutiny by the strictest of critics: other journalists. Some newspapers themselves have also engaged in exercises of self-criticism: for example, a newspaper in the State of Idaho in the late 1970s published a full page of criticism of its staff and possible conflicts of interest (Lambeth 1992: 112). The executive editor had done the publicity for a US Senate candidate; the business reporter wrote stories linked to her husband's work for a forest-products firm; the publisher was president of the State board of education and may have influenced the paper's education coverage. These exercises in self-flagellation, however, are more the exception than the rule.

University journalism programmes

The period from the publication of the Hutchins Report until the end of the 1980s was a time of expansion for journalism education in the nation's colleges and universities.[7] There are about 400 schools or departments of journalism in the United States and about 100 have been approved in a national accrediting process. Since the 1970s, instruction and research in media ethics have expanded greatly and most academic units provide their students with ethics instruction. The academic literature on journalism ethics and responsibility has also expanded greatly, with many new titles being published each year. Several universities sponsor institutes for research and assessment of press performance. A number of independent or industry-sponsored institutes also provide research studies, training workshops and other activities that monitor and analyse media performance.

Press councils

The Commission's call for the establishment of an independent agency to appraise and monitor the press was answered in 1973 when the National News Council (NNC) was founded. However, the self-appointed council, supported by foundation money but with no official standing, lasted only eleven years, voting itself out of existence in 1984. The NNC accepted public complaints about news coverage, but only in cases in which the news media themselves declined to respond to the complaints, and only if the complainants signed a waiver of rights to file a lawsuit in the matter in question. The council aimed to stimulate discussion of media responsibility through publicity. Altogether, 242 complaints were brought to the NNC during its eleven years: 82 were found to be warranted, in whole or in part; 120 were found to be unwarranted; 37 were dismissed, and three were withdrawn (Lambeth 1992: 109–12). The NNC was handicapped throughout its history, however, by the lack of cooperation of major newspapers, such as the *New York Times*, and the unwillingness of many media organizations to publicize its deliberations or findings. Minnesota is the only American State with a press council, which has been in existence since 1971.[8] A number of local press councils have been tried since the 1960s, with varying degrees of success.

Ethics and the problem of public accountability

The impact of the post-Hutchins examination of the press's responsibilities should not be underestimated. It is unquestionably true that American newspapers are now more careful of problems such as correcting errors or potential conflicts of interest, that journalists' professional societies pay more attention to ethical issues in their publications and at conventions, that more news media staff have received instruction in making ethical judgements. It might even be argued that American newspapers are more sensitive to ethics transgressions – their own and those of others – than ever before. But all this seems to illustrate is the difference between trying to act responsibly and maintaining the public trust. For repeated opinion surveys and scattered pieces of evidence seem to suggest that the public has little confidence in the ethics of 'the media', which itself seems to have become a pejorative of the 1990s. And more ominously in a market economy, news-oriented media organizations – especially newspapers, but network news to some degree – are losing audiences. Members of the public are simply not paying attention as they once did, in the same way as they are not voting in presidential elections, joining political parties or attending church on Sunday.

There is no shortage of critics who link a perceived erosion of American society with the press's performance. James Fallows, then Washington editor of *The Atlantic Monthly* magazine, published a book in which he said:

> Americans believe that the news media have become too arrogant, cynical, scandal-minded, and destructive. Public hostility shows up in opinion polls, through comments on talk shows, in waning support for news organizations in their showdowns with government officials, and in many other ways. The most important sign of public unhappiness may be a quiet consumers' boycott of the press. Year by year, a smaller proportion of Americans goes to the trouble of reading newspapers or watching news broadcasts on TV. This is a loss not only for the media but also for the public as a whole. (Fallows 1996: 3)

The consequence, according to Fallows, is that members of the public do not obtain the sort of information they need to make intelligent, informed decisions on public issues.

A similar conclusion had been produced by the Kettering Foundation

some years earlier as part of a long-term study of the relationship between American citizens and government. Its report, 'Citizens and Politics:
A View from Main Street America', found that contrary to conventional
wisdom, Americans are not apathetic about politics, but feel impotent –
that they do not matter in an increasingly impersonal system. The report
concluded:

> this report does not offer specific approaches for how the media can engage
> the public – only optimism that the public holds the desire, and is ready, to
> enter the debate. But will the media help citizens sort through the maze of is-
> sues they face? Will they provide a context for understanding those issues?
> Will they increase the emphasis they place on covering policy issues, even at
> the possible expense of covering political gossip, mudslinging, and scandals?
> Is now the time to expand what appears to be an emerging debate on the role of
> the media in the civic life of communities? (The Harwood Group 1991: 59–60)

Paul H. Weaver, a political scientist and former journalist, contributed
another book which argued that the press, political officials and public
relations-oriented corporations have banded together to create an artificial reality with an insistent focus on a sense of crisis and needed
emergency responses:

> the credibility of the culture of lying is practically nil. In the view of the large
> majority of the American people, the public discourse is a pasticcio of cheesy
> fabrications, the highest officials in the land routinely lie to the public they're
> supposed to serve, and fundamental processes of communication and
> answerability that make liberal democracy a reality have broken down.
> What's more, they're mad as hell about it. Public opinion surveys reveal
> massive public distrust of the élite and institutions involved in the culture of
> lying. (Weaver 1994: 19)

How can the press's post-Hutchins interest in responsibility be recon-
ciled with these analyses? If American journalists have a greater concern about ethical standards and accountability issues, how can they
also be seen as culpable for failing with something as basic as keeping
the public informed on the basic issues of the day? One answer to these
questions might lie in structural changes in the press itself. Most of the
post-Hutchins discussion has been concerned with micro-conceptions
of responsibility, supported by individualist theories of rights and
ethics generated by the Enlightenment. Questions about the reporter's
relationship with news sources, matters of accuracy and fairness, objectivity, conflicts of interest, and economic temptations (such as accepting
favours, gifts, and travel from sources) have dominated the discussions.
These are important issues to be sure, but they do not begin to address
those raised by the changing structural arrangements of the press.

These structural changes can be reviewed here only briefly.[9] Many
are grounded in the continuing corporatization of the American news
media and the resulting redefinition of news and changes in the press's
relations with other institutions and the public. Increasingly, news outlets are owned not locally, but by national and international chains or

groups, or vertically integrated multimedia conglomerates which own several mass media forms (of the American TV networks, for example, ABC is owned by Walt Disney, NBC is owned by General Electric, and CBS by Westinghouse – all purchased in recent years). More than 50 per cent of all American newspapers, magazines and television stations are owned by twenty large corporations ('Big media got bigger' 1996: 43). These entities compete in an increasingly competitive marketplace, using sophisticated marketing data to fragment the population by audience desires. The entrance of electronic, specialized forms of communication and the loss of audience and advertising revenue by traditional forms, such as newspapers and television networks, has led to a redefinition of media fare based on a convergence between entertainment and information on the one hand, and persuasion and information on the other. The result is a daily news menu increasingly based on personalities, scandal, sensation and the interests of tabloid television.

Some of these changes were noted by Michael Fancher, the editor of a Seattle newspaper, in describing how the modern newspaper editor's job has changed:

> This does not mean that newspapers have ceased to be great businesses. They often are, especially in markets that offer limited competition and a monopoly niche. But notice how the terms of discussion have changed. 'Comfort zone' is a marketplace concept as much as an editorial one. Even in a 'comfortable' market, chain ownership and/or the need to maximize return on investment can lead to a new definition of what constitutes an 'acceptable' level of profit. And this in practical effect can be as revolutionary as the shifting definitions of 'news'. (Fancher 1987: 72)

These 'shifting definitions of news' may explain such preoccupations in the American press during 1995 as O. J. Simpson, Hugh Grant, Kato Kaelin, Mike Tyson, the marketing of Windows 95, Michael Jackson and Colin Powell, identified by news ombudsmen among the top ten 'junk food news stories' of the year (Jensen et al. 1996: 165). Among the major stories not adequately covered during the year was the writing and eventual adoption of a new federal telecommunications law which virtually ends telecommunications regulation in the United States, deregulates cable television rates, and permits if not encourages the growth of larger ownership entities in American broadcasting. Nearly every media-owning corporation was affected directly or indirectly by the law, which might explain the lack of news coverage about it (Jensen et al. 1996: 49–50).

Such structural changes were anticipated by the Hutchins Commission, but the accountability mechanisms developed since appear powerless to preserve the localism of the American press in the face of the corporatization of the news media, defend the objectivity ideal from the power of corporate greed, or reinforce the traditional separation between press and State in a political culture that links information and power.

Rediscovering the community

In the early 1980s, the sociologist Robert Bellah and colleagues embarked on a study of community in middle-class culture (Bellah *et al.* 1985). They were concerned that individualism as an American trait, already observed a century and a half earlier by de Tocqueville, had grown pernicious and was destroying the basis of American freedom. 'What has failed at every level – from the society of nations to the national society to the local community to the family – is integration: we have failed to remember "our community as members of the same body", as John Winthrop put it. We have committed what to the republican founders of our nation was the cardinal sin: we have put our own good, as individuals, as groups, as a nation, ahead of the common good' (Bellah *et al.* 1985: 285). *Habits of the Heart* ignited a renewed interest in the concept of community on many fronts across the United States. In 1990 a group of ethicists, philosophers and social scientists met in Washington and found they shared a 'distaste for the polarization of debate and the "sound bite" public life, the effects of teledemocracy' (Etzioni 1993: 14). Their meeting led to the establishment of the Communitarian movement, the name selected to 'emphasize that the time had come to attend to our responsibilities, to the conditions and elements we all share, to the community' (Etzioni 1993: 15).

Perhaps not coincidentally, several American journalists rediscovered the community at about the same time. They also recognized that corporate journalism, with its emphases on detachment, inflexibility and uniformity, was separating journalists from their traditional foundation: readers in the local community. Their response was to reform reporting and editing to something they called 'civic journalism' or 'public journalism'. 'Public journalism' opens the possibility that journalists can serve their communities in truly useful ways that go beyond telling the news. 'It also offers us a chance to regain our lost credibility,' wrote Davis ('Buzz') Merritt, the editor of the Wichita, Kansas, *Eagle*, one of the pioneers of the movement (Merritt 1995: 131). Civic journalists do this by getting back in contact with the public, finding out what their concerns are, and structuring news coverage – especially during election periods – so it addresses their concerns. The aim is to reinvigorate democracy on the local level by reconceiving the form and function of journalism. By 1995 more than 170 public journalism projects had been initiated by newspapers and broadcast stations across the USA.

Will public journalism be the answer for the Hutchins Commission's call for journalistic accountability to the community? Perhaps it is too early to know. Already the movement has its critics, especially in the traditional press.[10] Some argue that public journalism introduces a new definition of news and discards the concept of objectivity and journalistic detachment by enlisting journalists on the side of citizen involvement. Others claim that the movement is business-office-oriented, a last-ditch effort by newspapers losing their subscription base to regain their readers: an allegation supported by the financial assistance provided for public journalism projects by wealthy newspaper foundations. Others say there is nothing new under the sun – that public journalism is nothing more that what good newspapers have done all along. Finally, we might question whether the community being rediscovered is more myth than reality, already having been surpassed by a new, high-tech commercial culture that is defining accountability in new and different ways.

Notes

1 The wording of the First Amendment is: 'Congress shall make no law respecting an establishment of religion, or prohibiting free exercise thereof; of abridging the freedom of speech, or of the press; or the right of the people peaceably to assemble, and to petition the Government for a redress of grievances.' Journalists in the USA work in the only private industry guaranteed a specific constitutional protection against government interference.
2 This is not to say that American politicians are not adept at manipulating the news media to obtain the sort of news coverage they desire. For an example of how the Reagan Administration orchestrated network news coverage, see Hertsgaard 1988.
3 Broadcasting in the United States is regulated by the federal government through the Federal Communications Commission. Radio and television stations are required to, among other things, operate 'in the public interest, convenience and necessity'. This provides the federal government with the authority to regulate broadcast content, but the FCC over the years has rarely intruded in content or news coverage matters.
4 Encyclopaedia Britannica later provided another $15 000 to complete the project. A good description of the work of the commission is provided by Blanchard 1977.
5 The composition of the commission was later criticized for being 'eleven professors, a banker and a poet' (Blanchard 1977: 31).
6 The reaction to the Hutchins Report is ably summarized in Blanchard 1977: 29–50.
7 The journalism schools of the 1940s had been criticized by the Hutchins Commission for their vocational-style training and the absence of informed criticism of industry performance (Commission on Freedom of the Press 1947: 78).
8 The Minnesota council has supported the news media in 42 per cent of its decisions, backed complainants in 38 per cent, and sided partially with complainants in the remaining 20 per cent (Lambeth 1992: 111).
9 Changes in the economic structure of the American press are ably reviewed by Demers 1996.
10 Many of these criticisms are reviewed in Fallows 1996: 260-4.

References

Bellah, R.N., Madsen, R., Sullivan, W.M., Swidler, A. and Tipton, S.M. (1985) *Habits of the Heart: Individualism and Commitment in American Life*, University of California Press, Berkeley.

'Big media got bigger' (1996) *Mother Jones*, Jan./Feb.

Black, J., Steele, B. and Barney, R. (1993) *Doing Ethics in Journalism: A Handbook with Case Studies*, The Sigma Delta Chi Foundation and The Society of Professional Journalists, Greencastle, Ind.

Blanchard, M.A. (1977) 'The Hutchins Commission, the press and the responsibility concept', *Journalism Monographs* **49**, May: 1–59.

Breed, W. (1958) 'Mass communication and sociocultural integration', *Social Forces* **37**.

Cirino, R. (1971) *Don't Blame the People*, Vintage, New York.

Commission on the Freedom of the Press (1947) *A Free and Responsible Press*, University of Chicago Press, Chicago.

Demers, D.P. (1996) *The Menace of the Corporate Newspaper: Fact or Fiction?* Iowa State University Press, Ames.

Dominick, J.R. (1996) *The Dynamics of Mass Communication*, 5th edn, McGraw-Hill, New York.

Etzioni, A. (1993) *The Spirit of Community*, Simon & Shuster, New York.

Fallows, J. (1996) *Breaking the News: How the Media Undermine American Democracy*, Pantheon Books, New York.

Fancher, M. (1987) 'The metamorphosis of the newspaper editor', *Gannett Center Journal* **1**, Spring.

Fatout, P. (ed.) (1976) *Mark Twain Speaking*, University of Iowa Press, Iowa City.

Graber, D.A. (1993) *Mass Media and American Politics*, 4th edn, CQ Press, Washington.

The Harwood Group (1991) Citizens and Politics: *A View from Main Street America*, Kettering Foundation, Dayton, Ohio.

Hertsgaard, M. (1988) *On Bended Knee: The Press and the Reagan Presidency*, Farrar Straus, Giroux, New York.

Jensen, C. and Project Censored (1996) *Censored: The News That Didn't make the News – and Why*, Seven Stories Press, New York.

Lambeth, E.B. (1992) *Committed Journalism*, Indiana University Press, Bloomington.

Lichter, S.R., Stanley Rothman, S. and Lichter, L.S. (1986) *The Media Elite*, Adler & Adler, Bethesda, Maryland.

Merritt, D. (1995) 'Public journalism – Defining a democratic art', *Media Studies Journal* **9**, Summer.

Siebert, F.S., Peterson, T.B. and Schramm, W. (1956) *Four Theories of the Press*, University of Illinois Press, Urbana.

Weaver, P.H. (1994) *News and the Culture of Lying*, The Free Press, New York.

CHAPTER 8

Media quality control in the USA and Europe

Claude-Jean Bertrand

My impression is that today people worry too much about cyberspace and not enough about the contents of the news media; too much about the information superhighway – and not enough about those media most people now use.

However, in recent years, on both sides of the Atlantic,[1] there has been a revival of public interest in media behaviour. A fundamental reason is that the market everywhere has been given more importance than public service. In Europe, a demonopolization, decentralization and commercialization of broadcasting has taken place; in the USA, an increase in competition, caused by deregulation and technology, has led to hypercommercialization, and hence infotainment.

But let's go back to basics for a while. The freedom of the news media is vital for mankind. Obstacles to that freedom are no longer technological; they are less political than they used to be; they are increasingly economic – and they also reside in the journalistic tradition itself.[2]

The measures taken to ensure good media service also differ somewhat on either side of the Atlantic. I perceive four types:

- Regulation: considered indispensable, even by free-enterprisers, it is entrusted to autonomous agencies like the American Federal Communications Commission (FCC), or the French Conseil Supérieur de l'Audiovisuel (CSA). Europeans trust laws more than Americans do, but even they do not wish to rely too much on the State
- Competition: for instance, the multiplicity of services on the Internet is forcing the media to provide more, like extra news and documents online
- Education in journalism (and in media ethics) is far more developed in the US than in Europe. Education includes the sensitization of the public to media issues
- Ethics and 'media accountability systems' (MAS): what is commonly grouped under the term 'ethics', I would prefer to divide into three levels:

1   Personal ethics: individuals and their moral conscience – if any
2   Professional ethics: the consensus on principles and rules, materialized in codes (which concentrate on sins to be avoided) and enforced through peer pressure
3   Quality control: a far wider concept, including both what should and should not be done. It has no moral connotations: the aims here are good public service *and* good profits. Together owners *and* news people *and* the public are involved. Corporations cannot be expected to have a moral sense, but their managers can be made to understand that quality pays – by those who do the paying, the consumers. Since consumers are an amorphous mass, their power needs to be focused by the professionals. Together they could become irresistible

On either side of the north Atlantic newspeople and scholars love to talk about the media and ethics. Their earnestness can only be evaluated by how they turn words into action, the ways and means to make ethical rules respected, to 'control quality' – what I call the MAS (see Box 8.1).

Box 8.1   Media accountability systems

The MAS

A MAS is any kind of non-governmental means used to ensure that the media are 'socially responsible'. They come in more than thirty different shapes. The concept of MAS is global – and hence nebulous – as it includes individuals, groups of people, regular meetings, single documents, small media, a particular approach, or a long process.

MAS have several immediate purposes

- *criticism* – the oldest method to better the media, the easiest and most common
- *monitoring* – needed now because media products are so numerous and shortlived; and because the media sin more often by omission than by commission
- *access to the media* – both in the sense that all media need feedback, and in the sense that every group in the population must be able to broadcast information
- *training* – the long-term solution to most media problems; both the education of professionals and the sensitization of citizens

---

Some MAS consist of texts or broadcasts

- very visible correction boxes
- pro and con opinions presented on all public issues
- letters to the editor and open forums
- on-line message boards and forums for immediate feedback
- accuracy and fairness questionnaires mailed to people mentioned in the news, or published for all readers to answer

- codes of ethics which media professionals have discussed and agreed upon – with (preferably) input from the public
- regular media sections in newspapers and magazines, or programmes on TV and radio
- journalism reviews, local or national, devoted principally to media criticism
- books written by professionals or by expert observers to expose media failings and recommend improvements
- movies and television series dealing with the media, sometimes critically, like *WKRP in Cincinnati* or *Murphy Brown*, or a satirical programme like the daily *Les Guignols* on Canal Plus or *Drop the Dead Donkey* on Channel 4

Some MAS consist of individuals or groups

- in-house critics, staff review groups[3], or content evaluation commissions (like those established by Japanese dailies as early as the 1920s) to scrutinize their own newspapers for possible violations of ethics
- media reporters who keep a critical eye on a whole sector of the media industry and report on it to the public; and (when the occasion warrants it) courageous whistle-blowers
- press ombudsmen, paid by a newspaper or broadcast station to deal with complaints from customers; and an ethics coach operating in the newsroom

- liaison committees set up by the media and some group with which they may occasionally clash; for example, the legal profession or the police
- citizens appointed to the editorial board[4]
- local press councils – regular meetings of professionals from the local media and representative members of the community
- regional and national media councils (composed of representatives of media owners, professionals and citizens) created by the media both to adjudicate on complaints by media users and to defend press freedom against government threats
- special 'quality control' projects by media-related groups, such as labour unions, professional associations, NGOs (like Reporters sans Frontières)
- consumer associations, especially associations of media users using awareness sessions, mail campaigns, opinion polls, evaluations, lobbying, even boycotts

- the 'société de rédacteurs', an association of newspeople which usually owns shares in the company they work for, and hence has a voice in the setting of editorial policy.[5] Similarly, the employees who own their own medium[6]
- the even rarer 'société de lecteurs', an association of readers which buys shares in the capital of a medium and demands to have a say, even a very small one, in the general policy of the company

Lastly, some MAS are processes

- the crucial MAS: higher education
- the continuing education of working journalists through one-day workshops, one-week seminars, six-month or one-year fellowships at universities
- internal awareness programmes to increase the attention of media workers to the needs of citizens

- regular opinion surveys; and, better perhaps, surveys of panels of citizens after they have been briefed by experts and have debated a given issue
- the regular encounter of newspeople with citizens in some kind of press club or at town meetings
- non-commercial research, done mainly by academics, often in 'media observatories' or foundation-funded think-tanks, on such topics as the perception of media messages by the public, or the contents of the media, or the absence of content

Europe

The old continent differs from the New World in that it has faith in laws to protect the freedom of the press, and to force the media to serve the public: laws like the very remarkable Swedish law, or the French General Press Law of 1881. There is also a long tradition of public service in broadcasting. Nevertheless, all over Europe in recent years media ethics has become a hot issue. At the beginning of 1993 and at the end of 1994, I conducted a survey of two different sets of twenty-six journalists and media observers in seventeen nations.[7] All respondents, without exception, agreed that the interest in ethics had increased. Three-quarters of them could cite at least one book on the topic recently published in their country.

The causes suggested for the concern show great diversity.[8] These included dramatic cases like the Timisoara 'massacre' hoax (France, Greece, Switzerland) and the Gulf War (Britain, France, Greece, Switzerland); the role of the media in a political crisis (Italy, Spain); serious violations of court rules (Britain), or of ethics by individual journalists (France, Germany, The Netherlands, Switzerland, Turkey); a general worsening of inaccuracy (Turkey), of sensationalism (Germany), of vulgarity (Turkey); the invasion of privacy (The Netherlands, Norway, Portugal, Sweden, Turkey) by the tabloid press (Britain, Ireland, Norway, Sweden), and especially against politicians (Britain, Finland, Germany, Spain); TV violence and reality-shows (Finland, Germany, Switzerland); and the mix of journalism and advertising (Switzerland).

That general trend is linked to the new means offered by technology (The Netherlands, Spain), and to the greater media commercialization and competition (Austria, Finland, The Netherlands, Norway, Switzerland), to the concentration of ownership (Sweden), or the non-media activities of media barons (Turkey); to the links between government and the media (Ireland, Spain), legal restrictions or the threat of such (Belgium, Britain, Denmark, Ireland, Spain); to the dwindling credibility and prestige of journalists (Belgium, France), the ethical awakening of journalistic organizations (Italy), or a higher profile assumed by the national press ombudsman (Sweden). There has been a general reaction to the *laissez-faire* of the 1980s (Denmark) by a public more aware of its rights (Norway), of the need for ethics (Italy, Finland), and of the media's increased role in society (Britain, Ireland, The Netherlands, Sweden).

So, for some years now professionals and non-professionals have talked and written abundantly about what the media do that they should not – and the consequent threats of State intervention. But have they sought practical means to remedy the situation? Do they even know what means exist in their own countries? Whoever is concerned about media behaviour must first try to define what is right and what is wrong for them to do. Do many European media outlets have an individual code of ethics? The reply was 'No' in nine countries out of ten. On the other hand, in thirteen countries out of seventeen the existence was noted of a generally accepted code of media ethics – the exceptions being Britain, Greece, The Netherlands and Spain.

Where did the codes originate? Unions or associations of journalists were most often responsible (as in Belgium, Finland or Switzerland), sometimes jointly with an association of publishers and editors (Norway, Sweden). In two cases (Austria, Germany) the code was written by the press council which itself had been set up by journalists' unions and associations of publishers.

Everywhere in Europe the unions have manifested an interest in ethics, most often by organizing conferences and workshops; by publishing items in their own bulletins or in books; by drafting a code of ethics (Belgium, Britain, Ireland, Italy); by creating a committee on ethics; and often by helping create a press council (Austria, Germany, The Netherlands, Norway, Sweden) or setting one up on their own (Switzerland). Occasionally, all of the above applied, as in Denmark and Finland.[9]

Once rules have been agreed, how are they to be enforced if recourse to the judicial system is rejected, as it must be? Since at least the 1960s an easy answer has been a non-governmental tripartite court of arbitration, a press council (PC), gathering representatives of owners, journalists and media users. Ten Western European countries (60 per cent) have a national council, and seven do not, the latter being located in the south,[10] with the exceptions of Ireland and Belgium. Nowadays, wherever PCs exist they tend to widen their membership (Finland) or their functions (The Netherlands, Switzerland) or both (Norway). The British, however, have narrowed both the composition and the scope of their PC, which became the Press Complaints Commission in 1991.

In a large country the national PC cannot deal with all the sins of all the media. A post-Second World War US invention and a Canadian invention of the 1970s was the regional PC. None of the European respondents had ever heard of either in their country, save in Switzerland where regional public radio stations are required to have something similar. However, liaison committees between local media controllers and their communities may exist under another name.[11]

Ombudsmen[12] are almost as rare as local PCs. Only seven countries report having one or more: Britain, France, Ireland, Italy, The Netherlands, Spain and Switzerland. Only the last has more than three or four: the new private radio stations (about forty) are each required to have one – a legal, not an ethical disposition. Discounting the Swiss, it adds up to fewer than twenty in a region that harbours about 1500 daily newspapers, more than 5000 radio stations and some 900 television networks and stations, not to mention thousands of magazines. The meagre compensation is that some of the best newspapers on the continent have one, like *The Guardian, Le Monde, El Pais* and *La Repubblica*.

There are many other MAS than PCs and newspaper ombudsmen, though the fact is not much publicized. MAS come in extremely diverse shapes, from visible correction boxes to a college education for journalists. Are such MAS to be found in Europe?

The most traditional means of improving the media, also the quickest and least expensive, is criticism; pointing out the errors of the media and also what they regularly do wrong, together with what they ought to do. As a first step, do all the European media ostensibly correct their blunders? The answer is a quasi-unanimous 'No'.[13] However, 60 per cent of respondents say that some media do; about 50 per cent say most print media do. But, except for Finland, all consider corrections to be 'discreet'.

The second step can be to use an 'in-house critic' on a part- or full-time basis, or a 'contents evaluation commission' (*shinshashitsu* in Japanese). They are unknown. Media reporters, who write critical pieces on all the media for the general public, seem to exist in more than half of the seventeen countries surveyed. Their numbers range from four or five (Austria, Norway, Spain) to 10–20 (Germany, The Netherlands, Sweden). In Britain, it is reported, every quality daily or Sunday newspaper now has one: a recent and remarkable development. The problem, however, is that some respondents tend to confuse media critics, who expose the unethical operations of the media, with the conventional TV or film critics who comment on particular media performances.

Are there any reviews that specialize in venting strictures? The answer is 'Yes' for a small third of the seventeen countries; for example, for Britain, Germany or Switzerland. For a large third, the answer is 'No': that is, Belgium, The Netherlands and Portugal. Respondents for the final third did not agree. It is worth noting that quite a few of the periodicals cited as examples of 'journalism reviews' are closer to trade magazines or to journals, such as the Spanish *Noticias de la Comunicación* or the British *Media, Culture and Society*. On the other hand, in more than two-thirds of countries media criticism is the object of regular (30 per cent) or occasional (40 per cent) programmes as part of public service broadcasting.

One means of finding out what media users like or dislike, is to ask them. A few US newspapers have in the past used 'accuracy and fairness questionnaires' – and the Brazilian *Globo* does it now. The European media never send or publish any. But in almost half of the seventeen countries surveys are done, or commissioned, by the media to discover what their clients think of their services – but they do not do it often or regularly. Only in Turkey is the answer unequivocally 'No'.

One way to give media users an opportunity to vent their opinions is to publish their 'letters to the editor'. This, in the French press, for instance, has become the norm only in the recent past, and in the prestigious daily *Le Monde* it is still a weekly feature. The answer to the question, 'Do most newspapers and magazines have such a section?' is a 100 per cent 'Yes'. In every country they devote a quarter of a page (33 per cent), half a page (55 per cent), or a full page to letters. However, in about 30 per cent of countries letters critical of the publication are not often published: they are in 40 per cent.

Undoubtedly the safest and most efficient media accountability system, but the slowest, is education. A journalist with a college education can be expected to be a more ethically aware and autonomous operator than someone trained on the job. What proportion of journalists have a college degree? What proportion of new entrants? How many of them have been through a journalism school?

As regards education, respondents from the same country gave different answers – with few exceptions, like France (69 per cent, an official figure). Often answers differed widely: 10 to 35 per cent for Austria; 30 to 100 per cent for Denmark; 48 to 85 per cent for Finland; 30 to 65 per cent for Germany, and so on. What it means is that few know and, alas, that most don't care. The same applies to the question of how many journalists have attended a university-level school of journalism. Respondents say 20 to 50 per cent in The Netherlands; 20 to 80 per cent in Spain; 40 to 75 per cent in Sweden; 10 to 50 per cent in Turkey, etc. One cause of confusion is that in some nations university-level journalism training is a must (Denmark), or was until recently (Spain), while in other countries it is a recent creation, as in Britain and Italy, or seemingly does not yet exist (Greece, Switzerland).

However, one, highly gratifying, trend is clear: in twelve responding countries out of fourteen the perceived proportion of professionals starting off with a college degree is between 70 and 100 per cent. Another interesting feature is that in ten out of the seventeen nations newspeople 'commonly attended workshops and seminars to improve their knowledge or skills'. Only in Italy and Turkey is this not the case.

Cynics look on ethics and MAS as useless and hazardous – and maintain that the improvement of the media (that is, better service of the public) is predicated not on noble principles but on power. One power that can be used is that of the purse. If consumers stop consuming the media, or the products advertised in them, media owners will get the message. However, the boycott is used in the USA but not in Europe. What of associations for the general defence of consumers which keep a close eye on TV sets and bank services: have they developed an interest in media contents? From seventeen nations only one clear 'Yes' was given (from Denmark). In thirteen nations the answer was 'No'. This is amazing: is popular welfare more threatened by mediocre VCRs or mediocre daily newspapers? Cannot violence on TV be analysed just as well as nitrates in tap water?

Fortunately, in almost half of European nations there are one or several associations of media users, mainly of television viewers, which strive to be heard. One, MTT in France, is fascinating because it was set up by forces which, traditionally, have been antagonistic: an association of school teachers and one of Catholic families.

Consumers and newspeople could also aim at the power that derives from ownership. Hence the last two, most unusual, MAS consist of journalists owning part of the medium or the whole of it[14] – or in citizens buying some shares so as to have a (tiny) say in setting the policy of a medium. Share-holding by journalists is found in ten out of seventeen European nations, but it usually involves only one publication (France, Switzerland) or two (Belgium, Germany) and seems not to have much impact.

Do European consumers buy stock in media companies? Out of a total of forty-nine respondents, only four (Britain, Denmark, Finland, Switzerland) found cause to answer positively. But the *société des lecteurs* of *Le Monde* should be taken into account: its purpose is to assist journalists in maintaining quality and independence.

Overall, what impression does such a survey inspire? A double impression: on the one hand, it confirms a growing awareness among the population that media behaviour is unsatisfactory; that something must be done to avoid both abusive commercialization and State intervention; that some of the best media do introduce 'quality control'; that enlightened citizens do organize themselves to obtain better service. On the other hand, the survey shows that respondents from the same nation quite often give different, even opposite, answers. In some cases, I knew some answers to be incorrect. This implies either that the concept involved (for example, a PC, a newspaper ombudsman) is not familiar to some of them;[15] or that the operation of MAS is not familiar even to experienced professionals or professors of journalism. Either way, the errors say much about the state of practical ethics.

The United States of America

While in the US the print media were entirely free to prostitute themselves, there used to be a relatively strict regulation of broadcasting with the FCC and the courts keeping watch. Thus, some amount of public service was forced upon commercial firms. Hence, the quality of news programmes. In the 1980s deregulation became rampant and the last existing rules are in the process of being abrogated

Over the last twenty years there has been a steady decline in the trust Americans have in their media. Among the many sins they stand accused of being manipulated, of mongering sexual scandals, of practising attack-dog journalism – while investigative journalism is dying. In the early 1990s the quality media were infected by 'tabloidization', while such popular media as MTV, *Larry King Live* (on CNN) or the weekly *National Enquirer*, started playing a political role. Typically, in 1994 AP judged the number one story of the year was the O. J. Simpson case, followed by a baseball strike – two entertainment items.

In parallel, and since the 1960s, a great passion for media ethics has developed, largely concerned with the behaviour of the individual journalist, not the responsibility of the media. Various associations have revised their codes – the American Society of Newspaper Editors, the association of managing editors of newspaper members of the Associated Press (APME), the Society of Professional Journalists (SPJ-SDX) and the Radio and Television News Directors' Association (RTNDA). By 1983 three-quarters of newspapers had a fixed policy in the matter of ethics, as opposed to about 10 per cent ten years before.

Much of the interest in 'quality control' originated in academe. The first school of journalism was that of the University of Missouri (1908). Since then the USA has created the largest, most efficient system of journalism schools, uniquely blending scholarship and professional training. They have played a major role in developing concepts, in applying research, in spreading the concern through books, textbooks, college courses, conferences, seminars, articles, even a *Journal of Mass Media Ethics*. And by offering continuing education to journalists. Media-related foundations, like the Freedom Forum and the Poynter Institute, participate in the effort.

As far as the better known MAS are concerned, the USA was the great pioneer. The first known press code was adopted in 1910 in Kansas; the first 'journalism review' was produced by George Seldes from 1940 to 1950; the firs known local PC was started in Santa Rosa, California in 1950; the first press ombudsman was appointed by the Louisville *Courier-Journal* in 1967. But the MAS have never been really accepted, save maybe in the rebellious period of 1967 to 1975. They seem to threaten the sacrosanct 'freedom of the press' which, strangely, US media people talk about a lot and use little. And since the late 1980s, the MAS have been in decline, largely because of the financial concerns of the media.

Criticism is the weapon mainly used. It has come from every direction: in the reports of federal inquiry commissions; in speeches from the White House; in the parallel press of Blacks, leftists, feminists, environmentalists, consumers; in research publications by academics, in their textbooks and their classes. Later, in the 1980s and up to the present, they were relayed by a coalition of conservative businessmen, evangeli-

119

cals, army leaders, Republican Congressmen – talking, writing, suing. More specifically, twenty-five journalism reviews were created between 1968 and 1975, and fifteen in the next twenty years. In 1995 there were about twenty left: three general titles (the *Columbia Journalism Review*, *American Journalism Review* and the regional *St Louis Journalism Review*) based on university campuses; most of the others were partisan, some radical, like *Extra* published by FAIR (1986), but mainly right-wing, like *AIM Report* (1972).

Trade reviews no longer avoid criticism, particularly the weekly *Editor & Publisher*. Besides, regular media have joined the fray. The movie industry never hesitated to satirize other media. Now television, mainly PBS, does a little scutinizing. Quality magazines, especially news magazines, have greatly increased their coverage, as have the metropolitan dailies (see *Media Studies Journal* 1995): in 1992 David Shaw, the media critic of the *Los Angeles Times*, was awarded the first Pulitzer Prize for media criticism.

As regards PCs, nothing much has been done. In 1967 the Mellett Foundation (run by the journalists' union) with the assistance of journalism professors experimented with six well-publicized community-media councils. There had been some before and there would be a few afterwards – twenty in all. But that strictly US[16] innovation, the local PC, no longer exists, at least under that name. A PC was started in Honolulu in 1970, which was almost State-wide, but there has been only one lasting regional council – the Minnesota News Council started in 1970, still alive and doing well. The National News Council, an original institution established in 1973 by foundations, died quietly in 1984 for lack of media support.

That other US invention, the newspaper ombudsman, has done a little better. In the mid-1990s some thirty daily newspapers employed one to deal with the complaints of readers and report on their work in a column. This is a small number for the existing 1600 dailies, but some of the greatest have one, like the *Washington Post* and the *Chicago Tribune*.

Going down the list of the less controversial MAS, we would find that many have become commonplace – like correction boxes, letters to the editor (often occupying a full page), media sections, opinion surveys – or are spreading fast (like online message boards). But in the 1990s many such MAS seem old hat. More interesting is the latest development (1990) in the campaign to better the news media, or rather to slow the decline of daily newspapers and public life. Called 'public' or 'civic' journalism (Merritt 1995), it has been illustrated by the *Wichita Eagle*, the *Charlotte Observer*, the *Seattle Times* and others. It implies a return to the 'social responsibility' ideas of the Hutchins Commission in the 1940s. For some years now it has generated intense interest at meetings of publishers, editors (APME), reporters (IRE) and professors (Association of Educators in Journalism and Mass Communications), in journalism reviews (such as the *American Journalism Review*), and in trade publications (*Editor & Publisher*). As early as 1974 (and again in its 1994 version), the APME code stated that:

The newspaper should serve as a constructive critic of all segments of society
... Editorially it should advocate needed reform or innovations in the public
interest ... It should provide a forum for the exchange of comment and criticism, especially when such comment is opposed to its editorial positions.[17]

Public journalism consists not just in serving the interests of advertisers,
business people and politicians or the owners – but, on the contrary,
in taking a real interest in the welfare of the community, in asking
people (all groups, not just the rich and men only) what is important for
them, what their problems are, and what are the possible solutions.[18] It
aims at helping alienated citizens to re-engage in public life, instead of
cynically entertaining them with crime, conflict and fluffy features.

Civic journalism has been called a mere marketing ploy – or, again a
crusade by left-wing militants, like the 'participatory' journalism of old.
But it is less controversial than the major MAS have been. After all, it re-
introduces the ideal of public service, as opposed to infotainment for
the masses, news-and-services for the rich, and boosterism for the community. Certainly, it cannot by itself cure all the ills of the news media,
but it could help to make them better.

Conclusion

So? So the situation is serious. Even though the media are better than they
have ever been, they are not good enough. And without good media,
democracy cannot survive. And without democracy, the survival of
mankind is not assured: the ecological catastrophes in the (former) Soviet
Union have proved the truth of such reasoning. Everybody now agrees
on the extreme need to get the media to serve the public well. This cannot be expected from total government control, as was shown in the
USSR. It cannot be expected from market forces, as is obvious in the US.
As I have already argued, the only body of people capable of curbing
media abuse is the public, i.e. consumers and voters. They are the ones
who must insist on being served better. The mobilizing and guiding of
such troops into action can only be done by media professionals who,
besides, have much to gain and little to lose in the endeavour.

Alas, not all media professionals are even agreed that firm ethical
rules should be set down. Not many media people are ready to accept
the intrusion of the general public; hence the fate of most MAS. There
are PCs and ombudsmen and other MAS a little everywhere, but in relation to the quantity of media outlets their numbers are tiny. And it
would be foolish to expect an extension in the near future, even in the
West. Why?

All methods to increase quality encounter huge resistance. There are
five insubstantial obstacles. It is often feared (especially in the USA) that
the government will use self-control systems to restrict freedom: a fear
never justified anywhere. Another argument is that MAS are useless:
good media don't need quality control, and bad media won't accept it.

A third accusation is that whatever the media do in the way of quality control is cosmetic, simply to fool public opinion.[19] A fourth is that quality control is nothing but a cover for anti-media militants, mainly left-wing, which is patently false. Fifth, both within and outside the media most people have simply never heard of the various MAS that have been tested and proved to be harmless and useful.

Then there are five real obstacles. First, the power instinct: media owners and professionals think they have power to influence, and they do not want to share it. Second, many media professionals refuse to acknowledge that they commit mistakes. Third, media people have fragile egos and find it very hard to take criticism. Fourth, many MAS, such as ombudsmen, are quite expensive: a good investment but one that some media sometimes cannot afford. Last, the most and least serious obstacle is time. Quality control consumes time, which in the news media is in short supply. And it requires time: education takes years to bear fruit. All systems also require that professionals and public get used to them, which takes years, too.

But all this might not be very important. The MAS are, it seems to me, not so much *factors* as *signs* of an evolution. Things are changing. Real change in human society is usually very gradual. More and more people are concerned about the media. A lot more people now write, talk and debate about media ethics, and are getting used to the concept of 'quality control' by the professionals and their clients.

One last point I would emphasize is that around the north Atlantic there *is* a concern for media ethics, and there *are* MAS of all kinds – which is also true of Japan (and, to a lesser degree, Korea), of Australia, New Zealand, and some nations in Latin America, like Brazil. Elsewhere, there is next to nothing: in Africa,[20] the Arab world and/or Moslem world, the former Soviet empire,[21] the Indian sub-continent (in spite of India's interesting PC), China and South-East Asia. The media are not worsening: with a few exceptions, they are everywhere better than they have ever been. Those who disagree are simply ignorant of the past. However, the media could be and should be better.

Notes

1 The first post-Second World War awakening dates back to the late 1960s and early 1970s.
2 As evidence of the interest in that particular obstacle, an article I wrote (Bertrand 1995) has been published in sixteen languages and twenty countries.
3 Monthly rotating panels of journalists acting as a grand jury on newsroom issues.
4 As at the Portland (Oregon) *Press-Herald*.
5 The first to attract attention was that of the French daily *Le Monde* in 1951.
6 Like the Peoria *Journal Star* in 1984.
7 Including Turkey, but excluding Eastern Europe.
8 A *Times–Mirror* poll in 1994 found the major causes of dissatisfaction

were sensationalism for Canadians, Mexicans and Germans; invasion of privacy for the French and British; and lack of objectivity for Italians, Spaniards and Americans (*Los Angeles Times*, 16 March).

9 In Italy the Order of Journalists has largely played the same role.

10 Portugal had one from 1975 to 1990, however.

11 Such would be the 'cercle de lecteurs', a readers' club, used by the Swiss *Journal de Genève/Gazette de Lausanne*.

12 In the USA the sense of a person employed by a media outlet to field complaints from the consumers. The Swedish press ombudsman serves merely as a gatekeeper for the PC.

13 The sole exception is Denmark.

14 As at the Peoria *Journal Star* in the USA.

15 When asked what 'other' MAS were operating in their countries, some respondents mentioned the marketplace, parliamentary threats (Britain), a statutory complaints commission for broadcasting (Ireland, Norway, Sweden).

16 Except for one in Windsor, Ontario, in Canada, and creations of a similar nature elsewhere.

17 *USA Today* (1982), the first national daily in the USA, has for many years systematically published opinions opposed to its editorial on the same page.

18 A *Times–Mirror* poll indicated that 71 per cent of Americans believe the press gets in the way of solving social problems.

19 For instance, admittedly the PC in Peoria was set up and run for many years by the public relations department of the *Journal-Star*; but if it is a good PR ploy, then why don't more media use it?

20 Although a PC was set up in Ghana and Nigeria in 1992, and in Malawi in 1994, not to mention South Africa which has a PC and ombudsmen.

21 With exceptions like Estonia which has a PC.

References

Bertrand, C-J. (1995) 'The media of 2045', *Public Relations Review*, Winter.

Media Studies Journal (1995) 'Media critics' issue, Spring.

Merritt, D. (1995) *Public Journalism and Public Life: Why Telling the News is Not Enough*, Erlbaum, Hillsdale, New Jersey.

PART III

People and processes in accountability

CHAPTER 9

Interpreting codes of conduct

Adrian Page

In Henrk Ibsen's play, *An Enemy of the People*, Dr Stockmann discovers that the waters of the spa town to which he has recently moved are polluted and represent a danger to health. He decides to inform the population. As a medical practitioner, he sees the health of the people as his prime concern, and an undeniable priority. The town officials and the newspaper proprietor, however, disagree with him and demand that he keep the news quiet. There is a fear that he will provoke a panic which will lead to a loss of the town's main source of income: visitors to the spa. It is by disagreeing with the population's decision that Dr Stockman becomes 'an enemy of the people' and opposes the majority will. How would the contemporary codes which are intended to regulate journalists' behaviour help to clarify the obligations of a journalist in a case like this? In such a case, the journalist could be personally responsible either for a major outbreak of disease or the economic collapse of a community. This is an ethical question which a journalist would undoubtedly have to account for, yet how do the codes assist in this reasoning?

In contemporary terms the concern over what is commonly known as mad cow disease is a similar, but more complicated example. If a journalist discovered the possibility of infection, would it be ethical to release this information before a full scientific picture is known if it led to the complete collapse of the British beef industry? Would it be more important to highlight governmental failure to inform the people of the risk or to save the beef industry?

There is no mention in current codes of conduct of the journalist's right or obligation to withhold information which might cause mass alarm and endanger a society. The Press Complaints Commission (PCC) code of practice (see Appendix 1), however, does contain clauses which empower journalists to publish if the matter is 'in the public interest'. One way in which this concept is defined is that it is in the public interest to know that they have been misled by any organization or individual. The example of the 'mad cow' scare is one where publication of a story about an official 'cover up' would be justifiable on these grounds.

The code specifies that the interests of the public take precedence. Although it may be in the interests of the nation that the beef industry continues, the publication of scares such as this can be justified on behalf of those who currently make up the population, and are the people who have been misled.

The press often acts according to this principle and in doing so it may expose important issues. The most telling example of recent times was the Matrix Churchill trial where the government tried unsuccessfully to issue public interest immunity certificates in order to suppress information. The press refused to accept this argument and maintained that it was in the public interest to know what had occurred. There can be little doubt that there is an overwhelming case that they were right (Leigh 1993). In court the defence solicitor representing the three men who were nearly wrongfully convicted referred to the philosopher Bentham's view that the independence of the judiciary was essential to ensure that judges did not align themselves with the State and the suppression of court proceedings flouted this principle (Leigh 1993: 75). The national interest has to be distinguished from the interests of State security, which may be dealt with by D-notices. These originated from a wartime need for security of information, yet are also theoretically voluntary forms of press regulation.

Appealing to the public interest does not provide a criterion which enables a journalist to decide easily whether or not to publish. Dennis McQuail cites three definitions of the public interest according to which journalists might take action over the above example: the preponderance theory, the common interest theory and the unitary theory (McQuail 1992: 22–3). According to the preponderance theory, the journalist would attempt to decide in accordance with the majority public opinion. The common interest theory would pose the question of how many people might suffer if the story is published. The reasoning here could involve a calculation of consequences. The unitary theory refers to general principles which are held to be in the interests of society on all occasions. Such a principle might be the free circulation of information. What must be noted in the case of press codes is that these definitions can conflict. A journalist who takes the view that the publication of a mad cow disease cover-up is essential to protect the free circulation of information would publish 'in the public interest'. A journalist who took the view that more people would suffer than benefit if the story was published, might, however, not publish. An interesting example which recalls this dilemma is the statement by Edwina Currie that all eggs in this country were infected with salmonella. Although there is a basis in fact for this, it appears in hindsight that it might have been better not to make this fact public. Because the notion of the public interest is so difficult to detail accurately, it follows that it can be used to justify different actions. It does not lead to a prescriptive code.

If a journalist can defend any action on this basis, does it, therefore, mean that the codes do not make journalists accountable? It might seem that all a journalist has to do is devise an articulate defence and this can exonerate them of almost anything. This situation is not, however, as serious as it sounds. To be accountable is not necessarily to be in a position to prove that you were right in what you did. Sometimes, it is enough to prove that you acted in good faith. To be accountable means that you are under an obligation to defend your actions according to previously agreed principles. What codes may specify is not what action is correct, but how to argue such a point within the principles. To be accountable, however, also normally means to be responsible for the consequences of what you have done. This may occasionally be in conflict with the view that journalists are not responsible for the effects of their stories.

A schoolteacher may be obliged to follow a code which says they cannot tackle students when playing rugby. This may be foregone, however, when the situation is such that injury to others could be caused. A tackle might be justified if a student was about to cause a collision that would result in many injuries. Any injury to the tackled student would then have to be justified. To be accountable does not mean that the teacher simply has to argue that they believed there might have been an accident if they had not tackled. Their judgement is also on trial and they must justify this claim. The teacher is accountable for all avoidable injuries on the pitch. A code of conduct for sports teachers might specify clearly how the decision to tackle or not can be justified. It may be impossible to prove that the teacher was correct, but their defence must nonetheless follow certain principles. If, in the end, it is a matter of opinion, the teacher may be judged on the consistency of their case.

This example is intended to highlight a major problem for the PCC code in that it does not clearly regard the consequences of publication as the concern of the journalist (see Appendix 1). The schoolteacher example is a case where the principle of Utilitarianism in ethics, 'the greatest good of the greatest number', is the underlying principle against which a justification would be made. The various definitions of the public interest can also be debated by reference to this theory. Utilitarian theories are normally divided into two kinds: Act and Rule Utilitarianism. Rule Utilitarianism specifies which acts are always wrong and Act Utilitarianism argues that each act must be judged on its particular consequences. The PCC code specifies that it is always wrong to identify children under the age of sixteen in sex cases, 'even where the law does not prohibit it'. This is an example of a rule. In the case of privacy, however, the individual's privacy may be invaded if it is 'in the public interest'. This is an example where each case must be treated individually.

The PCC, however, can be seen in its decisions to reason in a number of ways. In 1991, the Commission rejected a complaint against a regional newspaper on the grounds that it might have provoked a violent confrontation when it published an article on an influx of 'hippies' into the area. The defence was that newspapers were entitled to take a partisan view about the stories they published and there was no explicit incitement to violence. The adjudication, by its omission of the possible consequences of the report, made it clear that such consequences were not its responsibility. It would seem that the unitary theory was important here and that the principle of free comment took priority over individuals suffering harm (PCC 1991: 16). In another case, however, the *Manchester Evening News* was found guilty of having identified the juvenile victim of a gang rape at a children's home, contrary to the code. In this case, the interests of an individual outweighed the public's right to know of any cover-up. Whereas in the previous case, the welfare of 'hippies' was not a consideration, here the welfare of individual members of the public was paramount. The adjudication found that it was not defensible to argue that the public interest justified revealing the identities of the children concerned.

The combination of Act and Rule Utilitarianism leads to a confusing situation where accountability is concerned. If we wanted to check that a Rule Utilitarian had been consistent, we would only have to check that they had complied with the rule. If it is right or wrong to do something, then any agent is either justified or not. The rule that doctors must not have affairs with their patients is a blanket ban. If, on the other hand, an Act Utilitarian wanted to demonstrate consistency, we would have to check that each case had in fact been judged on its merits. If a journalist were to confuse this situation, it might be easy to regard the codes as rules. If so, when it came to infringing privacy, for example, the rule was that a defence which mentioned the public interest had to be produced on every occasion. To be accountable is not to produce a defence, however, but to do rather more than that. For an Act Utilitarian the code is a set of principles rather than rules. If the code is regarded as a set of rules then all that has to be checked to ensure compliance is that a defence of some kind mentioning the public interest has been made. There is no need to elaborate on it. In other words, the PCC code may invite journalists to forget the vital word in the National Union of Journalists' code of professional conduct that intrusions into privacy are only justified by *'over-riding* considerations of the public interest' (see Appendix 2: emphasis added).

Some adjudications by the PCC seem to imply that the onus is on the complainant to prove that the public interest does not apply. (See for example, the complaint against the *Grimsby Evening Telegraph* and the *Scunthorpe Evening Telegraph* by a woman who had had an affair with a doctor who was later struck off (PCC 1996: 13–14).) This judgement states that the complainant had not 'sufficiently demonstrated that the public interest defences by the newspapers did not apply'. The phrase 'in the public interest', can in fact be used ambiguously: it can mean that something is overwhelmingly in the interests of the majority, or that it is simply likely to be of some (unspecified) benefit to the public. It may be that it would be in our interests to know who will win the next election, but we do not have a right to know this. The case of the disclosure of MPs' financial interests is one where the public interest may well be served by a full disclosure, but an ethical debate rages over whether individual MPs have the right to conceal this information. As I have argued elsewhere, the debate over privacy is really a fundamental problem for Liberalism and is really a question of the individual's rights *vis-á-vis* those of society (Page 1994).

At the moment the PCC simply checks whether the defence offered by the journalist conforms to one of the three criteria it uses to define the public interest. It does not follow, however, that meeting one of the criteria is enough. In an extreme case, the criteria themselves might be in conflict. If the government had covered up an AIDS epidemic, for example, it might have done so to prevent widescale panic in which individuals might be assaulted or riots may result. The PCC public interest criteria would then be in conflict: to expose misleading statements might endanger lives. The PCC code does not openly acknowledge that conflicts of this kind have to be decided upon. Would specifying the codes in greater detail therefore be a good idea? Nigel G.E. Harris (1992: 67) writes in a chapter on codes of conduct for journalists that:

> The trend towards the introduction of longer codes carries some dangers with it. It might seem that when a code contains detailed specifications of what is deemed to be unethical, rather than having just a few vague general principles, this will increase the extent to which the code can offer protection to the public. However, one of the consequences of bringing out detailed sets of regulations is that it fosters a loophole-seeking attitude of mind.

For what appears to be this very reason, the Calcutt Report which looked carefully at the possible revisions of the law on press behaviour also declined to specify what the 'public interest' was. This example shows that no code can legislate specifically to proscribe certain actions. Harris refers to this as what Dennis MacQuail calls the 'elasticity' of the notion of the public interest.

The ethical dilemma which the codes present is as follows: if any action at all can be justified by the codes, then the journalists cannot be truly accountable, since they can justify all their actions in retrospect. If, on the other hand, the code specifies what they cannot do in greater detail, it will simply leave great gaps to be exploited and only token compliance will result. The following remarks suggest how this dilemma might be approached in order to address some of the issues mentioned above. First, the codes need to consider how they will reflect on consequences, since they must surely guarantee that journalists are accountable to the public who may be affected. This might enable journalists to recognize conflicts and to acknowledge the rights of individuals. At the moment the emphasis on codes of practice carries with it an implication that all that can be done is to regulate how journalists gather information, not its effects. This is really a Kantian ethical position where the intention is more important than the eventual outcome and a good action is one performed with good intentions. Journalists might reasonably argue that they cannot foresee the consequences of publishing an article at the time of publication. Second, I will argue that the mixture of Act and Rule Utilitarianism can be tolerated if the judgements on individual cases are used to abstract principles. In other words, individual judgements can harden into rules. Both these points have virtually been conceded by Lord Wakeham in 1996 (1996a). In a speech to the House of Lords on 21 December 1995, Lord Wakeham, speaking as the chair of the PCC, proposed a protocol which would mean that editors had to ensure that any publication of the evidence of court proceedings volunteered by participants in the trial had to be in the public interest and any payments were made known to the prosecution and defence. In this case, an argument must be produced before publication. Lord Wakeham (1996b) has also announced that the PCC code will be kept under review and that precedents and case-law will be taken into account. I will use two recent examples to illustrate the need for these changes and then indicate how the NUJ code is beginning to guide journalists in the direction I am endorsing.

The case of Selina Scott's complaint against the *News of the World* illustrates the kind of issue that might give rise to a principle. The newspaper published a salacious story about Ms Scott which was provided by a man claiming to have been her lover some fifteen years before. This was strongly denied by Ms Scott and a complaint was made to the PCC on the grounds of violation of privacy. Had there been a court case, an individual would first have to find the funds and second would face detailed questioning under oath about their sexual behaviour.[1] The PCC is the only form of redress available to the vast majority of citizens. In its adjudication the PCC commented that it was unable to investigate the factual basis of a story which related to an alleged affair so long ago. *The Guardian* (29 April 1996) described the PCC's judgement as 'remarkably fuzzy'. For Andrew Marr, the editor of *The Independent* this showed quite clearly that a privacy law was needed which differentiated between sexual lives (which should not be reported on) and business dealings (which should). Laudable though this attitude might be, it is clear that such a distinction will not work. What of the MP who passes legislation in favour of a business person with whom they are having an affair? This would immediately cut across this distinction, making it untenable. The PCC made a point of referring to the lack of corroborating evidence to support the article: 'No attempt appeared to have been made by the newspaper to check some of the background facts or to question independent witnesses . . . who might have a knowledge of the matter described' (PCC 1996: 6).

There are two issues here which are really matters of principle: the issue of the public interest and corroboration. It may have been misleading for Ms Scott to have portrayed herself as a celibate, but whether it benefited the public to know otherwise (if true) is another matter. In this case, it is difficult to see what definition of the public interest could prove this to be overwhelmingly important. Second, if an individual is allowed to swear an affidavit and then make unsubstantiated allegations in the press, no one is safe from malicious allegations. Since the PCC code also maintains that no inaccuracies should be published, it would be reasonable to say that this case has generated a principle: no individual's allegations against another person should be published if the accused has no opportunity to refute them and unless there has been a successful attempt to corroborate them by other legitimate means. Highlighting this principle would give guidance to journalists and establish precedents.

Precedents can assist in making the ethically correct decision. A system of stating precedents and refining them where necessary would enlarge on the guidance which the PCC code is able to give journalists. There may be cases where someone's word is all that can ever be provided as evidence, as in some rape cases. It would also be wrong to refrain from publishing items which could not be substantiated such as this, but it is not difficult to distinguish this case from that of Selina Scott. The qualification of the principles may have to continue *ad infinitum*, but that does not mean that it should not happen. In this case the PCC decided that the *News of the World* was wrong, but it did not elaborate on this fundamental principle. The right of an individual to make an accusation cannot take precedence over the right to privacy. Such decisions could be made explicit to establish how reporters are to interpret the code.

The NUJ code avoids the possibilities of allowing loopholes to develop, specifying that newspapers should not process items which may 'encourage discrimination' (see Appendix 2). Rather than attempting to detail the types of material, the code calls for a vigilance to establish the consequences of certain news items. By specifying the consequences rather than the specific content, the code encourages an accountable attitude. The 'loophole defence' is no response to this kind of accusation.

At the moment there is a sleight of hand which is called secondary reporting where, for example, an issue can be featured as a matter of concern about burglary when it sells newspapers because of a prurient interest in the subject matter which was stolen. Lord Wakeham (1996a) has stated that secondary reporting comes within the jurisdiction of the PCC. The Paddy Ashdown burglary is a case in point. Papers that revealed his naming in a divorce case were stolen from his solicitor. It would not be explicitly unethical at the moment for a newspaper prevented by a court injunction from publishing the stolen papers to recommend to the would-be seller of the stolen Ashdown papers that he should take them to *The Scotsman* (a publication which was not legally obliged to keep quiet about the story). This would ensure that the English papers can eventually report the matter by reporting what was said in *The Scotsman*. Again, an emphasis on the consequences for the individual and whether they might be worse than any good which accrued to the public, would make the publication of the details of the sexual liaison less acceptable under the code. It would seem very difficult indeed to see what benefit the public gained from this knowledge of the Ashdown affair.

The question of competing claims raises the issue of fair comment. The PCC is vigorous in its defence of the right of newspapers to speak freely on all issues, and is not prepared to arbitrate on matters of taste. The right to comment freely on all issues may, however, lead to allegations of distortion, which is contrary to both codes. Whereas the PCC will take action against any misrepresentation of other people's published opinions, it will not prevent a newspaper from making its own comment on the available facts. There are occasions when issues such as matters of taste shade into matters of public disgust. No clear borderline exists between the two. Thus, a PCC report dismisses claims against descriptions of killings by an American 'cannibal killer' on the grounds that they were 'matters of taste', but complaints against a newspaper for publishing photographs of cannibalism in Thailand were upheld because they were offensive. The dividing line that has been crossed here is difficult to define.

In a similar manner, complaints against newspapers which represent homosexuals in an unfavourable light have been told that the expression of personal opinion is justified, however unpopular, but inciting people to hatred of minority groups such as gays is not. In many cases, the distinction between misrepresentation and free comment can be blurred by clever sub-editing, in order to give the same impression but escape censure. For example, *The Sun* once reported on the Clintons' apparent 'obsession' with giving White House jobs to gays and Blacks. In describing Janet Reno, the US Attorney-General, she was not said to be gay, but the following facts were given: 'Her name is Janet Reno and she smokes a pipe. She is six foot tall, with a short shapeless hairdo and has never married.' The implication is clear, but this selection of facts does not obviously infringe any code. It is arguably an example of misleading by subtle means which will lead to adverse social consequences. Not all people who fit the description of Janet Reno are lesbians, and this could lead to persecution. The NUJ code rules out discriminatory statements based on the selection of specific facts. The implication here is that the arbitrary selection of facts such as this can be misleading although superficially accurate. It is a frequent ploy used by journalists to select facts which have a clear underlying theme and imply what cannot be openly stated. The facts do not allow people to make up their own minds if they are not seen in perspective along with all other relevant facts.

The possibility of rephrasing a report in order to circumvent the codes illustrates the fact that the codes cannot, as Nigel Harris points out, be made watertight to exclude all abuses as they stand at present. The possibility of exploiting loopholes makes it necessary to see the existing codes as guidelines and to begin to require bodies such as the PCC to become more rigorous in debating the public interest defence. In a democracy it is essential that the press can occasionally violate privacy in order to defend our collective rights. It is also appropriate that there should be a continual tension between individual and collective rights, which characterizes the liberal democracy in which we live. A key example of this is the use of subterfuge to enable a journalist to discover that two Conservative MPs were prepared to take cash for asking questions in the House. A complaint was made to the PCC, but the journalist's actions were upheld. This seems to be a case where the public's right to know was paramount and the press rightly invaded privacy 'in the public interest'. This case shows how the press may sometimes be an essential element in an open democracy, and that the codes are defending some absolutely fundamental principles in an accountable manner. The issue of accountability, however, hinges on whether the press can demonstrate that it does not secretly believe that it has a right to publish any information if it can find the right justification. This would mean that it entirely disavowed the consequences and this could be seen as irresponsible. The codes might currently be seen as an invitation to select the justification that fits. The real question which neither code addresses, however, is what obligations a journalist has to society in general. Should they be held accountable for the social effects which the press actually causes? Can we ever be certain what the effects of the press are? The view that the press simply reports the facts and society reacts, however, is one which the codes of conduct are beginning to undermine.

Lord Wakeham's latest proposal to ensure accountability of the PCC is to adopt a Citizen's Charter which specifies what standards the public can expect from the PCC in handling their complaints. It remains to be seen whether this will achieve the reputation which Lord Wakeham (1996b) whimsically expressed as 'tough on protecting the public: tough on protecting the public's right to know'. It is worth bearing in mind that the press has graver responsibilities than this.

Note

1   I am grateful to my colleague, Peter Darling, for this point.

References

Harris, N.G.E. (1992) 'Codes of conduct for journalists', in Belsey, A. and Chadwick, R. (eds) *Ethical Issues in Journalism and the Media*, Routledge, London, 62–76.

Leigh, D. (1993) *Betrayed: The Real Story of the Matrix Churchill Trial*, Bloomsbury, London.

McQuail, D. (1992) *Media Performance: Mass Communication and the Public Interest*, Sage, London.

Page, A. (1994) 'Privacy, technology and the freedom of the press', in Chadwick, R. (ed.) *Philosophy Today: The Newsletter of the Society for Applied Philosophy*, Jan.

Press Complaints Commission (1991) *Report* no. 4 (Nov.), PCC, London.

Press Complaints Commission (1996) *Report* (Jan./Feb./Mar.), PCC, London.

Wakeham, the Lord (1996a) Speech at St Brides Institute, London (23 Aug. 1995), in *Moving Ahead: The Development of PCC Policy and Practice in 1995*, PCC, London.

Wakeham, the Lord (1996b) The Harold Macmillan Lecture, Nottingham Trent University (23 Oct. 1995), in *Moving Ahead: The Development of PCC policy and Practice in 1995*, PCC, London.

CHAPTER 10

Teaching ethics to journalists in the United Kingdom

Barbara Thomaß

Ethics in journalism: critics ask whether they exist, and cynics may doubt if they are compatible with the reality of the media. And even more: media developments are in danger of creating a situation where ethics seem to be a luxury in a commercialized media landscape. On the other hand, the media rely on their credibility and trust. They have to do everything to gain this trust again and again from their public. There-fore, it is their responsibility to allow the journalists, who are the main actors in gathering, processing and distributing information, to main-tain ethical standards. Journalists themselves are often made to confront ethical dilemmas which emerge from the different concepts that prevail in the profession. We might even say that it is a part of journalism to live with ethical questions because underlying ideas, like freedom of the press, objectivity, truth, honesty or privacy, might conflict. Being famil-iar with the main issues of a responsible journalism means finding our way through the thicket of details of individual cases where decisions are necessarily made. Spotting the issue(s) and promoting sound debate to arrive at well-balanced decisions is the ethical responsibility of every single journalist. Defending these decisions will become more and more difficult as a market-driven journalism expands. The ability to find and defend ethical standards must be acquired and promoted within the in-stitutions where journalists learn their professional skills.

So we have to ask whether journalism training in the United King-dom meets these demands; if prospective journalists are confronted with ethical reflection which might enable them to withstand the press-ures of the media system? Is it acceptable to consider the training of journalists as a real, although informal, contribution to press account-ability in the United Kingdom? To answer these questions, this chapter will give a short overview of the education and training of journalists, and will present some results of interviews dealing with the role of ethics in journalism courses to come to a conclusion on how far the teaching of ethics contributes to the accountability of the British press and how this interconnects with other forms of accountability.

Journalism training in the United Kingdom

For a long time the education of journalists in the United Kingdom took place exclusively in newsrooms. Learning by doing, without any regulation of what the young journalists had to learn, was the generally accepted practice. It was not until 1965 that moves were made to define and impose concepts and outline syllabuses for the training of journalists. The University of Cardiff offered an academic training of journalists for the first time in 1970, but it was largely ignored by the publishers and journalists' unions (Stephenson and Mory 1990: 197). Even today there are only a few journalism studies courses offered by universities. Most of the non-industrial education of journalists takes place in a variety of courses at colleges, institutes or other non-university places. Nevertheless, an analysis of the contents of the syllabuses, as they are taught, and the answers of experts indicate that these institutions have started to integrate ethical reflection into their courses.

Traditionally, the National Council for the Training of Journalists (NCTJ), and with less decisiveness and clarity, the National Council for the Training of Broadcasting Journalists (NCTBJ), have played an important role in the shaping of the curriculae of journalism training courses. Both councils, which are recognized and participated in by publishers and journalists, are interested in an extreme practically orientated training. They are important for the training market in so far as their formal awards are important for young journalists to secure employment. While on the one hand it is in the interests of publishers for the most effective practical education, without any academic padding, to determine the curriculae, there are two additional conditions which actually help make such short courses with a dominant focus on practical skills effective. First, most of the courses which are accepted and accredited by the NCTJ or NCTBJ form part of postgraduate diploma courses building on academic studies at first degree level. Students are obliged to finance their journalism courses for themselves, or they obtain only small grants, so they are interested in quick results, and acquiring knowledge which is useful for getting, and using in, paid employment. As the universities are dependent on the numbers of students they register, and are in competition with other universities, their orientation to the expectations of potential or prospective students plays an important role. These conditions have led to rather homogeneous syllabuses, within which universities and colleges have a reduced freedom to shape the teaching, according their own understanding of what is necessary.

The teaching of practical skills for broadcasting and print journalism accounts for between 50 per cent and 80 per cent of the total time allocated in all these courses. Besides, subjects such as national and local government, law for journalists and even shorthand – a rather unique element in comparison with journalism courses in other European countries – also form part of the practical training of journalists. Normally only one small module offers an opportunity to examine and acquire general media knowledge, and this is where it is felt that ethical questions can be covered.

Teaching ethics: the attitudes and opinions of experts

In May 1995 experts in eight journalism teaching bodies were interviewed about their opinions on the ethical standards in journalism in the UK and their ways of teaching ethics.[1]

When the experts were asked what they supposed to be the most critical aspects of British journalism, most of them denied that this would be the much-discussed privacy issue. Although some of those interviewed condemned the performance of the tabloid press, the majority of them spotted other problems but not always the same ones. Several times it was the lack of accuracy in reporting which was criticized. Others reproach journalism for the role it has played in the decline in deference in British society, particularly to its great and revered institutions such as the church, the body politic and the royal family. A lack of consciousness about the multicultural nature of the media audience and the orientation of journalists towards the higher socioeconomic levels were also criticized. Another expert blamed journalists for having no idea of their function in society. The following observation alludes to this motif of a social function for journalism being violated:

> I think that the worst part of the British press at this point is its political venality. I mean, its concentration of ownership . . . and the complete failure of the popular press to maintain any sort of connection with reality. (D23)

Furthermore, the belief that the press is fooling itself when it thinks it acts in the public interest by pursuing stories which specifically interest the public, and the critique that this represents – 'an ego-boosting trip with many editors and many journalists' (H16) – also reflects the idea of the journalist's function in society.

Most of the questions in the interviews were centered around the weight, the content and the methods of teaching ethics. A first hint as to the role ethical questions have in the courses concerned was given by the way in which the experts questioned decribed the general aims pursued by the institutions they represented. Those general aims are rather strongly dominated by the chances of the students on the labour market, as expressed in the following quotation:

> The fundamental aim is to get people jobs. It's as simple as that. I mean this is a vocational course . . . It has always been our intention to turn out people who can get jobs. That has been our aim and we have been fairly successful at that. (E3)

Other similar comments included: 'to prepare people to be fully effective working professionals' (D2); 'to teach them how to be journalists and how to operate as journalists, certainly to start with the provincial newspapers' (B3); 'to train people to get a job in broadcast journalism' (F1); 'to enable students to be equipped to be employed in the broadcast industry' (G1). So the focus of the declared aims of such courses lies in the intention to adapt the students as best as possible to the demands of the labour market in journalism. There are differences about the hierarchy of aims, but not in the lack of ethical components in the descriptions of general aims.

Only a few experts wanted to create competences by which future journalists are able to reflect on their practice in the job and within the structures in which they work. The desire to connect a practical education with a critical analysis of society and the role of journalists in it was unique:

> So, it's a slightly different breed of journalists that we are hoping to produce. The kind of people who will no longer passively enter an organization that has very clear conventions, that have been laid down over many many years, but someone who is prepared with reflection to be a little more subversive and in that way to be able to create the ways of reporting and reflecting the life around them. (C2)

The aims of teaching ethics

When the experts talk about the aims they pursue in the teaching of ethics it is possible to characterize two main areas: the competence to act in a given situation and the competence of reflection. Competence of action is concerned with the potential performance of the students when an ethical dilemma is discussed, when the legitimacy or amorality of certain actions are debated, or with training by discussion or consideration of concrete cases in the ability to make decisions in situations of conflict:

> What I think the university does, what I try to do, is to present students with situations that they could encounter while they are working as journalists. Where there are not any legal sanctions, where there aren't any punitive measures that can be taken, but where they have to decide themselves as a matter of conscience, whether they will do or not do certain things such as revealing sources of information. (H4)

The exploration of the behaviour of students and their experiences is also orientated to action in relevant ethical situations:

> What we do is to encourage them to discuss it in a more open way, not to posture, not to say, 'Well, I am not a racist.' We would say, 'How do you actually apply that on a day-to-day basis?' So we go so far. But this is very much based on their experiences, that is the key element. (A10)

The second aim of teaching ethics, the competence of reflection, was mentioned by the experts on different levels. On one level the goal is to sensitize students to think about their behaviour (D9) and to stimulate reflection on ethical questions (D5). This may be set within, and shaped by, a consideration of the cultural context of the media and journalism, which – as one expert stipulated – can itself be looked upon as unethical:

> There is a real craziness about it; there is a so amoral a tradition of the press in Britain, so you have to acknowledge that background. So you can't then systematically approach the question in that specific cultural context where there is such a hostility to any ethical questions, industrially speaking. (D4)

The following quotations make allusions to contexts which should be considered through a reflection of journalistic decision making:

> What is news about? What purpose does it serve socially? If it's going to serve that purpose how should you go about doing it? How do we deal with the compromise of not having as many staff as we would like to cover the stories, having to produce information in a form that fits the requirements of my employer and also if it fits the requirements of the listener? You know, I think ethics goes to those points. (E13)

> So what we are saying to the students is, as journalists you are making your own decisions about ethics, but not always in circumstances that you can choose. So you have to understand the media contacts, media structures, political economy and all that kind of thing . . . in order to then understand what constraints there are on you making your own decision. (A8)

> We look at the National Union of Journalists' code of ethics. We look at the Press Complaints Commission's code of ethics. But for comparison purposes we look as it happens at the Scandinavian countries and we look at the Norwegian code of ethics. We have an American code of ethics which we look at as well . . . I think this increases the awareness of potential journalists as to their own reponsibility of what they write. They then have the consequences and the implications of what they write. (B5)

> Because the part of the course that I teach from media institutions and practices . . . would deal with questions of ethics and the questions of whether there are easily defined parameters in contemporary society with crises of faith and belief being quite pervasive in that postmodern fashion . . . And so I would look at this very much in terms of embedding of ethics in the whole contemporary debate . . . because otherwise you could have a very closed view of journalistic practice. (F6)

So the experts intend to create a place for reflection on journalistic practice (E13); to implement knowledge about decision making and opinion-forming processes in journalism, and to impart the idea that journalists have to make their own ethical decisions under the given conditions (A8). The intention is to raise the consciousness of prospective journalists of the consequences and implications of what they write (B5), and the subject is embedded in a wider social debate (F6). In this way ethical reflections are separated from normative appeals to do the 'right thing', and instead there is the intention to create the idea of conditioning for ethical decision making and acting.

Given this stance, which considers the whole system of the media, one consequence may be that the postulation of 'right' norms and values is neglected, and that what is aspired to is qualification for autonomous ethical decision making, which is to be defended even against resistance. The understanding of ethics is one of a continuous process of decision making, and this is the reason why no defined values are taught but students are encouraged to make up their own minds about practical ethical questions.

So in the main the experts want to achieve a competence of reflection, which ought to develop a consciousness about the conditions and structures that determine the performance of the individual professional. The orientation to, or the searching for, guidelines or binding norms or values is of no great importance.

The representation of ethics in syllabuses

In deciding whether ethics is a special subject in syllabuses, or is integrated into different courses and seminars, the role of the NCTJ is quite important. As this organization fixes the standards of training for print journalists, develops examples of curriculae, accredits the journalism courses and administers the examinations, its decision against there being an identified subject of ethics in the curriculae carries substantial weight. This decision is heavily criticized by some experts:

> The NCTJ is a body which was established some time ago by the journalists' union and the publishers and it has a very old-fashioned, a very limited view on what education for journalists should be. And therefore we are constrained by that tradition and don't do as much background scholarly academic work in the diploma as we would like or as our students are capable of. (D2)

Similarly, the NCTBJ and its ideas about ethics in the training of journalists were not well received by the following expert:

> I think it is fair to say that the way we teach journalistic ethics would not be at the top of their [the NCTBJ's] list. I think their concern will be more that we are turning out people who are actually able to do the job. But it would be most unusual if a course in journalism did not, some way or other, deal with journalistic ethics. (G21)

The other experts neither seem to appreciate this reduction of knowledge or orientation in favour of a high concentration on teaching practical skills, because they all – with one exception – defended the fact that their institutions had found more or less well-defined ways of dealing with ethical questions in special seminars besides the integration of ethics in practical training.

There is one module in all the syllabuses which is dedicated to several aspects of media analysis, concerning the performance as a whole of the media in society. While the naming of practical modules is rather similar, this has different titles which try to catch the attention of the students who are estimated not to be very interested in such rather academic subjects: 'Media analyses'; 'Media topics'; 'Media and society', or 'The reporter and the reported': these courses are the place where issues of journalistic ethics may be addressed according to the interests and commitments of the teaching bodies and lecturers. The NCTJ does not suggest a specific subject called ethics, but it demands that ethical aspects are installed in everything, and that the students acquire a knowledge of the code of practice of the Press Complaints Commission. In a similar way the NCTBJ expects the teaching bodies to present the BBC's Producer Guidelines and similar codes of the Broadcast Standards Council or Broadcast Complaints Commission[2] to the students.

In one instance practical–ethical problems were debated regularly one hour each week; another course offered single sessions or lectures on ethical topics. Only two of the courses accredited by the NCTJ offered special courses named 'Ethical issues in journalism' or 'Duties and dilemmas' which lasted ten and thirteen weeks respectively.

Besides the guidelines of the NCTJ and NCTBJ, it is the students themselves whose motivation is not to answer positively to an expansion of ethical subjects in the curriculae. The experts mainly think that they only want to achieve practical skills:

> My experience over a couple of years that I have run this course now is that journalism students tend to come into this course with a kind of notion that all they need from the course is to acquire practical skills that can then lead them to get employment in the industry. In a sense you can't blame them because that is what the industry itself emphasizes. (E35)

> I think an important thing to stress is that . . . the students do not come on to a course like this in order to learn journalistic ethics. They would not see that as the main reason why they would come on a course like this, it is still to acquire the skills. (G22)

The relevance of ethics for examinations

As all the modules in the curriculae are normally compulsory and not optional so, too, are the ethical elements. Ethics is of more or less importance in the final examination of students, however. It is possible that ethical subjects are an element of the exam, depending on the role of the lecturer (D23); if the weight of the ethics module has been equalized to the other modules (F19); or the fact that the ethics module is one-twelfth of the whole course is reinforced by applying ethical criteria in the assessment of other student work (C29). Most weight is given to the subject at a university where ethics counts for one-eighth of the course (A22). Such assessment of the ethics-related parts of the curriculae is greater than that required by the NCTJ which desires only that students prove that they are aware of ethical aspects of the profession throughout their courses and during final examinations.

Changes in the curriculae?

There are several statements in the interviews which show a certain discontent about the quantity and the quality of journalistic ethics in college and university courses. One expert explained that this has arisen because of the dominant role of the NCTJ:

> We are really constrained in terms of the development of the course by the National Council for the Training of Journalists who are already hostile towards teaching an extra course at all, which they don't care about. I have accreditation meetings with them which drive me crazy. Because I say to them: 'What do you think about ethics? Or what do you think about teaching some of that or some of this?' and they say: 'Oh, wasted time, don't do this.' (D24)

Others are looking for possibilities to deal more intensively with ethics not only in teaching but also in supporting research:

> We will, I hope, be given money for research. And one of the areas that I would personally be very interested in and encourage is, whether it's me or somebody else, will be ethics. When I was in the States I was fascinated to see the length and the depth of the research that has been done into ethics by the academic server there. (B22, similarly C30 and E34)

This appreciation of US research and also methods of teaching can also be found in the following quotation:

> There is a lack of kind of expertise in diversity teaching, I think there is a lack of materials, relevant British material, or even European materials ... the bulk of materials are American ... but they are not terribly accessible by the students. They tend to get turned off, and there is always an excuse, 'Well, that is American.' So we do need materials. And some of the techniques the Americans have I think can also be useful. So I am off to the States in June to begin sort of finding what we can learn, what we can use and what we can doubt. (A23)

Cooperation

The efforts, evidenced in these answers, to approach ethics more intensively in research and teaching have not yet reached the phase where cooperation in projects seems to have been suggested or deemed necessary. The majority of the experts give the impression that they feel – about ethics – like lone voices in the wilderness:

My experience of this is a perfectly personal experience and direct one. I spent ... years in America, and when I came back ... one of the things I wanted to do, because I was appalled by the quality of the debate about press freedom, that was going on, and I really wanted to start it and all attempts that I have made to sort of interest people like the *UK Press Gazette*, you know, the trade newspaper. I had a conversation with the editor, and I said 'Why don't we raise the ethics flag?' and he said: 'Not interested ... Ethics? It's not an issue.' ... It's just not a major issue within the socialization of the profession except as seen as a threat. (D31)

Another expert denies that other insitutions would be interested in ethics:

I know of no evidence that we, the professional bodies, are interested in that thing. If you look at their agendas they might be interested in the teaching of shorthand or they are interested in whatever. You can talk to them but I would like to see on what agendas or what things they send around to people like me do actually increase the teaching of ethics ... There are obviously very vigorous people who are writing books and researching things. ... but I think that they feel that they are swimming against the tide. (E40/41)

There were only a very few cases where partners in cooperation were named; for example, the National Union of Journalists or the European Journalism Training Association.

Methods of teaching ethics

Considering the methods used in teaching ethics it is remarkable that there is hardly any systematic approach. 'As it comes up' is the oft-repeated formula for the handling of ethical issues which seems to be the answer of the experts to the difficult situation they have to defend. They see their intention to teach ethics confronting so many difficulties. Or as one expert put it:

I think it is fair to say that despite the haphazard nature of the input on ethics none of our students leaves here without an understanding at least that there are ethical concerns in the field ... It is not that we have singled out ethics for this treatment. It is that we do everything within the context of the practical workshop. And this is obviously a very strange way of doing things but it is very British. (D9/32)

It is obvious that the experts interviewed avoid a systematic approach to and a theoretical framework for ethical topics within journalism. There are several reasons for this: the practical orientation of the courses; a lack of opportunity to teach ethics; the constraints of the curriculae; the lack of British teaching materials; and the expectations of the students. On the other hand, there is the prevailing haphazard way of dealing with ethics, according to the necessities of practical work and often

144

stimulated by case studies. Two different forms can be observed.

1 Students are presented prepared case studies which contain a specific ethical problem towards which they have to find their own position and argue within a debate or a written essay. The advantage of this method is seen in the fact that the teachers can give clear input on the subject and that the students are confronted with real subjects from the world of the media. The main areas of conflict in these cases are issues of privacy and conflicts of interest. These advantages are also cited when representatives of media-accrediting bodies, journalists or other experts come in and discuss cases from their own practical work. The disadvantages are seen in the fact that these cases do not always emerge from the experiences of the students, and therefore do not stimulate reflection on their own behaviour. Another disadvantage seems to be that reflection on underlying norms and values is left unaddressed when the concrete circumstances of a case tend to dominate.

2 An experienced-orientated approach utilizes what happens with the students when they produce their practical work during the courses, and takes these incidents as a starting-point for discussions about the ethical dimensions of what they have just gone through. This method is defended as having the advantage that students are highly motivated, because they grapple with their own practice, their interests and values, and such ongoing reflection is likely to be more effective. It has to be added that the haphazard nature of this method, when it is the only one to be used, is a serious disadvantage, because there might be many subjects which do not come up during the studies and so are never discussed.

The media topics of the day and the experiences of students during their internships are other possibilities which are used to motivate considerations of ethical issues in the courses.

Conclusion

The evaluation of the interviews shows that the ethical issues of journalism have begun to enter the curriculum. Although notions of responsibility do not normally form part of the general aims of the education of journalists, the intensity with which the experts plead for the necessity of the competence of reflection as a teaching aim demonstrates how strongly they perceive the problem. Ethical aspects can be found more or less explicitly located in the syllabuses; they are to a certain degree relevant for examination and there are clearly defined desires to incorporate them even more in research and teaching. There is great interest in looking at the experiences and practices in this field in the USA, although it is clear that there are limits in transferring them. A great problem seems to be that most experts give the impression they are the only ones who care about the issue of ethics.

In this situation where there is a hostile rather than an open atmosphere for ethical reflection it is understandable that teachers choose methods which are overall dominated by the idea of stimulating the motivation of the students. It seems to be the best that can be done in the given conditions. Systematic approaches, theoretical foundations and ethical reflection which overcome a subjective judging of concrete behaviour might lead to a more sound understanding of what journalism has to be in a democratic society. On the other hand, ethical education always has to bear in mind the conditions under which individuals are actually acting, a consideration which is rather common among the experts. But the job-orientated character of lots of the courses conceals the danger that a critical reflection of these conditions cannot command a commensurate place within the curriculae.

When students enter jobs they must be prepared for what they find there, but they must also be prepared not to willingly accept circumstances as they are. Journalists thinking this way might be able to create a job culture which is open to ethical debate and self-regulation. It is the collective process of a profession which leads to ethical standards, not individualistic heroism. But the smallest unit of the profession of journalism is the single journalist. The training of journalists in the United Kingdom has started to consider the notion of responsibility as an integral part of what a journalist has to learn.

Notes

1   As the differences between the various colleges and universities are not important for the purpose of exploring the main ideas of the experts from the journalism-teaching bodies, the sources of the quotations will remain anonymous. Four of the eight colleges and universities whose experts participated in the interviews are accredited by the NCTJ (A–D); four are working according to the guidelines of the NCTJ (E–H). The numbers represent the sequence of the interviews.
2   The two bodies merged in 1997.

Reference

Stephenson, H. and Mory, P. (1990) *Journalism Training in Europe*, European Journalism Training Association and Commission of the European Communities, Brussels.

CHAPTER 11

'Watching the watchdogs'? The role of readers' letters in calling the press to account

Michael Bromley

Introduction

Many Western, liberal, capitalist nation-states were thought to be experiencing crises of participation in their democratic processes in the 1980s and 1990s (for example, see Rosen 1996; Aitkenhead 1997). The media are regarded as essential components of, and 'the right to communication' as fundamental to, these processes (Habermas 1989; Platform for Cooperation 1996); and there has been much speculation that the development of electronic delivery systems (EDS) in communication (the 'information superhighway') will resolve these crises by enabling more effective interactivity which will bring a 'significant ... change in the provision of electronic democratic capabilities to enhance the quality of citizenship more broadly' (Rabb *et al.* 1996: 284).[1] Simultaneously there has been widespread concern in the media that their futures might be made more insecure by such direct, interactive communication via EDS, possibly leading to the formation of 'new citizen practices' which the traditional forms of mediation are less capable of promoting (Friedland 1996).

Readers place a high priority on interactivity in their relationships with the traditional newspaper press (Elenio 1995: 14); but they may feel that the available participatory mechanisms, such as writing letters to newspaper editors, are ineffective (Hacker 1996: 215–17). Twenty years ago Tunstall reached a similar conclusion about the role of newspaper correspondence columns in acting as fora for interaction between readers and the press over the latter's own performance (1977: 226). In the intervening period much of the press has declared its intention 'to get closer to ... [its] readers' as an expression of a business orientation founded on a faith in marketing practices (*UK Press Gazette*, 26 Dec. 1994). Has this newly empowered the authors of letters to newspapers as 'watchdogs of the watchdogs' (Tunstall 1977: 226)?

The development of correspondence columns

The term 'letters to the editor' should be interpreted broadly and within its historical context. In the early eighteenth century such letters, it has been argued, played a role in establishing the distinctive sphere of journalism, and redefining notions of 'public' and 'private', by mimicking and parodying the epistolary novel (Goldgar 1994: 24–5). A 'massive' increase in the numbers of letters printed in the press followed in the period 1760–80. These supplemented the pamphlet as the chief means for putting across political viewpoints, and were constitutive of an increase in the amount of space devoted to politics by the press. It became important to have such views aired in this way (Harris 1996: 38–40). The protracted development of the press towards serving a readership beyond a very narrow élite led to changes in both the form and function of letters sent to the press.

By the mid-nineteenth century the Sunday newspaper was a 'centre of organization, agitation and involvement'. Columns devoted to letters received by the editor were manifestations of a dialogue conducted between a paper and its readers. Correspondence was also a way in which the expanded, largely working-class Sunday newspaper readerships could seek advice, often about their new roles as consumers (Berridge 1978: 252–3). By the closing decades of the nineteenth century readers' letters had been fully co-opted into the commercialization of the press: for example, Northcliffe's *Answers to Correspondents* was begun as an enterprise ostensibly devoted entirely to responding to readers' inquiries (Engel 1996: 53; Taylor 1996: 14–21). The long-established function of the press as 'popular educator' was made to serve speculative capital (Williams 1961: 202–3).

At the same time, correspondence columns reflected the press's parallel tendency to turn its attention increasingly to a redefined private sphere. The debate on prostitution prompted the *Daily Telegraph* to carry a lengthy correspondence on the topic 'Marriage or celibacy?' in 1868, and the issue 'Is marriage a failure?' supposedly attracted 27 000 letters to the paper twenty-one years later (Engel 1996: 35–6, 42–3). Not surprisingly, by the end of the nineteenth century the 'agony aunt', who responded in print to readers' intimate personal problems, dilemmas and questions, was becoming an established figure in much of the press (Van den Bergh 1997). Williams (1961: 199–206) emphasized the extent to which the late nineteenth-century 'revolution' in the press was an economic one: readers were drawn into a relationship with newspapers as consumers susceptible to 'the new kind of "mass" advertising' which addressed their personal needs as consumers.

Correspondents' intentions, and the power of letters to the editor, to influence and shape public debate remained, however (Jackson 1971: 169–73; Tunstall 1977: 223–4). To cite only two examples indicating the range of the impact letters published by the press could have throughout the twentieth century (see also Tunstall 1977: 212): in 1916 a letter in the *Daily Telegraph* from Lord Landsdowne, a former viceroy of

India, governor-general of Canada and foreign secretary, urging the British Government to explore the possibilities of opening peace negotiations with Germany, rallied support for the idea across the country in the face of opposition at the highest political levels (Robbins 1976: 149–54); while in 1980 a letter from a *Guardian* reader complaining that the names of magistrates sitting in local courts were being withheld prompted a campaign group to lobby the Lord Chancellor, whose office subsequently instituted the necessary changes to make JPs' identities available to the public (*The Guardian*, 6 Jan. 1997: 14).

The ecology of correspondence between readers and newspapers is relatively complex, therefore, incorporating several overlapping contours – public and private – in terms of at least both the subject matter and the nature of the correspondence; seeking to convey opinion and to solicit advice and guidance; articulating 'protest' and 'debate' (Jackson 1971: 153). This is suggestive of a relationship of real interdependence, however unbalanced in terms of the holding of power.

An attempt to fuse some of these approaches can be detected in the introduction in the 1940s of readers' advice services by the *Daily Mirror*[2] and the *News of the World*, the newspapers which after 1945 came to dominate, respectively, the national daily and national Sunday sectors. Intended to provide 'serious' guidance – more often than not privately, although a relatively small number of letters was published – these services addressed a range of readers' concerns across both public and private areas, from housing legislation to marriage guidance (Lamb 1989: 183). They were to some extent detached from the editorial sections of the papers. The *News of the World*'s bureau was located in Cambridge rather than Fleet Street, and Tunstall noted that in the case of the Mirror Group (by 1975 the service worked on behalf of the readers of the group's three national papers) the 'air of social purpose . . . [was] markedly at odds with the deliberate triviality' of some of the content of the *Daily Mirror*. Contrary to what might have been expected, the Mirror Group's service was 'less well known than it perhaps deserves' (Tunstall 1977: 219–21).

In the provincial press the idea prevailed of the correspondence column as 'an open platform for protest and debate' (Jackson 1971: 154). This seems to have been reflective more of the traditional approach of the 'serious' broadsheet national press than the view taken by the London tabloids of letters as principally a form of 'entertainment' (Tunstall 1977: 209). An editorial in the Darlington *Evening Dispatch* in the mid-1960s opined:

> In its columns its readers should be encouraged to express their opinions, their fears, their hopes – and, just as important, air their grievances. In short, readers should be encouraged to participate in the newspapers (quoted Jackson 1971: 152).

Nevertheless, provincial newspaper correspondence columns tended to be dominated by readers 'letting off steam' (Tunstall 1977: 216), indicating that among the readerships protest may actually itself have been used to initiate more 'serious' debate (Jackson 1971: 173–4).

All correspondence columns are highly mediated, and publication has always been subject to editorial discretion. The fabrication of letters has been, at times and in some instances, common practice; and genuine contributions tend to be selected and edited for publication in accordance with editorial policy, or with an eye to political and commercial interests, including advertising (Jackson 1971: 153–5; Tunstall 1977: 225–6; Royle 1990: 54; Goldgar 1994: 21–2). Moreover, Tunstall (1977: 221) calculated that in the mid-1970s the letters appearing in newspapers were written by less than 1 per cent of the population, and came predominantly from white, middle-class men. Despite this, these columns were often projected as manifestations of the genuine voice of the public, however narrowly defined: 'bulletins on the temper of civilization', according to one *Times* journalist (Gregory 1976: 19).

Indeed, the appeal to readers of published correspondence in its various forms is potentially far wider than the narrow base of letter-writers might suggest. In the 1960s and 1970s evidence was available to newspapers that letters were more interesting to readers, especially women readers, than the space normally given over to them implied (Bogart 1981: 73ff; Tunstall 1996: 2160). The importance of this was that, above all, the generation and publication of letters was tied to circulation, both as a reflection of a paper's sales and as a means for maintaining and increasing sales (Tunstall 1977: 211ff). All the same, it has been argued that it was possible for both readers and newspapers to benefit mutually from the arrangement.

Readers as participants

From the late 1930s the *Daily Mirror* began to utilize its multiplex contact with its readership to establish a true 'dialogue'. As well as the readers' advice service, the *Mirror* ran orthodox correspondence under the title 'Viewpoint', its 'Live Letters' feature and a column contributed by the 'agony aunt', Marjorie Proops. Readers' letters were also introduced into, and used to originate, the work of the paper's news and features journalists. Correspondents tipped-off the paper about potential stories, which suggests they became adept at spotting what made a *Mirror* story. They also began imitating the paper's style, particularly when writing to the 'Live Letters' column. Through such devices the *Mirror* facilitated, although perhaps only for a relatively brief period in the 1940s, the meaningful participation of a growing readership on the basis of 'a daily rehearsal of . . . everyday life, of Us, the neighbours' (Cudlipp 1953: 265–70; Smith 1975: 99–101ff). As late as the mid-1970s Tunstall (1977: 215) described 'the whole letters operation' at the *Mirror* as 'a kind of working-people's-club-by-correspondence'.

The charge has been levelled at the *Mirror* that the opportunity to make commercial gain out of exploiting this relationship quickly supplanted any commitment to providing a platform for popular dialogue (Smith 1975: 234). In any event, the means of addressing newspaper editors began to change, particularly among working-class readers. In the 1970s most letters received by national newspapers were typewritten, although some were dictated over the telephone – both factors indicating a heavy middle-class bias among correspondents (Tunstall 1977: 223). Within perhaps a decade the telephone was providing greater and, coincidentally, more immediate – opportunities for working-class readers to correspond with the papers (Tunstall 1997: 222).

Following its acquisition by Rupert Murdoch in 1969, *The Sun* consciously aped the *Mirror*, not least in adopting a similar approach to correspondence from readers – even going as far as calling one column 'Liveliest Letters' after the *Mirror*'s 'Live Letters' feature (Lamb 1989: 178). The company's commitment to interactivity with its newspapers' readers was even less altruistic, however: the *News of the World* readers' advice bureau (which also served *The Sun*) was first sharply cut back, then closed altogether (Tunstall, 1977: 215, 219). The paper's claim to be 'the people's newspaper' was based on its ability to define for itself what it rather misleadingly called 'YOUR [the readers'] place in *The Sun*' (Lamb 1989: 25–6: original emphasis). It did not take long for those running the paper to discover that a reworking of the 'popular educator' role of the press could serve this purpose. The paper's serialization of the American book *The Sensual Woman* not only stimulated readers to write in their hundreds, but demonstrated to *The Sun*'s editor that:

> how-to-do-it books, and especially how-to-do-it-in-bed books, were guaranteed to put on sales . . . There was a clear hunger for knowledge about these things which no one had previously sought to satisfy. *The Sun*, obligingly, stepped into the gap. (Lamb 1989: 129)

In the 1970s and 1980s the great expansion in correspondence from readers of *The Sun* occurred in letters seeking advice on personal problems from the paper's 'agony aunt'. Figures supplied by the newspaper to the third Royal Commission on the Press suggested that its 'agony aunt' received 250 letters a week in the mid-1970s: by 1988 the number had reportedly grown to a weekly average of 1100. Over the same period, the number of letters to the editor remained static at between 2500 and 3000 each week (Tunstall 1977: 233; Grose 1989: 76).

The Sun also took advantage of the increasingly commonplace availability of the telephone to provide interaction with its mainly working-class readers in he form of telephone-polling. The technique was a kind of obverse of the market research which at this time began to play a more important role in newspapers' business strategies, and it was introduced against the backdrop of the development of the 'phone-in' format in radio. The relative immediacy of the method permits a more precise synchronization of editorial values and judgements with wider public opinion. Editorial coverage, leading articles and readers' views can be combined to establish an almost self-perpetuating cycle. For example, in May 1996 the *Mirror* used its 'Hotline' to solicit readers' views on its editorial campaign in support of improved pay and conditions for hospital nurses, and then reflected these back to its readership in its leading articles.[3] The impact might even extend beyond the closed circle of the newspaper and its readers: a telephone poll conducted by *The Sun* in April the same year on the issue of British membership of a more federal European Union provided a database of 58 000 readers which was used to found the Referendum Party (Donegan 1997). Most newspaper telephone polls were conducted on quite spurious topics, however (Tunstall 1996: 222–3).

The broadsheet 'quality' newspapers stood aloof for much of this kind of activity. Their approach seemed quite different: while Tunstall (1977: 215) observed that *The Sun*'s correspondence column read as if it had been 'sub-edited by a computer', the editor of *The Times* spent 45 minutes a day with the letters' editor going through the correspondence received from readers. Nevertheless, the variety of correspondents to the paper widened considerably in the 1960s and 1970s (Grigg 1993: 177–8), and the first anthology of letters to *The Times* published in the mid-1970s consciously discriminated against reproducing correspondence from 'the Establishment' (Gregory 1976: 21–2). Other broadsheet newspapers developed policies of encouraging and printing letters from particular sections of a still relatively narrow public – the *Daily Telegraph* 'young and prominent people'; *The Guardian* the 'counter establishment'. For this group of papers correspondence columns were also a means of conferring prestige (Tunstall 1977: 211, 213–14). In itself this could be seen, however, as providing 'an incomparable channel of communication with ... readers' (Grigg 1993: 176). Yet the 'serious' press was not immune to the cumulative background effects of radio phone-ins, audience-participation television and cheaper, more efficient telecommunications (including, in the 1990s, e-mail). Additional sections for letters outside the traditional correspondence columns were developed from the 1960s (Tunstall 1977: 222). These included advice columns – even of the 'agony aunt' genre (Van den Bergh 1997) – and in *The Guardian* a sort of reborn *Answers* called 'Notes & Queries'.

While the bulk of correspondence published in the broadsheet papers could still be categorized under the heading of 'debate', there were indications that these newspapers did not eschew the idea of stimulating their readers to engage in less carefully considered, and presumably more entertaining, 'protest'. The proliferation of columnists' work can be expected to have given rise to additional correspondence of this kind (Tunstall 1977: 218–19; 1996: 222). As by way of incitement, in the mid-1990s the *Observer* ran the work of two columnists alongside its correspondence column under the general heading 'Opinion: theirs and yours'; and *The Independent* published a letter *from* the editor with letters more traditionally addressed by readers to him.

Newspaper correspondence in 1997

The quantitative differences in letters published in four national daily newspapers (*The Sun*, *The Mirror*, *The Times* and *The Guardian*) surveyed over one week in February–March 1977,[4] were in many respects unsurprising. Both *The Times* and *The Guardian* ran recognizably standard broadsheet newspaper correspondence columns, immediately adjacent to their leading articles, on each of the six days. The average numbers of letters carried each day (15 in *The Times* and 14.33 in *The Guardian*) and the weekly aggregate numbers of letters (90 in *The Times* and 86 in *The Guardian*) were almost identical. So, too, was the average length of each letter published – 31.5 column lines in *The Times* and 29.5 column lines in *The Guardian*. The main letters' columns appeared less frequently in the two tabloid papers: *The Sun* published its main correspondence column on only four days (not Thursday or Saturday) and the *Mirror* on five days (not Saturday). In less space they carried fewer readers' letters (overall, 71 in *The Sun* and 76 in the *Mirror*), but not few enough to allow their correspondents as much space to air their views as the broadsheets did. The average length of a letter in both tabloid papers was about 10.5 column lines, or nearly two-thirds less than a correspondent to *The Times* or *The Guardian* was granted.

To the numbers of letters appearing in the main correspondence columns of *The Times* and *The Guardian* should be added a number (four in *The Times* and eight in *The Guardian*) published in the paper's Saturday magazines. All four papers published additional letters outside their main correspondence columns. The two broadsheets carried readers' letters in specialist sections, such as the business pages (*The Times*) and the education supplement (*The Guardian*), and some seeking advice on a range of subjects (for example, personal finance, gardening and pet care). This type of letter was far more common in the *Mirror* and *The Sun*, however, particularly in the form of advice sought from 'agony aunts'. Each paper ran such a column more frequently than it did even its main letters page.

The format in the *Mirror* was the same on each of the six days the column appeared, but *The Sun* devoted more space in its Thursday editions to the 'agony' column (about one-and-a-half pages) than to any other correspondence in a single issue of the paper. Each of these columns published a small number of letters, a great deal of space being given over to the advice offered by the 'agony aunt'. The format in the *Mirror* was two letters a day, except on Tuesday when there was an additional short letter nominating someone for the 'bouquet of the week'; while *The Sun* usually carried four letters each day. Where the *Mirror* devoted more space to the column, it simply published longer, more complex letters and replies. On the other hand, *The Sun* doubled to nine the number of letters published in its Thursday issue. In total, the *Mirror* carried 13 'agony' letters and *The Sun* 25. On Thursday when *The Sun* did not publish its main correspondence column, the space was also given over to letters requesting 'youth counselling' – a kind of junior 'agony' item.

Furthermore, *The Sun* published even larger numbers of letters in other parts of the paper. Like the broadsheet newspapers, it carried readers' inquiries (about personal finance and gardening, too, but also sport), and readers' letters in specialist sections (the women's and the

Table 11.1 Numbers of letters published in selected national daily newspapers, 1975–1997.

Newspaper	1975	1975	1997	1997
	No. of letters appearing in main letters column	No. of letters appearing elsewhere in paper	No. of letters appearing in main letters column	No. of letters appearing elsewhere in paper
The Times	60	30	90	16
The Guardian	70	10	86	11
The Sun	75	40	71	70
The Mirror	75	25	76	13

Source: Tunstall, 1977.

sports pages). It was clear, however, that while the tabloid papers published fewer readers' letters on Saturday, *The Times* and *The Guardian* published more. About a quarter of the letters published over the six days in each of the broadsheets appeared on Saturday, compared to about 10 per cent in *The Sun* and only two actual letters in the *Mirror*. In all, *The Sun* published 141 readers' letters in one form or another throughout the week; the *Mirror* 86, *The Times* 106 and *The Guardian* 97.

These figures may be compared, even allowing for Tunstall's caveat, with those produced twenty years ago for the Royal Commission (Tunstall 1977: 209–10). All these newspapers, with the notable exception of the *Mirror*, published more readers' letters in 1997 than they did in 1975. The numbers of letters appearing in the main correspondence columns appear not to have changed markedly in the tabloid press, while they have risen in the broadsheets. On the other hand, the practice of publishing readers' letters in other parts of the papers has grown in the tabloids, but probably remains much the same in the broadsheets (see Table 11.1). Such broad descriptions mask the significant difference in individual papers, however.

No doubt of qualitative significance is the fact that only the broadsheet titles maintained the concept of readers writing directly to the actual editor of the paper. Correspondents to the two tabloid newspapers were invited to write to named letters' editors (Sue Cook in *The Sun* and Jo Dipple in the *Mirror*) in obvious imitation of the practice employed in 'agony' columns. Furthermore, the main letters' columns in the two papers were closely juxtaposed with these other columns: both were normally published on the same page in *The Sun*, while both types of letters appeared in the *Mirror*'s television guide section. The idea that letters in the tabloid press were meant to be chiefly 'amusing ... nostalgic, and ... naughty' (Tunstall 1977: 214) appeared to be even more deliberately pursued in the 1990s. There were also indications that the process of interaction with readers was itself being commercialized.

The various personal advice columns in *The Sun* were linked with commercial activities, and promotions for these appeared among the readers' letters. The 'agony' column was used to promote telephone 'helplines' for which calls were charged at 50p a minute. The 'youth counselling' column included a promotion for telephone 'Teenlines' which pointed out that calls would cost up to £2.38 each. On two occasions readers with personal problems were advised that they could take part anonymously in a phone-in programme broadcast by the commercial television station GMTV. This contrasted with the practice of paying readers for letters published. In 1997 *The Sun* still offered readers money for correspondence published, but at £10 each for selected letters (usually on a predetermined topic) the fee, allowing for inflation, was not significantly more than the £1 for published letters (£5 for lead letters) offered more than twenty years before (Tunstall 1977: 234). The *Mirror* did pay £25 for its chosen 'letter of the day' and, unlike *The Sun*, provided a freepost address for readers wanting to write to its 'agony aunt'. This apparent generosity may have had more to do with commercialism than first appears: at this time the *Mirror* was making a concerted effort to challenge *The Sun*'s supremacy in the national daily tabloid newspaper market.

The tone of the main correspondence columns of the two tabloid newspapers may be gauged from the sub-sections featuring within them. Readers of *The Sun* were invited to 'get something off your chest' and urged to 'Have a go': one column was designated the 'Friday free-for-all'. Similar 'protest' letters also littered the *Mirror*'s letters columns. Not unexpectedly, only two letters out of nearly 150 published in the two correspondence columns were identified as written by anyone other than an 'ordinary' reader. One was a letter to the *Mirror* signed by the director-general of the National Lottery. Its publication was prompted by the only example in either column of anything approaching a 'debate', and which arose from the *Mirror*'s own news coverage of the lottery. (The other was a letter in *The Sun* from a British Airways executive making a factual correction to an article previously published by the paper.)

Anecdotal letters were also encouraged with special sections for 'kids [sic] talk' (the *Mirror*) and 'funny stories' (*The Sun*). The *Mirror* ran sections dedicated to 'forces [sic] pen pals' and for readers who thought they had noticed close physical resemblances between celebrities: both papers included 'where are they now?' items. Although the *Mirror* published more letters on issues of public interest (even allowing for its concentration on the lottery), the range of topics covered in the two columns was much the same, and about one-third of these issues were common to both papers. These included the royal family, crime, miscarriages of justice, political advertising and tax exiles. Again, with the exception of the lottery issue (where, in any event, all the letters published supported the *Mirror*'s editorial 'line'), no more than one or two letters were published on any single topic: neither paper attempted to present genuine debate in its correspondence column.

The number of issues addressed over a week in the correspondence column of *The Guardian* was, perhaps surprisingly, only marginally greater than that covered in the tabloid papers. By comparison, *The*

Times covered about twice as many topics as either tabloid, and almost twice as many as *The Guardian*. Correspondence published in *The Guardian* returned more often to the same issues day after day, and in each day's column one or two debates were established, each made up of five or six letters. *The Times* published fewer letters daily on any single topic (usually no more than three). While almost every letter published by *The Guardian* addressed itself to public matters, *The Times* ran a number of letters of the 'first cuckoo' type. *The Times*'s correspondents included a predictable number of peers (six); former Cabinet ministers (three); directors of charitable and voluntary bodies; editors; a cardinal; bishops; dons; novelists, business people, and one acting High Commissioner. If anything, *The Guardian* drew correspondence from ever more rarified strata of society – two serving Cabinet members (the Home Secretary and the Chief Secretary to the Treasury); the Brazilian Ambassador; the director-general of the prison service; a couple of MPs, plus a sprinkling of dons, writers, business people and clergy.

Towards an analytical framework

The differences in the correspondence and adjunct columns of the national daily newspapers, and therefore potentially in the nature of the relationships between those papers and their readers, appear to be more nuanced than a simple set of dichotomies ('quality' or tabloid; serious or trivial; public or private; 'debate' or 'protest'; commercialism or prestige) would suggest. The broad differences between the 'quality' and the tabloid press noted by Tunstall have been maintained over the succeeding two decades. Nevertheless the more popular press has consciously developed a more intimate relationship with its readerships, chiefly founded on (rather than in spite of) addressing them as individual, private consumers. As part of this project, this press has also provided more opportunities for interaction with its audiences. The broadsheet papers appear to have been far less innovative and imaginative in this respect, relying instead on expanding the traditional correspondence columns and, possibly, even narrowing the constituency from which they draw correspondents.

It is clear that in the national daily press as a whole the idea of what is suitable for publication in readers' letters of all types (as well as definitions of, and the balance between, what is considered 'public' and 'private') has changed over time, and that the main staple of eighteenth- nineteenth- and earlier twentieth-century correspondence – political debate – has been largely superseded by the assertion of opinion and the receiving of advice (sometimes on at least a quasi-commercial basis) as a function of the longer term development of the press as an advertising-driven medium. It has been proposed in another, but related, context that the effectiveness of any such mechanism in promoting participation may be measured in six ways: access; the exercise of editorial control; the (self-) selection of the participants; the genuineness of the activities;

external assessment (the value associated with the activities); and influence (Jankowski and Malina 1996).

To some extent overlapping this approach, Goldgar's (1994: 22) analysis suggests that the generation, use and reception of letters for publication by the press may be critically determined by five factors: the extent to which they are (or are accepted as being) unedited, unchanged letters from ordinary readers containing their own views; or letters sent by ordinary readers but 'shaped' by the editor(s); or phoney letters written by the editor(s) but masquerading as genuine; or fake letters which are not obviously so but contain jokes which can be decoded to reveal their true nature; or, finally, obvious and deliberate fake letters not intended or likely to deceive.

Given the difficulty in establishing beyond doubt whether published letters are 'concoted in the office' with the intention to deceive (Tunstall 1977: 223), and that none of the letters surveyed appeared to be a spoof, it would seem reasonable to concentrate here on the extent to which the contents of correspondence columns are influenced editorially; whether these columns are genuine expressions, even if mediated, of the readership and are likely to be received as such; and how influential such columns are and with whom. Some factors may counteract each other: for example, ease of access offered by *The Sun* and the *Mirror* setting up telephone lines to receive letters may be offest by the small amount of space allocated in the tabloid papers for any individual letter.

The degree to which the letters published in all four papers shared a common core agenda of about fifteen different public interest issues suggests that this is not a crucial area in which editorial control is exercised at the level of each newspaper. What was far more distinctive were the differences in length, language and tone of the correspondence columns, and the extent to which the *Mirror* and *The Sun* published letters of no obvious immediate public interest. To echo Tunstall (see above), the letters published in these two papers faithfully replicated the highly stylized journalism of the tabloid press and dealt with areas, such as personal problems and sexual practices, reflecting its editorial priorities. Nevertheless, the experience of the *Daily Mirror* in the 1940s illustrates how much readers may at least temporarily share the journalistic values and lexicon of the tabloid press (Engel 1996: 257). Even where letters are 'ruthlessly' cut, some correspondents may welcome editorial intervention and see it as improving their contributions (Tunstall 1977: 218). *The Sun* in particular foregrounds the supposed, and mediated, ordinariness of its correspondents and continues to attract large numbers of letters from its readers (Grose 1989: 74–6).

Watching the watchdogs

While the larger question of the influence of readers' letters published in newspapers lies beyond the scope of this brief analysis, there is one area where any such influence ought to be immediately apparent – in the press itself. Tunstall (1977: 226–7) believed the letters' columns to be unsuitable as watchdogs on the press. The main factor militating against correspondence columns performing this function was editorial control, and its subordination to advertising and other economic and political interests (Tunstall 1977: 211–12). In the 1980s and 1990s for both *The Sun* and the *(Daily) Mirror* these interests were chiefly their own direct self-interests, as they vied with each other for circulation and advertising revenue: *The Sun* in particular boosted itself as the '*Sun*-stoppable' and '*Sun*-beatable' paper (Engel 1996: 270). Such a publication was unlikely to carry in its own correspondence columns 'sustained, reasonable and informed criticism' of its performance (Tunstall 1977: 226).

It might be expected that letters to the editor selected for publication would instead be unreflectively self-congratulatory. In fact, in the sample surveyed there were no such letters in *The Sun* and only one in the *Mirror*. (One also appeared in *The Guardian* but it was mainly ironic in tone.) A minority of letters appearing in the main correspondence columns (fewer than 25 per cent in *The Sun* and just over one-third in the *Mirror*, a figure inflated by the paper carrying 13 letters on its lottery story in one issue) even referred directly to news and feature stories which had previously appeared in either of the two respective papers. All the same, neither paper published a letter of criticism of its own performance, or even its own editorial views. The only critical tone came in the two letters submitted by representatives putting the views of commercial organizations (mentioned above). By comparison, letters published by both *The Times* and *The Guardian* criticized and corrected, *inter alia*, the papers' leading articles; news and feature stories; columns and commentaries; reviews; headlines, and even an advertisement. There was little in these letters, however, which amounted to 'general criticisms of the overall operation of . . . [either] publication', and most concentrated wholly on the details of the individual topics (Tunstall 1977: 226). A striking feature of both papers' correspondence columns was the numbers of letters which referred to other previously published correspondence, particularly in *The Times* where this kind of letter accounted for nearly one-third of all those published.

This evidence points to the published correspondents of newspapers, the tabloids neither less nor more than the broadsheets, being comprised of largely self-identifying, more or less closed groups, whose influence is chiefly exercised within each group itself. Because of the crucial role played by the editing process, the potential exists then for the newspaper also to play its distinctive role, thereby establishing interactivity. This occurs in some instances, as when letters to the editor may be mobilized for the purposes of self-promotion, or to validate an editorial 'line'. For the most part, though, the editorial functions – principally, the desire of the tabloid papers to edit letters heavily to conform to their editorial values, and the inclination of the broadsheet press to restrict access to its correspondence columns to maintain their prestige value – work against such an arrangement. Editors prepared to embark, and even enthusiastic about embarking, on editorial campaigns and crusades on a wide range of issues feel powerless in the face of critiques of their own papers' performances (Tunstall 1977: 226). This need for permanent self-referential validation renders newspapers incapable of accommodating a full interactivity with their readers in which there is naturally space for systemic reader criticism of the performance of the press.

Conclusion

Tunstall's scepticism about the role of correspondents as watchdogs of the press remains valid more than twenty years later. Setting aside the question of the fabrication of letters, for which no evidence was found, the key factors are the extent to which newspapers 'shape' the correspondence they publish; the access to their columns they facilitate, and the interconnectedness of these processes of editing and gatekeeping which promotes genuineness. The terms on which readers are addressed, whether as apparently more passive consumers or as actors in the public sphere, have a largely internal importance: for example, there is little evidence that a telephone poll conducted by *The Sun* is extrinsically less influential than a letter published in *The Times*, but this area deserves more attention. The potential exists for this form of mediation to promote the authentic participation of readers on the basis of interactivity between newspapers and their audiences, but this is most normally blocked by the interposition of superior editorial power.

This occurs most obviously, but far from exclusively, in the case of readers' criticisms of the performance of the press itself. Given that readers want not only to 'let off steam' but also to receive advice and guidance, the alternative of a seemingly unmediated interactive participation via electronic delivery systems is likely to be attractive. A substantial number of sites dedicated to media criticism already exist on the worldwide web, although mainly outside the UK. The majority of these sites, however, are run by, and mainly oriented towards, professional media practitioners and media users rather than the general public.[5] While it is too early to analyse these supplementary outlets for press criticism, in the 1970s the underground press performed a similar function (Tunstall 1977: 226). That it was relatively short-lived possibly illustrates, as well as the shortcomings inherent in the 'alternative' print media, the flexibility in the letters-to-the-editor feature of the mainstream press. In other words, newspapers were to a considerable degree successful in the 1980s in adapting their correspondence columns to meet the changing demands and expectations of readers. All the same, it is clear that these responses were tactical rather than strategic. Tunstall argued that a strategic change would occur only if letters of criticism of the press were removed from routine editorial control. This has clearly not happened – in fact, the opposite might be true. The value of the tactical adjustments that have been made must not be underestimated, however. The only paper of the four surveyed here not to adopt the albeit limited tactic of expanding both the scale and scope of readers' letters was the *Mirror*: in many ways the accessibility and authenticity of the paper are more restricted than they were fifty years ago. It is tempting to associate this with the decline of the *Mirror* from its position of pre-eminence in the national daily newspaper sector, and in the standards of its journalism and editorial judgement (Pilger 1997).

If the newspaper press marginalizes its audiences through an excessive exercise of editorial power at the point where large numbers of readers expect authentic interaction, the seemingly unmediated, anarchic openness of cyberspace, if it proves capable of meeting audience expectations more authentically, it may offer an alternative locus where 'ordinary people' can more effectively and more satisfactorily call the press to account. For the press, the longer term implications are enormous.

Notes

1 I am grateful to Howard Tumber for directing my attention to a number of works on EDS.
2 The newspaper was called the *Daily Mirror*, and was known as the *Mirror*, until 1997 when its title was changed to *The Mirror*. All three are used here.
3 I am grateful to Belinda Simmelink for drawing my attention to this example. An account is included in her thesis, 'The tabloids exposed: the sociocultural, political and economic reality of the downmarket newspapers in Great Britain', (1996) Institute of Higher European Studies, The Hague.
4 24 Feb.–1 March. The editions were those circulating in central London.
5 Web sites are maintained by, among others, the Australian Centre for Independent Journalism; Project Censored; Center for Media and Democracy; Reporters' Committee for Freedom of the Press; Institute for Alternative Journalism; Fairness and Accuracy in Reporting and Index on Censorship.

References

Aitkenhead, D. (1997) 'Election? What election?' *The Guardian* 2, 10 Mar.: 2–3.
Berridge, V. (1978) 'Popular Sunday papers and mid-Victorian society', in Boyce, G., Curran, J. and Wingate, P. (eds) *Newspaper History: From the 17th Century to the Present*, Constable, London, 247–64.
Bogart, L. (1981) *Press and Public: Who Reads What, Where, When and Why in American Newspapers*, Lawrence Erlbaum, Hillsdale, NJ.
Cudlipp, H. (1953) *Publish and Be Damned: The Astonishing Story of the 'Daily Mirror'*, Andrew Dakers, London.
Donegan, L. (1997) 'Party pooped', *The Guardian* The Week, 8 Feb.: 1–2.
Elenio, P. (1995) *Capturing Readers: The Battle to Keep and Attract Consumers of Newspapers*, Reuter Foundation Paper 27, Green College, Oxford.

Engel, M. (1996) *Tickle the Public: One Hundred Years of the Popular Press*, Victor Gollancz, London.
Friedland, L.A. (1996) 'Electronic democracy and the new citizenship', *Media, Culture and Society* **18** (2): 185–210.
Goldgar, B.A. (1994) 'Fact, fiction and letters to the editor in Fielding's essay-journals', in Harris, M. (ed.) *Studies in Newspaper and Periodical History 1993 Annual*, Greenwood, London, 19–26.
Gregory, K. (ed.) (1976) *The First Cuckoo: Letters to 'The Times', 1900–1975*, Times Books and Allen & Unwin, London.
Grigg, J. (1993) *The History of 'The Times': The Thomson Years, 1966–1981*, Vol. vi, Times Books, London.
Grose, R. (1989) *'The Sun'-sation: Behind the Scenes of Britain's Bestselling Daily Newspaper*, Angus Robertson, London.
Habermas, J. (1989) *The Structural Transformation of the Public Sphere*, trans. T. Burger, Polity Press, Cambridge.
Hacker, K.L. (1996) 'Missing links in the evolution of electronic democratization', *Media, Culture and Society* **18** (2): 213–32.
Harris, B. (1996) *Politics and the Rise of the Press: Britain and France, 1620–1800*, Routledge, London.
Jackson, I. (1971) *The Provincial Press and the Community*, University of Manchester Press, Manchester.
Jankowski, N.W. and Malina, A. (1996) 'Community building in cyberspace: theoretical considerations and proposals for empirical study', paper to the conference of the International Association for Mass Communication Research, Sydney, Australia.
Lamb, L. (1989) *Sunrise: The Remarkable Rise and Rise of the Best-Selling Soaraway 'Sun'*, Papermac, London.
Pilger, J. (1997) 'Breaking the *Mirror*: the Murdoch effect', *Network First*, dir. D. Munro, Central Television, 18 Feb., Birmingham.
Platform for Cooperation on Communication and Democratization (1996) communiqué (31 Oct.–1 Nov.), *PCR-Newsletter* **5** (1) Winter: 32.
Rabb, C., Bellamy, C., Taylor, J., Dutton, W.H. and Peltu, M. (1996) 'The information polity: electronic democracy, privacy and surveillance', in Dutton, W.H. (ed.) *Information and Communication Technologies*, Oxford University Press, Oxford.
Robbins, K. (1976) *The Abolition of War: The 'Peace Movement' in Britain, 1914–1919*, University of Wales Press, Cardiff.
Rosen, J. (1996) *Getting the Connections Right: Public Journalism and the Troubles in the Press*, Twentieth Century Fund Press, New York.
Royle, E. (1990) 'Newspapers and periodicals in historical research', in Brake, L. and Jones, A. (eds) *Investigating Victorian Journalism*, Macmillan, London, 48–59.
Smith, A.C.H. (1975) *Paper Voices: The Popular Press and Social Change, 1935–1965*, Chatto & Windus, London.
Taylor, S.J. (1996) *The Great Outsiders: Northcliffe, Rothermere and the 'Daily Mail'*, Weidenfeld & Nicolson, London.
Tunstall, J. (1977) 'Letters to the editor', Royal Commission on the Press, in *Studies on the Press*, Working Paper No. 3, HMSO, London, 203–48.

161

Tunstall, J. (1996) *Newspaper Power: The New National Press in Britain*, Clarendon Press, Oxford.

Van den Bergh (1997) 'Agonizing decisions', *Press Gazette*, 27 Jan.: 16.

Williams, R. (1961) *The Long Revolution*, Chatto & Windus, London.

CHAPTER 12

Democracy under threat

Andrew Calcutt

Summary

Many commentators have argued that democracy is under threat from cross-media ownership and the excessive influence of tabloid news-papers and television. They also argue that the proliferation of media will contribute to this anti-democratic trend by making regulation more difficult. This chapter looks at the current concern over the effects of media on politics, and reveals the common ground between novel notions of 'virtual politics' and the long-established élitism of 'mass society' theories. In both instances it is assumed that the mass of the viewing public cannot read between the lines of press and media cover-age. The ordinary voter, it is said, stands mesmerized by media images like a child in a sweet shop.

Media monopolies are undoubtedly a hindrance to democratic de-bate. However, in suggesting that the majority of the electorate is 'vul-nerable' rather than rational, the proregulation camp gives expression to a form of élitism which is more insidious, and probably more danger-ous, than the explicit threat to democracy posed by the media moguls.

Introduction

On 28 September 1994, BBC2 broadcast an edition of *The Late Show* en-titled 'Berlusconi: Mussolini of the Media?' This was before the media-mogul-turned-politician was unceremoniously kicked out of office towards the end of December 1994. The programme described how Silvio Berlusconi ('the great seducer') used his own media empire to sell him-self to the Italian electorate. His election to the office of prime minister was described as 'a terrible situation for democracy ... verging on the totalitarian'. A contributor to the programme concluded 'television is the breeding ground of a new dictatorship and television is the instru-ment of that dictatorship'.

On 3 December 1994, the cover story of *The Guardian*'s Weekend supplement began with a pastiche of *News At Ten* headlines:

> Booing. Uproar in the Commons. The leader of the house, Richard Littlejohn tells Opposition MPs – put up or shut up . . . Good evening, after this morning's Fraud Squad raid on News International, the prime minister Rupert Murdoch is tonight meeting with his coalition partners John Tyndall and the Reverend Ian Paisley . . .

'It is not easy,' explained *The Guardian* feature writer John Hooper, 'to convey what it is like to live in Berlusconi's Italy . . . his grip on television is greater than anything experienced in a democratic State . . . This is not simply a government run by a TV mogul, it is an authentically televisual administration of a kind not yet experienced even in the United States.' Hooper seemed to agree with the *Late Show* thesis that Berlusconi's Forza Italia had inaugurated a new era of 'virtual politics for the age of virtual reality'. The use of the term 'virtual politics' is here intended to connote the unprecedented primacy of presentation and imagery in a new political context defined by proliferating media and the collapse of Big Ideas along with the Berlin Wall. But is 'virtual politics' as unprecedented as it is made out to be?

Virtually new

'In this book I describe . . . the thicket of unreality which stands between us and the facts of life. The making of the illusions which flood our experiences has become the business of America . . . The Grand Canyon itself became a disappointing reproduction of the Kodachrome original.' This is a description of what would now be described as 'the age of virtual reality'. Except that it was written nearly a quarter of a century before anyone had ever heard of virtual reality. In 1962, the American commentator Daniel Boorstin described 'the age of contrivance' as a world dominated by the 'pseudo-event'. Boorstin was particularly concerned that the 'pseudo-event' had already begun to exercise a distorting effect on the real world of politics.

In *The Image* (1962), Boorstin developed some of the themes introduced by Theodore H. White in *The Making of the President 1960* (1961). White assigned overwhelming significance to the televised debate which was a novel feature of the presidential election campaign of 1960. According to White, the mass audience was influenced, not by the policies advanced by Richard Nixon or John F. Kennedy, but by the combination of television technology ('the X-ray effect') and Lazy Shave make-up which rendered Nixon 'haggard and heavy-bearded' in contrast to the 'pert and clean-cut' appearance of the victorious Kennedy.

Boorstin and White suggested that the US presidential election of 1960 was unprecedented in that it was the first major political event in which the candidates' image on TV was of such importance that it turned the image-reality relationship inside out. But the Kennedy–Nixon election predates the election of Berlusconi and the 'new era of virtual politics' by thirty-four years. This would indicate that the era of 'virtual politics' is only virtually new.

Far from being a new development, the suggestion that media images have created their own political (un)reality has been advanced by a long succession of writers and pundits. In 1991 Baudrillard declared that the Gulf War was only a figment of 'the delirium of communications'. In 1988 Ira Glasser referred to 'televison and the construction of reality'. In 1983, Umberto Eco pre-empted the Berlusconi thesis in an essay entitled 'Towards a semiological guerilla warfare': 'Not long ago, if you wanted to seize political power in a country, you had merely to control the army and the police . . . Today a country belongs to the person who controls communications.'

J.G. Ballard, in the course of a talk which he gave in central London in the early 1990s, looked back to the 1970s and his own first use of the term 'media landscape' to describe the marketing of Ronald Reagan in the gubernatorial elections in California. In 1967, the late Guy Debord maintained that 'the spectacle is the heart of the unrealism of the real society . . . the spectacle is the present form of socially dominant life'.

The absorption of reality into representation is even said to predate the advent of TV. Throughout the 1960s, Marshall McLuhan repeated his claim that the Great Crash of 1929 was caused by jazz and the radio. In *One Dimensional Man* (1964), Herbert Marcuse complained of the 'overwhelming concreteness of newspaper copy' and warned that the self-marketing of the *status quo* through the media had rendered it impenetrable to all but a handful of creative artists.

The élitist tradition

The recognition of the 'media landscape' by a variety of commentators presupposes that they themselves have not been subsumed by it. Most of them regard themselves and their associates as the last bastion of the democratic tradition, holding out under a constant bombardment of media images. The corollary of this supposition, however, is that nearly everyone else has succumbed to the proliferation of media. The underlying assumption – more often implied than clearly spelt-out – is that the vast majority of the general public has been rendered incompetent by the disorienting influence of tabloid newspapers and satellite TV.

As applied to the political arena, this outlook is profoundly anti-democratic. It raises the question 'Are they fit to vote?' and implies a negative answer. Formally expressed as a criticism of media moguls and the air of unreality arising from their manipulative practices, the underlying content of this approach is to raise a question mark over the universal franchise and demean the critical faculties of the overwhelming majority of the electorate. In this respect the 'virtual politics' thesis should be seen as the latest development in the élitist tradition of 'mass society'. For a century and more, 'mass society' theorists have shown their contempt for the allegedly low culture of the masses as expressed in the mass media.

In *Culture and Anarchy* (1869), Matthew Arnold redefined the entry of the English working-class on to the stage of history as a problem of culture. Friedrich Nietzsche (1961) declared that the masses 'vomit their bile and call it a newspaper'. T.S. Eliot (1938) claimed that the effect of newspapers on their readers is to 'affirm them as a complacent, prejudiced and unthinking mass'. In *The Revolt of the Masses* (1930) (*The Revolting Masses* might have been a more appropriate title), Ortega Y. Gasset complained of the corrosive effect of mass culture, in contrast to the minority pursuits of art, rationality and good government. F.R. Leavis counterposed mass culture with minority civilization. Gustav Le Bon (1896) and Vilfredo Pareto (1926) also subscribed to the notion of mass culture as a debilitating consequence of atomization and the erosion of 'organic community': stripped of the ties of community, mass man was highly suggestible and would travel along almost any political route that was laid out by the mass media.

After the Second World War, the notion of 'mass society' was given a new guise by the left-wingers of the Frankfurt School. Their critique of the 'culture industry' combined Marxist terminology with the élitist tradition. Theirs was the first of many attempts to blame the working-class – alleged to have been bought off by the stupefying jee-jaws of mass culture – for failures which were largely the responsibility of the left.

'I didn't vote Tory and I don't read "The Sun"'

'I do not like to sit next to a *Sun* reader on the tube.' In the aftermath of Labour's fourth successive defeat in the 1992 general election, the Labour Euro MP Anita Pollack expressed her resentment towards *The Sun* and its readership. Among Labour's middle-class activists, this mood was widely shared. Letters to *The Guardian* claimed that *The Sun* readership was 'not interested in articles that argue cogently'; Essex Man was said to be 'unfit to hold the franchise'. The working-class voter, allegedly mesmerized by the copy of *The Sun* rolled up in his back pocket, was scapegoated for the Labour Party's lack of political credibility. It seemed there was more than a germ of truth in columnist Richard Littlejohn's claim that an attack on *The Sun* is a covert attack on the working class.

Some of the sentiments expressed in the letters pages of liberal newspapers after Labour's fourth successive electoral defeat subsequently appeared, somewhat modified, in a theory of sorts. In a feature article called 'Heads on the chopping box', published in *The Guardian* on 10 June 1993, which pre-empted the 'virtual politics' thesis of *The Late Show*, *The Guardian*'s political editor Michael White combined Fabian-style high-handedness towards the electorate with postmodernist theorizing about media proliferation.

White cited Michael Foley's *The Rise of the British Presidency* (1993), and complained that 'marauding gangs of tabloid newsmen and TV crews' have created 'leaderland', a political cyberspace inhabited by 'designer populists' such as Ronald Reagan and Margaret Thatcher. According to White, the new technologies are inherently inimical to serious politics and quality journalism· 'TV demands a focus on personality which diminishes policy and party ... satellite, cable TV, faxes and mobile phones have created a pseudo-global hook-up ... a global Tower of Babel in which newspaper accounts of Major's "fightback" speech are as fragmented as TV soundbites. Result: no one knows what's going on' White depicted a delirium of communications in which even senior journalists like himself had to struggle to maintain 20/20 vision. For others, the struggle was over before it had begun. There was one group of people in particular whose vision, according to White, would inevitably be distorted to the point of total blindness. Step forward, Essex Man. 'With jaundiced eye, Essex Person surveys political leaders whose powers – and potential perils – are amplified by the pervasive presence of television.' (Note that White considered the term 'Essex Man' an affront to women. But he is entirely at ease with the idea that the majority of the electorate is unable to see through media-hype. Expressing such a view of the mass audience is entirely in keeping with the new etiquette of equal opportunities.)

Where *The Guardian*'s White utilized the image of 'Essex Person' as a caricature of the majority of the British electorate, BBC2's *The Late Show* demonstrated a similar attitude toward its Italian counterpart. In 'Berlusconi: Mussolini of the media?', the masses were symbolized – and misrepresented – by prolonged sequences of a blue-collar family sitting in passive submission to the phantasmagoria of Berlusconi's TV channels. 'The TV has literally hypnotized Italians,' said the voice-over. Opposition spokesmen claimed that the voters were 'dazed and bedazzled' by a cocktail of 'consumer dreams and carnal desires' broadcast through 'the small screen temple to popular culture'. Berlusconi was 'the great seducer' who had taken advantage of 'teenagers and housewives'.

It is interesting to note that the Italian left were the prime-movers of the idea that the masses who did not vote for them had allowed themselves to be duped by Berlusconi's 'virtual reality'. The Democratic Party of the Left had expected to take office in 1994, and the 'virtual politics' thesis provided a convenient excuse for its failure to win enough votes on that occasion. Meanwhile the liberal-left in Britain added their voices to the complaint that Berlusconi sold himself to the electorate on the basis of a false image of prosperity for all who aspire to it. Ironically, these were the same voices who praised the artificial image of the Labour Party in Hugh Hudson's 'Kinnock: The Movie' – an exercise in 'virtual politics' which failed in its pitch to the British electorate in 1987.

The limited influence of the media

Noting that the Berlusconi administration had already run into trouble, the September 1994 edition of *The Late Show* opined that 'he probably has enough power to ensure the show stays on the air'. But the credits had hardly stopped rolling on *The Late Show* before Berlusconi's administration was taken off. If the 'virtual politics' thesis was not so clearly out of touch with reality, its anti-democratic assumptions might be harder to argue against. However, this is not to say that television played no appreciable role in the Italian elections of 1994 in which Berlusconi was victorious, or again in April 1996 when he was defeated. In a society where collectivity is in sharp decline – and this is increasingly the case even in Italy – the individual voter has little or no means of finding out about the rest of the world except through the press and broadcasting media. In so far as the media are now the sole conduit of information about the wider world, they do enjoy an unprecedented significance. Yet individual voters, isolated as they are, have not lost the ability to measure media images against direct experience. They maintain the intellectual capacity to criticize the former when they do not tally with the latter. Indeed, it is the popular recognition of this discrepancy that accounts for the fact that politicians and journalists always come joint-bottom whenever pollsters ask the public 'Who can you trust?'

Nowhere is the regard for politicians lower than in Italy. As far as the Italian electorate was concerned, in 1994 Berlusconi's selling points were his lack of a track record as a politician combined with his apparent disdain for existing political arrangements. The negative experience of the existing political order, and the hope that Berlusconi the political virgin had not been sullied by it, were more important to the Italian electorate of 1994 than the media fantasy of Berlusconi, the great seducer. Yet as far as the Italian establishment was concerned, Berlusconi was far from being an unknown quantity. An old friend of former socialist prime minister Bettino Craxi and erstwhile member of the infamous masonic lodge P2, Berlusconi was a reliable backroom boy of long standing. Here was an insider whose lack of political profile enabled him to appear as an outsider with no connections to a discredited political order. At the same time, his reputation as a highly successful entrepreneur and consummate pragmatist chimed in with the trends in Italian society away from collectivity and ideology.

At this point – and only at this point – Berlusconi's influence over the media came into play. It faciliated the establishment of a substantial political profile for Berlusconi the nonpolitician; and this was achieved in a three-month period which was short enough for Berlusconi not to be revealed and discredited as a wheeler and dealer like all the rest. After a few months in office, however, Berlusconi was seen to be just like any other political operator; and all the television channels in Italy could not have saved him from the inglorious exit from government which occurred in late December 1994. Once again, political and economic realities overtook the airbrushed images of politicians and other public figures.

Regulation of the media

Liberal-left criticisms of Berlusconi and *Sun*-owner Rupert Murdoch nearly always end in calls for the increased regulation of the media. The prospect of new media technologies has brought a new urgency to this discussion. There are dire warnings of Murdoch's satellite stations ravaging the sensibilities of the West and upsetting the environmental balance of the Third World. It is certainly galling to think that Rupert Murdoch might become the gatekeeper of cyberspace. But equally it remains to be seen how the freedom of the information superhighway could be guaranteed by government regulation.

While there is no such thing as a 'free market', at least the 'free market' ethos assumes that consumers who can pay their way are also capable of making their own decisions. The theory behind increased government control, on the other hand, suggests that the masses cannot cope with media images unless such images are sanitized on their behalf by professional regulators. Nothing could be more alien to the spirit of democracy.

Postscript

In the run-up to the 1997 general election, the 'virtual politics' thesis did not get much of an airing. *The Sun* shone on Tony Blair, and those who might have otherwise have complained about tabloid 'pseudo-events' opted to keep mum on this occasion. There was, however, a media candidate in the form of ex-BBC foreign correspondent Martin Bell, who stood against Tory Neil Hamilton in the Cheshire constituency of Tatton. Billed initially as the 'anti-corruption' candidate (the ballot-paper wording subsequently became the subject of legal proceedings), Bell was held up as a man of good character standing out against the sleaziness of politics.

The pro-Bell notion that a political virgin (demonstrated by his wearing of a white suit) with roots in the media would be more trustworthy than a politician, had much in common with the dynamic behind Berlusconi three years earlier. Except that in Britain, Bell's base of support was largely comprised of the domestic counterparts to Berlusconi's opponents in Italy: his backing came primarily from the liberal-left, and in particular, *The Guardian*.

The events in Tatton were an expression of anti-democratic trends. When the Labour and Liberal Democrat candidates stood down in his favour, the voters of Tatton were restricted to returning a Conservative MP or electing Bell. Although the latter was presented as a people's champion against the tyranny of corruption, Bell's candidature was fully in line with the wider attack on the democratic tradition of political contestation. Instead of a contest between competing interest groups, i.e. political parties, voters were invited to back a morally robust candidate who stood above politics and self-interest. The overall effect was to suggest that the electorate should reciprocate by suspending self-interest in favour of moral rectitude. This too is alien to the spirit of democracy.

References

Arnold, M. (1869/1969) *Culture and Anarchy*, Cambridge University Press, Cambridge.
Baudrillard, J. (1985) *The Ecstasy of Communication*, trans. John Johnston, in Foster, H. (ed.)
Postmodern Culture, Pluto Press, London.
Baudrillard, J. (1991/1995) *The Gulf War Did Not Take Place*, trans, Paul Patton, Power Publication, Sydney.
Boorstin, D.J. (1961/1963) *The Image*, Penguin Books, Harmondsworth.
Carey, J. (1992) *The Intellectuals and the Masses*, Faber & Faber, London.
Debord, G. (1967/1983) *The Society of the Spectacle*, Black & Red, Detroit.
Eco, U. (1967/1987) *Towards a Semiological Guerrilla Warfare*, in *Travels in Hyper-reality*, Picador (Pan), London.
Eliot, T.S. (1938) in *Criterion*, xvii, Faber & Faber, London.
Foley, M. (1993) *The Rise of the British Presidency*, Manchester University Press, Manchester.
Gasset, O.Y. (1930/1961) *The Revolt of the Masses*, Allen & Unwin, London.
Glasser, I. (1988) 'Television and the Construction of Reality in Television as a Social Issue', *Applied Social Psychology Annual*, No. 8, Oskamp, S. (ed.), Sage, London.
Hughes, H.S. (1958/1988) *Consciousness and Society: the Re-orientation of European Social Thought 1890–1930*, Harvester Press, Brighton.
Kornhauser, W. (1960) *The Politics of Mass Society*, Routledge & Kegan Paul, London.
Le Bon, G. (1896) *The Crowd: a Study of the Popular Mind*, Fisher Unwin, London.
Leavis, F.R. and Thompson, D. (1933) *Culture and Environment: the Training of Critical Awareness* Chatto & Windus, London.
Lukacs, G. (1962/1980) *The Destruction of Reason*, trans. Peter Palmer, Merlin, London.
Marcuse, H. (1964/1972) *One Dimensional Man*, Abacus (Sphere), London.
McLuhan, M. (1964–1967) *Understanding Media: the Extensions of Man* (1964), Abacus (Sphere), London.
Nietzsche, F. (1961) *Thus Spoke Zarathustra*, trans, R.J. Hollingdale, Penguin Books, Harmondsworth.
Pareto, V. (1902/1926) *Les Systèmes Socialistes*, Giard, Paris.
White, T.H. (1961/1962) *The Making of the President 1960*, Cape, London.
Wolfe, T. (1969) 'What if he is right?', in *The Pump House Gang*, Bantam, London.

The Press Complaints Commission Code of Practice, 1995

The Press Complaints Commission is charged with enforcing the following Code of Practice which was framed by the newspaper and periodical industry and ratified by the Press Complaints Commission.

All members of the press have a duty to maintain the highest professional and ethical standards. In doing so, they should have regard to the provisions of this Code of Practice and to safeguarding the public's right to know.

Editors are responsible for the actions of journalists employed by their publications. They should also satisfy themselves as far as possible that material accepted from non-staff members was obtained in accordance with this Code.

While recognising that this involves a substantial element of self-restraint by editors and journalists, it is designed to be acceptable in the context of a system of self-regulation. The Code applies in the spirit as well as the letter.

It is the responsibility of editors to cooperate as swiftly as possible in PCC enquiries.

Any publication which is criticised by the PCC under one of the following clauses is duty bound to print the adjudication which follows in full and with due prominence.

1. Accuracy

(i) Newspapers and pediodicals should take care not to publish inaccurate, misleading or distorted material.

(ii) Whenever it is recognised that a significant inaccuracy, misleading statement or distorted report has been published, it should be corrected promptly and with due prominence.

(iii) An apology should be published whenever appropriate.

(iv) A newspaper or periodical should always report fairly and accurately the outcome of an action for defamation to which it has been a party.

2. *Opportunity to reply*

A fair opportunity for reply to inaccuracies should be given to individuals or organisations when reasonably called for.

3. *Comment, conjecture and fact*

Newspapers, whilst free to be partisan, should distinguish clearly between comment, conjecture and fact.

4. *Privacy*

Intrustions and enquiries into an individual's private life without his or her consent, including the use of long-lens photography to take pictures of people on private property without their consent, are not generally acceptable and publication can only be justified when in the public interest.

Note: Private property is defined as (i) any private residence, together with its garden and outbuildings, but excluding any adjacent fields or parkland and the surrounding parts of the property within the unaided view of passers-by; (ii) hotel bedrooms (but not other areas in a hotel) and (iii) those parts of a hospital or nursing home where patients are treated or accommodated.

5. *Listening devices*

Unless justified by public interest, journalists should not obtain or publish material obtained by using clandestine listening devices or by intercepting private telephone conversations.

6. *Hospitals*

(i) Journalists or photographers making enquiries at hospitals or similar institutions should identify themselves to a responsible executive and obtain permission before entering non-public areas.

(ii) The restrictions on intruding into privacy are particularly relevant to enquiries about individuals in hospitals or similar institutions.

7. *Misrepresentation*

(i) Journalists should not generally obtain or seek to obtain information or pictures through misrepresentation or subterfuge.

(ii) Unless in the public interest, documents or photographs should be removed only with the express consent of the owner.
(iii) Subterfuge can be justified only in the public interest and only when material cannot be obtained by any other means.

8. Harassment

(i) Journalists should neither obtain nor seek to obtain information or pictures through intimidation or harassment.
(ii) Unless their enquiries are in the public interest, journalists should not photograph individuals on private property (as defined in Clause 4) without their consent; should not persist in telephoning or questioning individuals after having been asked to desist; should not remain on their property after having been asked to leave and should not follow them.
(iii) It is the responsibility of editors to ensure that these requirements are carried out.

9. Payment for articles

Payment or offers of payment for stories, pictures or information should not be made directly or through agents to witnesses or potential witnesses in current criminal proceedings or to people engaged in crime or to their associates – which includes family, friends, neighbours and colleagues – except where the material concerned ought to be published in the public interest and the payment is necessary for this to be done.

10. Intrusion into grief or shock

In cases involving personal grief or shock, enquiries should be carried out and approaches made with sympathy and discretion.

11. Innocent relatives and friends

Unless it is contrary to the public's right to know, the press should generally avoid identifying relatives or friends of persons convicted or accused of crime.

12. Interviewing or photographing children

(i) Journalists should not normally interview or photograph children under the age of 16 on subjects involving the personal welfare of the child in the absence of or without the consent of a parent or other adult who is responsible for the children.

(ii) Children should not be approached or photographed while at school without the permission of the school authorities.

13. *Children in sex cases*

1. The press should not, even where the law does not prohibit it, identify children under the age of 16 who are involved in cases concerning sexual offences, whether as victims or as witnesses or defendants.
2. In any press report of a case involving a sexual offence against a child:
    (i) the adult should be identified
    (ii) the term 'incest' where applicable should not be used
    (iii) the offence should be described as 'serious offences against young children' or similar appropriate wording
    (iv) the child should not be identified
    (v) care should be taken that nothing in the report implies the relationship between the accused and the child.

14. *Victims of crime*

The press should not identify victims of sexual assault or publish material likely to contribute to such identification unless, by law, they are free to do so.

15. *Discrimination*

(i) The press should avoid prejudicial or perjorative reference to a person's race, colour, religion, sex or sexual orientation or to any physical or mental illness or handicap.
(ii) It should avoid publishing details of a person's race, colour, religion, sex or sexual orientation unless these are directly relevant to the story.

16. *Financial journalism*

(i) Even when the law does not prohibit it, journalists should not use for their own profit financial information they receive in advance of its general publication, nor should they pass such information to others.
(ii) They should not write about shares or securities in whose per-

formance they know that they or their families have a significant financial interest without disclosing the interest to the editor or financial editor.

(iii) They should not buy or sell, either directly or through nominees or agents, shares or securities about which they have written recently or about which they intend to write in the near future.

17. Confidential sources

Journalists have a moral obligation to protect confidential sources of information.

18. The public interest

Clauses 4, 5, 7, 8 and 9 create exceptions which may be covered by invoking the public interest. For the purpose of this code that is more easily defined as:

(i)   detecting or exposing crime or a serious misdemeanour
(ii) protecting public health and safety
(iii) preventing the public from being misled by some statement or action of an individual or organisation.

In any cases raising issues beyond these three definitions the Press Complaints Commission will require a full explanation by the editor of the publication involved, seeking to demonstrate how the public interest was served.

Source: Press Standards Board of Finance.

National Union of Journalists' Code of Conduct

1 A journalist has a duty to maintain the highest professional and ethical standards.

2 A journalist shall at all times defend the principle of the freedom of the press and other media in relation to the collection of information and the expression of comment and criticism. He/she shall strive to eliminate distortion, news suppression and censorship.

3 A journalist shall strive to ensure that the information he/she disseminates is fair and accurate, avoid the expression of comment and conjecture as established fact and falsification by distortion, selection or misrepresentation.

4 A journalist shall rectify promptly any harmful inaccuracies, ensure that correction and apologies receive due prominence and afford the right of reply to persons criticized when the issue is of sufficient importance.

5 A journalist shall obtain information, photographs and illustrations only by straightforward means. The use of other means can be justified only by over-riding consideration of the public interest. The journalist is entitled to exercise a personal conscientious objection to the use of such means.

6 Subject to justification by over-riding considerations of the public interest, a journalist shall do nothing which entails intrusion into private grief and distress.

7 A journalist shall protect confidential sources of information.

8 A journalist shall not accept bribes nor shall he/she allow other inducements to influence the performance of his/her professional duties.

9 A journalist shall not lend himself/herself to the distortion or suppression of the truth because of advertising or other considerations.

10 A journalist shall neither originate nor process material which encourages discrimination on grounds of race, colour, creed, gender or sexual orientation.

11 A journalist shall not take private advantage of information gained

in the course of his/her duties, before the information is public knowledge.

Source. National Union of Journalists.

Index